The Art
Of Happiness

The Art
Of Happiness

Teachings of Buddhist Psychology

Mirko Frýba

Translated from the German by Michael H. Kohn

Foreword by Claudio Naranjo

Shambhala
Boston & Shaftesbury
1989

Shambhala Publications, Inc.
Horticultural Hall
300 Massachusetts Avenue
Boston, Massachusetts 02115

Shambhala Publications, Inc.
The Old School House
The Courtyard, Bell Street
Shaftesbury, Dorset SP7 8BP

9 8 7 6 5 4 3 2 1

First Edition
Printed in the United States of America
Distributed in the United States by Random House
and in Canada by Random House of Canada Ltd.
Distributed in the United Kingdom by Element Books, Ltd.

Library of Congress Cataloging-in-Publication Data
Fryba, Mirko, 1943–
   [Anleitung zum Glücklichsein. English]
   The art of happiness: teachings of Buddhist psychology / Mirko
Fryba: translated from the German by Michael H. Kohn; foreword by
Claudio Naranjo.
     p. cm.
   Translation of: Anleitung zum Glücklichsein.
   Includes index.
   ISBN 0-87773-466-6
   1. Spiritual life (Buddhism)   2. Buddhism—Psychology.
3. Abhidharma. I. Title
BQ5620.F7813 1989   88-38444
294.3'444—dc19   CIP

Contents

Foreword

Dr. Frýba has reminded me, when we last saw each other, that during the First Conference of the European Association of Humanistic Psychology in Geneva, Dr. Arnold Keyserling and I presented contrasting views of transpersonal psychology: Dr. Keyserling (then president of the Association) had opened the reunion with a talk in which he showed transpersonal psychology at the apex of an evolutionary "pyramid." I had pointed out in my own talk, which followed, that while sophisticated bodies of knowledge most appropriately called "transpersonal psychology" have existed as part of Asian traditions long before the advent of Western psychology, today's transpersonal psychology is more the expression of an interest and an intent than a label designating an original body of knowledge. I called it an "umbrella" for contributions proceeding largely from the Asian heritage, and proposed that its originality—largely potential—was that of an emerging synthesis between spiritual insights and scientific knowledge, a synthesis to which many are contributing from the perspective of their individual and experiential explorations into the vast domain of the spiritual traditions.

On seeing Dr. Frýba again recently, I was pleasantly surprised to hear that this view of transpersonal psychology as an invitation to creativity rather than a novel body of theory and methodology was a stimulus to him while writing this book. This—in addition to my appreciation for him—justifies my writing these lines as a preface to the original German manuscript the content of which I only know through his account.

The Abhidhamma constitutes one of the three "baskets" of books into which is divided the Pali canon of Buddhist scriptures, the other two being the Suttas or discourses and the Vinaya or rules of monastic life. The Abhidhamma contains the psychology which is implicit in the Suttas and has been amplified throughout the centuries by many commentaries. In contrast to the books on Abhidhamma that have been available in the West—compendiums, essays reflecting traditional understanding, and works that can only be meaningful in the context of meditational experience—the present volume contains an interpretation of Abhidhamma for the modern world and constitutes an embodiment of that process of East-West synthesis which, according to Northrop, is one of the major tasks of our time.

Dr. Frýba, who was analyzed by one of Freud's direct disciples, explored psychedelic therapy in Prague, and trained in psychodrama with the Morenos, may well be the most knowledgeable Abhidhamma scholar among Western psychologists and psychotherapists. A disciple of Venerable Nyanaponika Thera—great light of Buddhism in Sri Lanka—he is also a former monk who has renounced renunciation to embrace the life of a householder and professional. May his perceptive and humorous analysis of modern situations in terms of old wisdom stimulate an appreciation for the way of nonattachment in a world that seeks transformation, yet suffers as ever from the consequences of greed, hate and spiritual obscuration.

CLAUDIO NARANJO

Introduction

The solutions to our contemporary problems require more than new pictures of the world. In order to be able to live in the world happily, we need skills that are rooted in the reliability of our personal outlook. Therefore, this book teaches first of all the art of seeing.

The purification of seeing is a methodical undertaking that is not just a matter of recognizing and eliminating the causes of unhappiness. The focus is rather on discovery and development of behaviors that promote happiness, behaviors that need to be cultivated in a framework of increased familiarity with outer and inner realities. Clear seeing, a connectedness with reality, and a joyful approach to life condition each other mutually. Happiness can be learned. The necessary guidance is found in the Abhidhamma, an ethical-psychological teaching presented in the body of ancient Buddhist scriptures of the same name. Related to various techniques of Buddhist mind-training, psychohygiene, psychotherapy, and meditation, the Abhidhamma represents the systematic knowledge of the Dhamma, or "good teaching," that is, the liberating, happiness-promoting way of life. The selection of themes from the Abhidhamma in this book reflects the practical requirements of everyday life in our civilization.

Our body, which is equipped with senses, feelings, and many latent abilities, provides us with the most reliable anchoring in reality. Through the body we experience direct encounters with the world; through the body we experience the joy of the freedom achieved through the liberation of the mind.[1] People who live free from fear and suffering reject every form of oppression and submission. At home in their own bodies and free in their minds from every external authority, they see reality as it is; thus they are able to bring about their own well-being and tolerate that of others. No guru, no scientist, no leader, no computer, no worldview, dear reader, can give you this kind of liberated, simple, and direct relationship with reality, this freedom and happiness. Even the Dhamma strategies explained in this book are only means, devices, and pointers, the application of which can broaden your own personal potential. Happiness is something we can achieve only for ourselves—only the person who really wants to can succeed.

Being happy is simple; however, the ways and means of achieving happiness have to be sufficiently multifaceted to accommodate people whose initial condition is complicated. The instructions for the Dhamma strategies leave each person the choice of whether to apply them in detail in their personal situation or to use them only as an inspiration. They are based on situations encountered by the author in working with friends, students, patients, and participants in public workshops and continuing education programs for managers, counseling personnel, educators, and therapists. Detailed instructions are given only for those exercises that have produced very good results either in groups or individual work; other exercises are merely mentioned.

It's simple to be happy if one possesses the key to the manifold complexity of life. Through an experiment in the first chapter you will soon learn of such a key that has been preserved for thousands of years. The next three chapters explain the social, cultural, psychological, and bodily experienceable conditions of our human existence in such a way as to make possible a personal breakthrough into a new area of experience. The last four chapters elucidate concrete strategies for increasing happiness and our capacity for happiness in the new circumstances—promising or menacing—that the future holds.

Our happiness is multiplied when we can share it with other people who have also attained a certain mastery of simple happiness. Through such sharing we can joyfully accomplish things together. At this point I think with joy and gratitude of those persons who helped to bring this book about—too many for all to be mentioned here by name. Above all, my thanks go to my wife, Beatrice, who patiently and creatively helped in the meaningful organization of the various drafts of the book and inspired me through illustrative examples from her psychotherapy practice. With Matthias Barth, a friend of many years and colleague in the Dhamma Group of Berne, I have repeatedly discussed questions concerning means of teaching the Abhidhamma in a popular form suitable to our time. Some of the formulations in this book came out of those discussions. Dr. Harald Brixel, Kay Burckhardt, Harald Fritz, Ueli Kornmann, János Morszinay, Claudio Raveane, Pavel Smrčka, Amadeo Solé-Leris, and Martina Streiff read parts of the manuscript and gave me valuable suggestions. Thanks to them and also to the translator, Michael Kohn, who managed even to render some of my German puns into English, and to my editor at Shambhala Publications, Kendra Crossen. Many thanks to the well-known contemporary psychotherapist Claudio Naranjo for composing the foreword.

By giving me lessons in Pali, Professor Lily de Silva of Peradeniya University made possible extraordinary discoveries in the canonical texts. Discussions with her and other Pali scholars in Sri Lanka helped me to clarify many an issue of the Abhidhamma tradition. The great Abhidhamma masters Nyanaponika Maha Thera, Piyadassi Maha Thera, Mahasi Sayadaw, and Rewatadhamma Sayadaw over long years, with wisdom and love, made the meaning of the Abhidhamma paradigms realizable for me in the concrete situations of life. The Venerable Nyanaponika pronounced himself favorably disposed toward my attempt, in the last chapter, to communicate some of the highest themes of Dhamma in a simple fashion—to him I am particularly thankful.

A Note to Social Scientists

You will soon note in your reading of this book that it in no way conflicts with the theories of Theodor Adorno, Gregory Bateson, Erich Fromm, Eugene Gendlin, C. G. Jung, Kurt Lewin, Jacob Levy Moreno, and Carl Rogers, but that it also does not lean on their work. Nor is this book directed toward elaborating one more theory; in this way it differs from those modern works of science and popularized science that offer only information and/or new worldviews. This book is written for intelligent persons, who, though they may not necessarily possess scientific training, nevertheless wish to develop their own personal potential in a practical fashion.

A considerable part of the book is devoted to instructions for some thirty exercises that can be carried out in everyday life on one's own, in the context of training groups, or in the practice of meditation. Theoretical knowledge is conveyed only to the extent that it is necessary for comprehension of the exercises and aids reflective evaluation of their results. What we have here, then, is an exercise book that gives instructions in concrete methodical steps, but nevertheless attempts to avoid the format usual in programmed textbooks.

The Art of Happiness concerns itself only peripherally with problems of psychopathology and psychotherapy. The psychopathology of everyday life, which is perpetuated by internalized guidelines for being unhappy, is the subject of a humorous book by Paul Watzlawick entitled *Anleitung zum Unglücklichsein* (literally "Guide to Being Unhappy"; published in English as *The Pursuit of Unhappiness*). Although our titles sound quite similar (the original German title of this book is *Anleitung zum Glücklichsein*, or "Guide to Being Happy"), the two books are neither conflicting nor complementary. We could, however, perhaps find another kind of connection. As a student and co-worker of Gregory Bateson's (whose *Steps to an Ecology of Mind* is discussed in chapter 4), Watzlawick has done much in his scholarly work to open conventional psychology to the teachings of the Abhidhamma. This will be a particular enrichment for modern psychotherapy.

Psychotherapists and others who do psychological counseling will find a number of the Dhamma-strategy approaches quite useful in their professional work. No matter what school of psychotherapy you associate yourself with—in practice, semantic classification of principles and methodology is of secondary importance in any case—try to respect the ethical criteria in the context of which those approaches were developed. The ethics of Dhamma strategies is far more than a mere professional code. This ethics is elucidated in detail in connection with the themes of "autonomous self-regulation" (*sīla*) and "questioning trust" (*saddhā*).

UNUSUAL EXPERIENCES—UNUSUAL WORDS

The manifoldness of human experience includes also those experiences that cannot be grasped through the rationality of everyday language. Our civilization has developed a very intolerant attitude toward extraordinary experiences. What cannot be easily understood is relegated to the realms of mysticism, magic, and mental disorder. It is true that a few extraordinary experiences from the domains of the great established religions of Christianity, Judaism, Islam, Buddhism, and Hinduism are socially acceptable. Others, however, are opposed. Modern psychology seems to be the only generally acknowledged discipline which strives to relate to extraordinary experiences with impartiality and which makes a point of not intentionally opposing them.

In a meeting with Erich Fromm in Prague in 1966, I was made aware of an ancient system of psychology, the Abhidhamma, which was capable of relating to extraordinary experiences nondogmatically. As a result, I was finally able after long searching to develop a unified vocabulary simultaneously applicable to my personal approach to life, my psychotherapy and counseling practice, and my work as a university lecturer. This vocabulary makes use of the ancient paradigms of the Abhidhamma[2] as expressed in the language of modern psychology.—So much for my personal background and the origin of various words and expressions in the text that may strike the reader as unusual.

In the text, foreign words like *sīla* and *saddhā* are used only when it is desirable to emphasize that English equivalents, which sometimes may include a number of words, correspond to a single Abhidhamma technical term. Thus, for example, the Pali term *sīla* contains the meanings character, art, nature, self-determination, self-regulation, morality, ethics, training, restraint, and protection and is usually rendered in this book as "a reliable subjective basis." Also, foreign words that are generally current today, as for example *samādhi* (concentration), *karma* (spiritual causation), *mettā* (universal kindness), and *ahimsa* (nonviolence), will appear (in parentheses) only in connection with their English equivalents. By contrast, many Pali terms will frequently be given in parentheses; the reader should pay no attention to these on the first reading. These technical specialized terms are given in the text only for those readers who may wish to investigate further the psycho-algebra of the Abhidhamma, so that they themselves can develop Dhamma strategies. For such readers, an index of technical terms is provided at the back of the book for rapid orientation in this manual, so that its technical material can be easily used for purposes of meditation and everyday activity.

How-to Instructions?

When you have a cold, get an aspirin. When you have a court case, get a lawyer. When you have a feeling, . . . what then?

Many people find emotions or feelings confusing. In our civilization they are still regarded as something not entirely decent. For a long time, we tried to control emotions and feelings and hide them in order to protect ourselves from the insensitive and hostile actions of others. Today's psychoboom tries to make a profit on this fact, and there are many recipes for working with emotions on the market. To "have the feeling that . . ." has become a fashionable expression and is unfortunately also often used by persons in positions of power to give emotional emphasis to their desires. Someone who says "I have the feeling that" (often continuing "that you . . .") goes on to express speculative points of view about others that are perhaps laden with fears, hopes, and even aspersions. In such a case, what is such a "feeling" really composed of?

There are, however, also people who really feel. They do not "have" feelings. Rather they experience through their emotions the qualities of their own state of mind and can also feel other people's situations. They experience the constant transformation of the world and of their own attitudes through their feelings. They value emotions as indicators of well-being. And yet we human beings are equipped with more than just feelings. It is the purpose of this book, in a dialogue with you, the reader, to discover, develop, and enjoy the inner factors leading to well-being and happiness. Thus your personal experiences and reactions as you read it are very much sought after.

The Art
Of Happiness

It's Simple To Be Happy

Yes, we all want to be happy. In accordance with our personal makeup and our level of spiritual development, we enjoy either more or less the tensions, problems, and dangers that we require as challenge and stimulus in order to find our lives interesting. Only a very few of us would be happy were they to suddenly find themselves totally calm and relaxed in the peace of a supposed nirvana.

We all want to be happy, and therefore we look for ways and means of achieving this happiness. Ultimately, striving for happiness is at the root of all human endeavor. It is not only the various psychological techniques, meditation practices, doctrines of salvation, religions, and psychotherapies that focus on increasing well-being and happiness. Also all economic, political, scientific, and technical undertakings have some conception of well-being and happiness as their goal. Unfortunately, the managers of such undertakings all too often behave rather stupidly and shortsightedly with regard to the means for realizing this goal. Many labor under the delusive belief that they can achieve happiness by ruthlessly exploiting the environment, by annihilating neighboring enemies with atom bombs, by using pressure and terror techniques on friends and family members who are unwilling to go along with their ideas of "should" and "must." In proverbial terms, they saw off the branch they are sitting on, they foul their own nests—because they fail to see that they too are dependent on this environment, that they are part of the same ecosystem as their enemies. They are shortsighted, their vision and foresight is impaired, for they do not see that they are cutting away at their own flesh and that they are calling down future blows upon themselves by harassing those to whom they are bound (whether by friendship or hostility). *Stop!*

What do I notice inside?

. . . is it really only "them," the others? Am I not (perhaps only rarely and for a short time) one of them? Perhaps. It would not, however, be particularly clever to begin with my own faults, to make my own stupidity my starting point. What would happen if I were now to lay my hand on my heart and begin an autocritique, if I were to put my own shortcomings under a magnifying glass and fervidly examine everything I have ever done wrong? An approach like this would only create a further sense of burden in my awareness of myself; it would discourage me, would complicate future action, would fill my whole being with malaise.

What can we do that is smarter?

How can we proceed in an easier way? There is a strategy for solving this very problem. However, I do not intend to come up with a lot of instructions and advice and, as happens all too often, turn the reader into a mere passive recipient of would-be superior knowledge. Instead, I am offering a challenge that I hope the reader will take up as an adventure. We are not going to work ourselves up to better, easier, and more interesting levels by dint of hard work; however, we are going to apply our mental abilities fully . . . until gradually things start to get easier. Reading this book is meant to stimulate the creativity of the reader, arouse unusual thoughts, and promote personal growth.

INVITATION TO AN EXPERIMENT

Dear reader, I invite you to take part in an experiment in which certain elements of our strategy will immediately be put to the test. Ready? Here we go:

Start!

What do we already know? We have already spoken about the shortsightedness and stupidity of leaders who are incapable of seeing things in terms of larger contexts. Although they do have well-being and happiness as a goal, they behave in such a way as to cause suffering to their fellow beings and to call forth reactions that they themselves will also have to suffer from. Then came a "stop!" which signified a shift in our level of thinking. To express this in a more contemporary fashion, this "stop!" made it possible to switch from our usual, ordinary kind of data-processing program over to another program. This second program of the computer in our head also took into account the ego of the reader. The shift by no means represented merely a change of theme; more important, it was a transition to another way of seeing. It was an alteration of consciousness.

We frequently experience such changes, transitions, and alterations of consciousness, not only in dealing with our everyday lives, but also in reflecting on things and in reading a book. However, we usually do not perceive them clearly and thus are unable consciously to make use of them and take advantage of their inherent power. Switching from the thinking consciousness to the feeling or the body consciousness is the most suitable for practice purposes. As we read, our consciousness goes along with the written word, then suddenly we switch over to an emotional reaction: "But this stuff is really ridiculous!" Or "Yes, that's true; I've always said the same thing!" Or "Aha, that makes things easier, that's a great idea!"

Sometimes a program switch happens when we are distracted by a bodily sensation. Our posture while reading may begin to create an unpleasant sensation; as a result our consciousness is altered and—perhaps without noticing it—we stretch a leg or sit up and take a deep breath. Although the program necessary for changing posture ran without our noticing it, we were nonetheless aware that what we did suited our physical circumstances. Does this sound strange to you?

Stop! . . . and *Start!*

Back to our theme: Other people, particularly leaders, are short-sighted and incompetent. They do plan good things (at least for themselves), but in point of fact they create suffering for their fellow humans and, further down the road, for themselves as well. Hopelessly caught up in the spell of a program that they are unable to interrupt with an intentional "Stop!", they carry on with projects that are doomed to failure. The problem is compounded if they are in charge of a whole group of people who follow them blindly! However, it is bad enough when we ourselves, as our own boss, start a program and then follow it through without ever interrupting the program to test it and possibly change it.

You also are in charge of an undertaking, one that may seem unimportant to you at the moment, but that will have weighty consequences later on. Like you, I too put my plans into practice, influence other people, my environment, our future, and I, like you—like all of us—will reap the results of these actions . . .

Stop!

New program: *What do you notice now inside?*

Start!

Just make a mental note of it for the moment. We'll come back to this point later. *Stop!*

Back to our subject: *Start!* The question is, is my orientation based on what I do wrong, or do I focus my cognitive abilities and energies on what I can accomplish skillfully and successfully, what I do that produces happiness? Like you, I can choose whether to develop myself into an expert on my own awkwardness and stupidity and short-comings, or whether I want to work on what is beneficial for me and makes me happy. Like me, you can make your skills, abilities, and potential the top priority for the dynamics and contents of your program. The result of this approach will be an ability to develop our capabilities into intentionally operable strategies. And not only that: the sole fact that we are directing our interest toward our capabilities and competence means that our mental energy will be drawn in this direction and that our attention will be increasingly easier to focus on the positive side. Positive abilities, programs, and strategies will become more easily accessible.

The positive and beneficial effects of Dhamma strategies do arise from the competent action of a mature person; however, the basis of them is a more comprehensive transpersonal reality. In any case, it is enough to begin with if I just learn not to cause suffering to others and do the best I can for myself. Sacrifices (which are most often called for in connection with proselytizing and imposition of a so-called compassionate outlook) are not at all necessary. Thus I do what is good for me and cause no harm, because I am capable of seeing a larger whole and of directly experiencing my solidarity with all other beings. I also do not force anything on anyone, because I know that even the good, when it is imposed through pressure or violence, creates a nonproductive reaction. Admittedly, I feel affinity with the New Age movement on several levels; I feel attracted, stimulated. Instead of preaching, converting, and arguing, I simply live in a way that corresponds with the New Age approach and let my peers know that life is easier for me this way and more rewarding.

If I apply what is beneficial and happiness-producing for me in my relationships with others, I can expect that those people who are mature enough to personally realize the promise of the New Age will catch on. All those who are not too obtuse or too lost in the muddle of their old programming will feel some kind of inner affinity. This inner resonance will promote in these open people an interest in what is beneficial. They will feel a quite intimate personal inclination, anchored in their own experience of their bodies, to cooperate, or better, to "participate in letting it happen" through a gentle sympathetic resonance within themselves. Such a sympathetic resonance manifests in a harmonization of rhythms on various levels, from biorhythms and the rhythmization of one's daily routine and manner of working to cellular rhythms and those of the subtle body. The rhythm of the breath (in which, by the way, the most subtle alterations of mood and consciousness can be discerned), when it is observed without interfering with it, is the best key to recognition of natural, beneficial processes. When my consciousness and my personal understanding of myself are attuned to my breathing, then I am well centered and integrated, and my experience is anchored in the organic reality. If I also perceive the organic reality of other beings and the breathing rhythm of the whole ecosystem, then a "con-spiracy," a breathing-with-one-another, is produced. To put it in one sentence: Pursuing one's endeavors for one's own personal well-being while being considerate of other sentient beings is the pith of the New Age strategies.

That sounds quite simple, doesn't it? So simple that you, the reader, immediately have the thought: "I know all that already; that's what the New Age is about." "Good," I reply, "I thought as much, and I'm glad you are aware of it."

Has something come to an end? Have we finished with the subject? Let's forget about the New Age for a moment. This could all refer as well to yoga, psychoanalysis, communism, ecology, the peace movement, or Buddhism. In other words, our experiment has not yet been concluded and evaluated. Something further is announcing itself in our minds, an important aspect of the object of our investigation, our *style of experiencing*. We are, after all, critical, thinking people, who express their just reservations. Maybe after the thoughts "It's simple" and "I know that already" further considerations come up, such as: "Yes, but . . . it's too theoretical for me. I don't see how it can be put into practice." Or "It's great all right, but in everyday life it would never work; I can come up with lots of examples from my own experience." *Stop!*

It is worth interrupting such a defeatist program if we do not want depression, despondency, and faintheartedness to set in. How does this "Yes, but . . ." lead to defeatism and negativity? In fact, it need not always. Let us include in our experiment an analysis of this second train of thought that followed the "Yes, but."

As we know, there are people who suffer from yes-but sickness. We shall not deal with this type of case here, because such a sickness cannot be counteracted by a book, but requires psychotherapy. However, let us presume that the seed of defeatism does not lie so deep in us as this. Let us say that here the "Yes, but" is an expression proper to the holistic New Age style: New Age people make it a practice as often as possible to consider the other side of any proposition. This only becomes dangerous if we fall into the absolutist approach of "either-or," "always-never," or "utterly–not at all." Such absolutism is valid only on the level of words, pure verbal logic, but not on the level of real life. So much for this problem at this point; later we will look into it more thoroughly. Yet even now we can note that there exists in the old linguistic programs a danger that they may hold us prisoner in absolutely closed thought-worlds.

So what do we hear in this second train of thought? Let's fill in the missing words: "It (the whole thing altogether) is too theoretical for me (since there is only the either-or of theory and practice)." This will suffice as an example. In the present phase of our investigation and process of learning new strategies, it is actually more important to recognize another threat imposed by this doubt and nip it in the bud, or at least put a stop to the unhappiness programs that proliferate from such buds. I am talking about the danger I mentioned at the beginning of this chapter of concentrating too much on what we do unskillfully and wrong. This style of negative self-evaluation seems to have established itself quite firmly in our geographical latitudes.

More Than Thinking

Dhamma strategies provide means to counteract negativity. In this respect, they have their forerunners in the self-help books that teach the power of positive thinking. However, they go a step further in that they overcome the split in objective thought-content—they train us in a way of seeing that bridges the gap between the experiencing and acting subject on one side and objects on the other. The psychology that is the basis of the Dhamma strategies is a relativistic psychology of experience,[1] hitherto little known in the academic world, which distinguishes itself from conventional psychological theories much as the Einsteinian theory of relativity distinguishes itself from the old theories of physics.

The objective data of everyday life do not exist as things-in-themselves in the world, separate from subjective experience. For the student of the New Age, the living relationships between self as subject and various objective realities are directly experienceable as living meanings. This allows the New Age student a creative development and a direct restructuring of his or her world without the alienation from the world that comes from manipulating it, as by the application of conventional technologies. The shamanistic and magical techniques of peoples close to nature and the psychological training methods of the great non-European religions have always made use of principles arising from the psychological knowledge that we are now rediscovering in our New Age. They also make use of the power of positive thinking, which is more to the point here than positive will or the spiritual wish for the welfare of all beings.

The capability of restoring the relationship between subjective experiencing and subjectively assigned objective significations must be stabilized through impartiality and bodily anchoring in reality if we wish to avoid drifting off to dream worlds of psychotic illusion. This is an extremely important point, to which we will return again and again. For the moment, let us simply note that through bodily anchoring in reality, we attain impartiality, unbiasedness.

This impartiality is a counterbalance to subjective experiencing of events and their implications. It makes it possible for us to maintain a certain remove from events that are too heavily emotionally charged. We are thus able to analyze such events with equanimity, without denying or repressing the fact that they concern us personally. In impartiality we maintain our relationship with external physical realities, but we do not identify ourselves with them or lose ourselves in them. Relationship means staying connected with what is happening—not identifying with it but also not separating and becoming alienated from it. Although physical realities continue to exist without our input, they are not experienceable by us as things-in-themselves. What we experience and know directly are our relationships to things and events, our participation in them through sense perception and bodily action. This is what is meant by the expression "anchoring in reality" (*yathā-bhūta*)—things act upon our senses, and we affect them through our action. Both are real in an "actual" operational sense. *Stop!*

Have I merely been reading, or have I also actualized what I was reading in my own thinking? Did I lose myself in the discussion of impartiality? I could actually reread this paragraph on impartiality to check and see how much I can maintain remove without losing connectedness. *Resolve* and *start!*

There are also other realities. Our emotional reactions, our thought-constructions, fantasies, and visions also have their actuality and effect and are real in this sense. However, before getting deeper into these other realities, it is a good idea to be quite familiar with the physical, bodily reality in which our fellow human beings and other living things also directly participate. Our feelings, thoughts, and doubts are, after all, not real in an interpersonal sense so long as they have not been expressed and apprehended by others. That all sounds so obvious. How often, however, do we actually apply these bits of obvious wisdom by expressing our unclear feelings and doubts (or even just write them down for ourselves) so that we can make them real, restructure them, and develop what is good in them?

In our experiment, we made major strides in this direction. Can you think back, dear reader, and recall something that you noticed inside, something that came up in you as a result of the experiment? Did you sometimes react strongly and sometimes less strongly? Were you offended when I addressed you in such a direct, personal manner? When I even included you among the stupid and incompetent leaders? In case the answer is yes and in case you noticed your emotional reactions as such and distinguished them from ordinary thought-consciousness as you were reading, then you have already gotten something out of this experiment, something that you can take advantage of in cultivating your own New Age strategies. Did you also notice switching over to body-consciousness while reading? Or even the structure of a program that you used without thinking about it to alter your physical posture? In that case, you are extraordinarily perceptive and have remarkably wakeful mindfulness.

You must now have some sense of what promising prospects are opening to you personally. But before we evaluate our experiment, there is a further principle that should be discussed, one that makes it easier for us to choose and actualize happiness and places conflicting perspectives into a context of workability. This is the principle of mental nourishment and elimination.

When in the course of self-investigation (for example, in our experiment), we give too much attention to failure and doubt, then we are, not very cleverly, nourishing these areas. That way our spiritual capacities and energies reinforce the negative areas and place them in a position of too much importance. This harmful attention and uncontrolled energy supply lets failure and doubt grow into defeatism and skepticism. Swelling in this way, the areas of malaise oppress and stifle our positive areas of confidence and self-trust, our feelings of our own strength and potential. When we feed the negative and occupy ourselves unreasonably with mistakes, we are training our attention in an unwholesome direction and will soon become masters of gloom and ineptitude.

One can avoid the dangers of negativity by learning to recognize its seeds. Without becoming occupied with the contents and processes of negative chains of thoughts, we simply note them and label them with the appropriate name. In this way we neither get into them nor take them into ourselves. The bad, the inept, the unwholesome do not pass through our experiential space unnoticed; thus we are not defenseless and at their mercy. When our critical faculty threatens to become damaging—for example, when doubt changes to skepticism—then we simply label this menace as skepticism (*vicikicchā*) and provisorily drop it. What remains with us is information and knowledge that can protect us against similar menaces in the future.

Negativity's potential for effectiveness is eliminated as a waste product. When we eliminate what is misleading and unhealthy, it becomes a thing, a thing that we can regard impartially, even knowing that it comes from us. It is also important here how good our digestion is, how much energy and knowledge we can take in from processing unwholesome material without being poisoned. From the description of these procedures, it can be seen that the elimination and "thingification" of unwholesome material is not a matter of repression. On the contrary, just these processes remain a controlled source of the most difficult and disturbing facts for impartial data-processing in our biocomputer.

OUR BIOCOMPUTER

During the experiment we began to discover in a direct way that changeovers, programs, and other elements from which the strategies are built are supported by specific psychophysical structures (sense organs, memory, inner experiential space, feeling, thought, etc.). Using the metaphor of a biocomputer further as a means of gaining insight into our experience, we could say that the data processing of content by our software system (programs, changeovers from one program to another, etc.) takes place through the support of the hardware of our psychophysical organism. It does not require any scientific theories to distinguish between the external world and the inner world, between hardware and software, since we can perceive them directly.

The data to be processed come into consciousness first from memory, second from the inner experience of the body and the feelings connected with it, and third, the facts of the external world are conveyed to consciousness by the sense organs. As soon as the data are apprehended perceptually, they can be stored in memory or processed by thinking. Although we will later see that these are not the only possible epistemological processes, they are nevertheless the essential ones for our orientation in the world. They consist of software routines and structures in our biocomputer and they also support the programs and strategies with the help of which we structure our lives.[2]

The following diagrams illustrate these structures and routines.

With the help of Diagram 1 (page 10), we can easily imagine how the picture changes when dovetailed programs are fitted with repetitive loops and switches and selection of the various programs and switches between them takes place through a higher-level program.

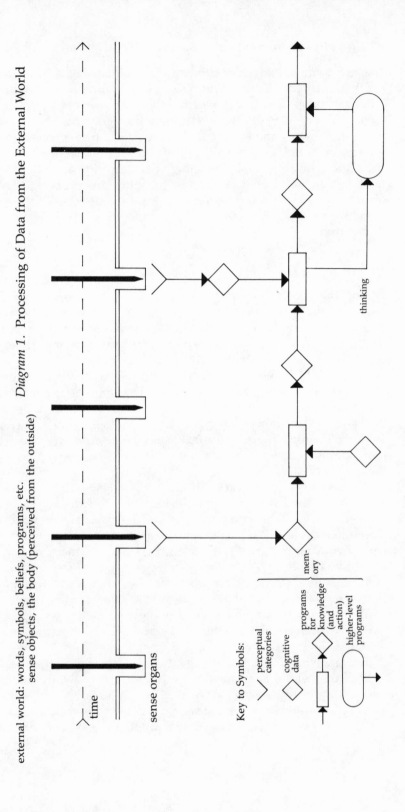

external world: words, symbols, beliefs, programs, etc.
sense objects, the body (perceived from the outside)

time

sense organs

Diagram 1. Processing of Data from the External World

thinking

memory

Key to Symbols:

perceptual categories

cognitive data

programs for knowledge (and action)

higher-level programs

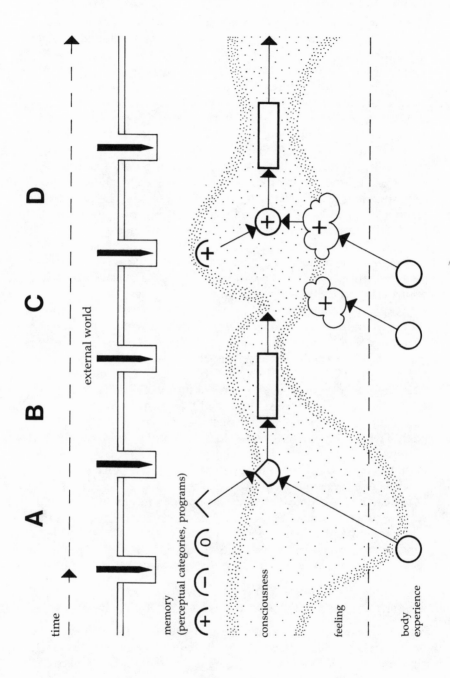

Diagram 2. Internal Cognition Anchored in Reality

The action and knowledge strategies include what is taken in perceptually and how it is taken in, what programs are applied and how and when they are halted or switched.

In Diagram 2 it is clear what happens when anchoring in reality through inner body experience and through feelings is the key factor in the epistemological process. Let us not forget that the anchoring in reality that is necessary for the effort toward liberation is characterized precisely by taking into account one's own body and feelings as sources and conveyors of knowledge.

Even in the kind of data processing that is purely related to our inner world (for example, meditation, dreams, visions, etc.), our bio-computer does not register all bodily processes and feelings. A certain amount of material is processed without being consciously apprehended. As can be seen from Diagram 2, consciousness moves back and forth between the areas of memory, thinking, feeling, and body experience. The mindfulness that notes changes of consciousness can be systematically trained so as eventually to be able to direct consciousness and the processing routines.[3]

In our experiment, even without training we have perhaps noticed certain alterations of consciousness, several of which are shown in Diagram 2. For example, during Time Period A, a physical posture is experienced internally and is apprehended perceptually via a memory category (for example, "leg fallen asleep" or "slouched sitting position"). Here, however, the pleasant or unpleasant feeling quality is not taken into account. At Time Point B, a program to plan and execute a change of posture starts, which if necessary also takes into account facts in the external world. At Time Point C, without any processing, a body-connected, pleasant feeling is experienced. In Time Period D, a similar pleasant feeling continues and is perceived as such in terms of a particular memory category.

You can now picture what further combinations are possible. In designing concrete strategies, knowledge gained by observation is definitely more helpful than theoretical constructions. Even knowledge concerning the structures and procedures of the software of our bio-computer is only of secondary help to our project.

ELEMENTS OF STRATEGIES THAT PROMOTE HAPPINESS

Now we are in a position to acquire an overview of the elements, programs, switches (changeovers), and principles that are used in the design and execution of Dhamma strategies. Clearly it is not necessary for you to limit yourself to the methods shown and made available in this chapter. If you feel like it, take a break now in your reading and recall the strategies, programs, and elements that you have already discovered and applied. Perhaps it would be helpful to make your own list of them. A "Start!" and a "Stop!" may help you to create the framework for it.

Start!

What elements of Dhamma strategies am I familiar with? What are their underlying principles?

Stop!

Now please take a look at the following list of main principles for personal Dhamma strategies that we have worked on so far:

1. Interrupting and halting complicated programs that we have learned from others but erroneously believe to be our own and apply uncritically.

2. Pausing and noticing what inner responses are occasioned by the command "Stop!" Are there among them any bits of personal wisdom that are anchored in the direct experience of our own organic relationship to ourselves and the world?

3. Learning to distinguish between various programs by noticing switches between them and the alterations of consciousness that accompany them (thought-consciousness, feeling, bodily experience).

4. Conscious resolve (will-building) to abandon programs that jeopardize happiness. This includes programs that, because of their complicated quality, are problem-prone, but refers especially to programmings based on outside suggestion, which senselessly bind our mental capability to preoccupation with our faults and failures and thus drains our energy.

5. Making sure experience is anchored in reality. Bodily reality is the surest basis for cognition and action. For persons who experience a situation or event in common, bodily reality provides the best basis for mutual understanding, because it is equally unequivocal for all. Bodily actualized and expressed inner realities make possible clear references and impartial judgments.

6. Elimination and "thingification" (in some cases, personification) of material that does not organically harmo-

nize with the development of well-being and happiness. Impartial, objective treatment of eliminated material through the application of suitable programs.
7. Development of strategies that are suited to the external situation, one's own state of mind, and consciously adopted goals. Using personal skills in the application of the six other principles.

How do the two lists compare? How many of the seven principles of Dhamma strategies were actually already part of your approach?

The principles and elements of Dhamma or New Age strategies determine how we manage personally in everyday life. To begin with, they represent mastery of concrete techniques that immediately increase our potential for happiness. After we have a certain amount of practice in carrying out the techniques, they lead to the elaboration of more complex patterns of action, which in turn culminate in a new way of living. This goes hand in hand with development and integration of the entire personality. Obviously, the Dhamma strategies also entail a thoroughgoing restructuring of one's life circumstances and bring about a whole new sense of meaning. Increasingly the contents of our thinking and experiencing changes in the direction of simplicity and beauty. All this is a result of an organic development, which takes time.

It is important to recall again and again that we have to be able to wait until things begin to get easier. Waiting and exercising patience do not, however, mean inactivity. When we are not specifically resting and enjoying the fruits of our good actions, the primary thing is to practice new skills. We should also continue to make our own decisions and purposefully change our inner conditions of life, that is, the contents of thought and experience. We can choose how we want to experience and what contents of our thinking we would like to cultivate and foster.

The contents of our doubting, pondering, fantasizing, and so on, even though they are less real, should not be ignored. We work in the right way with them when we keep them within a certain framework and relate to them as what they actually are—material that is only thought or imagined. As such, these contents can serve and help us, but we should not let ourselves be at their mercy. We must know the boundaries, and set them as well. Here the methods of stopping and pausing that we have already tried out can help us.

Naturally it is beneficial for us to reflect wisely about whether and to what extent we are making progress. Clear instructions and verbal transmission of strategic know-how are indispensable and also belong to the realm of thought and imagination. We test their effectiveness in action, by applying them experimentally. Thought experiments and doubting reflection are also helpful so long as they do not cross over into skepticism and negativity. Certainly no strategy works always and everywhere. It will be a particularly interesting and rewarding task during your reading of this book to find out which of your personal strategies can be applied successfully when and how, and which, on the other hand, have to be changed, and when and how.

PROSPECTS

Doubtless many of the thoughts you encounter as you read this book will seem quite familiar. Often you will pause and say to yourself that you have had the same or similar thoughts and wanted to act on them. Doubtless you will also read much that does not immediately make sense to you. Please persevere with such passages. If you read them a second or even a third time, they will no longer be the same! Repetition increases the joy of making a breakthrough.

For many who have tried to apply the seven principles of the Dhamma strategies, they have meant adventure, challenge, and joy. For many of those who have worked with the strategies, numerous questions and problems concerning mental energies, rhythms, and abilities have become clear for the first time. Probably in reading and pausing, a number of valuable or problematic ideas have occurred to you that call for proper investigation. There is now greater openness with regard to some things, and other things have become less clear: this is part of the dynamics of the spiritual adventure.

It is the purpose of the next chapter to provide further guidelines to enable you gradually to acquire a new, more comprehensive, and better thought-out overview. If you succeed in making this view your own in a completely organic way by understanding it in terms of your own experience—that is, if you develop this view out of your own anchoring in reality—then you will become increasingly able to evaluate critically all the other personal viewpoints that the authors of New Age books have reached through their efforts.

It would be good if during your further reading of this book, as well as in everyday-life situations, you could work on the exercise of learning to distinguish thought-consciousness, body-consciousness, and consciousness characterized by feeling and also to notice the transitions and changeovers from one to another. Mastery of this skill will, among other things, make you better able to manage your inner life and able to rely ever more on your personal judgment and emotional reactions. The host of other people's opinions will become less important. You will become more composed and see more clearly. You yourself will note how, as a result of the simplification arising from this mastery, your whole life will become simpler and happier.

New Age Politics:
Personally Experienced?

It's easy to be happy. Happiness and joy can only be lived, not theoretically thought out or technically produced. The more complicated the living situations we create and the more many-faceted and intricate our worldview becomes, that much more frequently do obstacles to welfare and happiness arise. True happiness requires clarity. Clarity is not achieved by shutting one's eyes to everything that runs counter to happiness, contentment, and well-being. Thus there is an essential strategy that consists of dealing properly and skillfully with the facts of life that are not conducive to well-being.

Before we look the unwholesome facts of life in the eye and seek out possibilities for dealing with them skillfully, we have to create a *reliable subjective basis* and make some useful basic distinctions. What is most reliable here is something that is not subject to the power of others and that no violence can take away from us. Neither political ideologies, nor doctrines of salvation, nor dogmas are suitable as starting points for New Age strategies. No belief, no submission to an authority can bring about security. What is most reliable is something available to us in all circumstances—our own capabilities, our own potential and skills. We possess capabilities in relation to various aspects of life, and not all of them are conducive to a reliable subjective basis (designated by the technical term *sīla*) for our strategies of liberation. Here I can say no more without getting ahead of my exposition, because the aim of this chapter is a deeper understanding in the technical sense of this kind of reliable subjective basis.

Whoever wishes to acquire a clear overview in order to be able to cultivate what is essential in life and effectively counteract the unwholesome side of it must learn to make unequivocal distinctions. For this purpose, we will separate objectively cognizable obstacles from those obstacles that are conditioned by the particular nature of our way of experiencing, that is, by our subjective attitude toward the world and ourselves. The last kind is hard to grasp and even harder to change. We will come to grips with obstacles of this type again and again from different angles in the next chapters. External dangers and obstacles, and even some in our inner world, are objectively cognizable once they have been subjectively experienced. The obstacles to a liberated attitude toward ourselves and the world are subjectively experienceable, but they are only objectively cognizable to a person who is familiar from his own experience with moments of overcoming them. Such liberated moments of experience provide us with a subjective basis for making wholesome distinctions and choices.

Some useful distinctions related to the basis for Dhamma strategies are already familiar to us. They are empirical and free from all theory, because they are based on clear, direct experience. Most important are distinctions according to the fourfold key that we became acquainted with through our experiment in chapter 1: body-experience, feeling, state of mind, and mental contents. These four objects for mindfulness (*satipatthāna*) become objectively cognizable in observing our inner world, even though they initially represent our subjective responses to external objects. Our experience does not consist solely of reactions; it is determined only partly by our situation in the external world. What is most deeply our own increasingly determines our way of experiencing when we begin to advance on the Dhamma path to liberation. Our own knowledge, made certain through direct experience, is what makes it possible for us to make distinctions and choices and to find our anchor in what is wholesome and conducive to happiness. This is a fundamental aspect of *sīla*, the reliable subjective basis, an aspect to which we will return again and again.

We find the reliable subjective basis in everyday life by pausing and becoming aware of our own competence. Through recalling ourselves, we become newly aware that we have the ability to make a "Stop!"—which in turn makes anchoring in bodily reality possible. In addition, in the face of all the real suffering that exists in the world, we flee neither into the gloomy forebodings of a pessimistic worldview nor into the optimistic fantasies of science and religion. Through our anchoring in reality and our ability to make distinctions, we make present in our mind the direct knowledge that both pessimism and optimism are dangerously one-sided ideologies that would distort our perception.

Optimistic self-encouragement can be helpful in times of crisis. As an overall attitude toward life, however, optimism is harmful. People who are not trained in New Age strategies, and who adopt a naive faith in happiness merely in reaction to the "no-future" outlook that has been so widespread lately, inadvertently reduce the New Age movement to cheap optimism. An optimist who simply ignores bad things becomes increasingly alienated from reality, because he or she is not capable of perceiving problems and dealing with them properly. The optimist is like a person going barefoot through the countryside, delighting in its beauties but heedless of the sharp stones and thistles underfoot.

The Facts of Suffering and Transcendence

Adversity, pain, distress, and malaise are familiar to all of us. And whoever is honest and strong enough to accept them is also familiar with feelings of profound grief, perhaps also lengthy periods of depression. These are natural reactions of the psychophysical organism to outer and inner situations of conflict. It would be futile to label them as good or evil. Evil and good, or better put, the unskillful and unwholesome and the skillful and wholesome, are actually a matter of how we *deal* with the facts of life. Perceiving these facts without value judgments does not, however, mean that we fail to pay attention to whether painful facts and the unwholesome way of dealing with them increase or decrease at certain times. And how is it right now? How do you perceive suffering in your immediate environment and in the world as a whole? To what extent do you experience it as directly touching you personally, subjectively? (This is perhaps a suitable moment to stop once again, to pause and consider these questions internally.)

Even fanatical optimists who succeed in pushing negativity out of their experience for long periods of time cannot deny the fact that our times are mainly characterized by a steady increase of aggression and suffering. Anyone can see that behind the aggression that creates so much pain in the world most often lies the totally ruthless greed of a few power possessors, which drives them avidly to seek even more power and, in their hate-filled delusion, to destroy whatever seems to stand in their way.

Pain, affliction, distress, adversity, frustration, sorrow, misery, wretchedness, and despair are not just empty words. Everyone is familiar with the nonverbal reality of suffering that these words indicate. So: suffering, entanglement, greed, and aggression in the external world; suffering, confusion, desire, and hate in the inner world. Beyond those, there is the suffering inherent in an unliberated way of experiencing, which also causes negativity and discontent even at times when we are temporarily not beset by problems from the outer world and in the inner world everything seems harmonious. Again and again there is suffering. In the terminology of the Abhidhamma, the experience of suffering is called *dukkha*. What should we do about it?

The outer-world problems that cause suffering are merely palliated by economic, juristic, and political measures based on scientific and social-scientific knowledge. Of course, external facts do have their effect on our inner world—and vice versa. The inner world can also be scientifically, objectively investigated up to a certain point. That is exactly what is done by the conventional psychology of Western universities. How valuable such investigations are is a question all by itself. There have been very few attempts on the part of academic psychology to develop an understanding of the nature of the different ways of experiencing that correspond to the various stages of spiritual development. Following the model of the various—meanwhile outdated—natural sciences, psychology is still attempting to attain the impossible ideal of scientific freedom from valuation; this, however, has simply ended up in a loss of value.

On the other hand, several new directions in research, which have largely been inspired by the psychological knowledge of non-Western cultures and are making a place for themselves in American universities under the name "transpersonal psychology," [1] claim to be investigating phenomena connected with the higher stages of spiritual development and providing guidance for actualizing such development. There is talk of peak experiences, self-realization, ultimate meaning, cosmic awareness, and spiritual realms. Semantically, however, the exponents of these schools stay close to the terminology of the old psychology, and they emphasize the extraordinariness of the themes under study. Can we hope for a solution from transpersonal psychology? It would be naive to expect that all those who have attached themselves to the transpersonal psychology industry will thereby become spiritually advanced on the spot and put aside their old prejudices and the programming that has been hammered into them by their conventional training. On the other hand, we often forget that some of the founders of experimental psychology and behaviorism, fields that today are so conservative and scientifically limited, were seriously concerned with spiritual questions. For example, Wilhelm Wundt, the father of experimental psychology, was thoroughly devoted to transcultural questions related to spirituality. Gustav Fechner, who pioneered physiological psychology and psychophysics, described his mystical experiences in detail (his work *Das Büchlein vom Leben nach dem Tode* appeared as early as 1836). No psychology student today learns about these facts. Academic lectures pay tribute to the two scientists with strong emphasis on their exact scientific methodology.

The pioneers of psychoanalysis were as open to the transpersonal as some contemporary psychoanalysts are. Freud himself grappled repeatedly with mystical phenomena, and he taught his method of meditation to several of his personal students.[2] One student in particular, C. G. Jung, devoted himself to this area; in the United States, where Jung is presently being rediscovered, he is celebrated as one of the most important forerunners of transpersonal psychotherapy.

It is remarkable that European academic circles as well as the broader European public have historically tended to begin to appreciate their foremost scientists only after those figures have been discovered in America. This is also true of various effective psychotherapies and self-realization techniques that are currently winning adherents to the New Age. The American professor of anthropology Agehnananda Bharati,[3] an Austrian who lived many years as a monk in India and who is considered an expert on social questions related to modern spirituality, has referred to this phenomenon as the "pizza effect." Pizza was for a long time an ordinary peasant food, ignored, even despised, by better circles in Italy. But in America it received an up-market restyling at the hands of parvenu Italian immigrants as a symbol of their national origin. It was then discovered by the entire world, acquired a new value, and was imported back into Italy. Of course this phenomenon functions with regard to many other elements of culture. How often does each of us experience the pizza effect on a personal level? How often does somebody else have to discover and use good things that we have always used and are an essential part of our inner world before we ourselves can affirm them as valuable? (*Stop . . .*)

From America, Europeans heard the well-moderated voice of Erich Fromm, whose work is perhaps the most important of all for the New Age. Fromm not only brought a new outlook, but also earnestly confronted the outer and inner terror of our times. With the help of the conventional disciplines, he analyzed the function of social and psychological pathologies in his *Anatomy of Human Destructiveness*, a book of great importance for the New Age. Fromm's greatest contribution was that he not only provided an analysis of our existing society and the basis for a new one, but beyond that showed us applicable means and methods for achieving a better life. Since his books are still widely read, we need not discuss them further here. For the development of New Age strategies, *Anatomy of Human Destructiveness* only interests us in broad outline, insofar as it is helpful for our psychological training on the path of liberation. Here I would primarily like to remind the serious reader of Fromm's repeated suggestions concerning pos-

sible ways of overcoming suffering, suggestions that are quite appli-
cable in our culture. Fromm has constantly called our attention to *The
Heart of Buddhist Meditation* by Nyanaponika Thera, a German living in
Sri Lanka who is well known in the English-speaking world.[4]

Psychologists and those communicating Asian methods of mind
training are not the only ones who have made practical methods available to us. Also very valuable for New Age strategies is the work of
the epistemologist Gregory Bateson. Together with his colleagues
from the so-called Palo Alto School, Bateson elaborated knowledge acquired through his research into "primitive" cultures, the world of the
mentally ill, and the scientific process, into a practical methodology.
The exposure of "double-bind" interactions and the uncovering of
state-specific skills and paradoxical interventions, described particularly in the works of Paul Watzlawick (an Austrian living in California),
are some of the fruits of the labors of the Palo Alto School. This group of
scholars also helped to demystify schizophrenia.

Among the ethnologists, Carlos Castaneda, with his fascinating
style of presentation, is surely a foremost figure. His works, which are
based on the liberational psychological knowledge of the North American Indians, enjoy a worldwide audience because of their literary
beauty. The main principles of the teaching transmitted by Castaneda,
as he recently explained them to a friend of mine and as they are most
clearly presented in *The Fire from Within*, coincide with the principles
of the Abhidhamma. That a connection between the findings of the
ethnologists and those of modern psychology is possible has been
shown by Claudio Naranjo and Robert Ornstein in *On the Psychology
of Meditation*.[5] Naranjo, a psychoanalyst and Gestalt therapist who
was originally inspired by Sufism, even makes reference to the four
foundations of mindfulness, a central teaching of the Abhidhamma, at
the end of his book on medical pharmacotherapy, *The Healing Journey*.

A Common Denominator: Abhidhamma

A growing number of transpersonal psychologists now refer in their
work to the paradigms of the Abhidhamma. These paradigms have
transcultural validity and are thus also present in non-Buddhist systems of knowledge. The Abhidhamma concept of pathology as *kilesa*
or *klesha* was adopted by C. G. Jung.[6] And it is self-evident that Fritz
Perls and Karlfried Graf Dürckheim, like all who draw the inspiration
for their psychotherapeutic approach from Zen Buddhism, have built
on the principles of the Abhidhamma. The voluminous manual of the
Chinese and Japanese Zen masters, the *Gedatsu do ron*, which teaches

the Abhidhamma, is available in English translation under the title *The Path of Freedom*. The still more detailed manual of the South Asian *theras*, the *Visuddhi Magga*, which corresponds to the *Gedatso do ron* almost exactly, is also available in English under the title *The Path of Purification* (Berkeley: Shambhala, 1976).

In a handbook of the methods of modern psychology edited by Hilarion Petzold in 1984,[7] the existential analyst Ales Wotruba calls attention to the fact that at the time of the writing of the Christian Gospels at the end of the first century, Abhidhamma writings from Sri Lanka were available in Rome; he also points out that the pre-Christian Germans and Slavs, as archaeological finds have shown, were familiar not only with the use of silk and spices but also with material from the Buddhist teachings of China and India. Wotruba also mentions an introduction to the study of the Abhidhamma that was extremely popular in China and India, written in the form of a dialogue between the Greek King Menander and a teacher of the Abhidhamma, and which appeared in English translation under the title *Questions of King Milinda*.

The American psychology textbook *Theories of Personality* by C. S. Hall and G. Lindzey[8] refers to the Abhidhamma as the prototype of Asian psychology altogether. The Abhidhamma definitively influenced the teachings of the Islamic Sufi masters, whose traditions transmit anecdotes and instructions of the Abhidhamma school that date back twenty-five hundred years. An example is the Sufi teaching story about the blind men who give entirely different descriptions of an elephant after having touched different parts of it. A fairly exact rendering of a teaching used by Abhidhammikas from the *Udāna* of the Buddhist canon, this teaching story is especially important for students of New Age strategies. We will discuss it in detail in chapter 8 under the heading "The Path of Seeing and the Path of Power."

When we consider that Sufism arose in exactly the same geographical areas that were previously dominated by Buddhism, the fact that the two religious traditions have things in common becomes easily understandable. It is also clear how it came about that the Abhidhamma is contained in the teachings of yoga. Whatever traditions of spiritual training survived the Islamic conquest of India in the eleventh century were called "yoga." Everything non-Islamic that continued to be practiced beyond the Indus River—whether Brahmanic, Buddhist, or from shamanistic local cults—was designated by the Arabic word *hindu*. Thus the English term *Hinduism* arose and was adopted also by some of the anglicized Indians. Not so easy to understand, on the other hand, is the almost sensational report of the ethnologist Frank Waters,[9] who is considered one of the foremost experts on the cultures of the American Indians and especially the Hopis. Waters has shown that some of the paradigms of Hopi wisdom are identical with material from the Chinese *I Ching* and the Tibetan Abhidharma. These facts in turn lend plausibility to the observation that even Carlos Castaneda teaches the Abhidhamma in his works.

The Abhidhamma is only indirectly concerned with the contents of thought and with cultural ideas. Its subject matter has more to do with ways of experiencing and psychological laws. For that reason, one can no more call the Abhidhamma Asian or Buddhist than one can call the relativity theory of physics or psychoanalysis Jewish, even though their creators were Jewish.

MYTHS, STORIES, SCIENCES

It is interesting that not only the laws of thought processes but also certain thought contents exhibit transcultural characteristics. All cultures, those of primitive peoples as well as of highly developed civilizations, create myths that are concerned with certain basic questions of human existence. There is much in common from culture to culture in these mythical perceptions of basic themes, as we know from the work of Mircea Eliade or Joseph Campbell. In his book *Hero with a Thousand Faces*, Campbell attempts to unify all transculturally relevant mythical themes into a single whole valid for the spiritual development of all men. This evolutionary whole, which he calls the "monomythos," is made up of encounters with various beings under changing circumstances.

In all myths, psychic and cosmic forces and beings are personified, and it is also in this way that they come to us in dreams, visions, and inspired works of art. Calling them archetypes, Jung investigated such phenomena psychologically and thereby made their existence acceptable to science. Sensitive people draw on these personified psychic and cosmic forces as sources of energy and information. To the extent that these personifications exhibit a higher level of consciousness, we regard communication with them as revelation. Such revelations play an important role, not only in Christianity and for Asian seers and Native American shamans, but also in the contemporary history of the New Age. Thus, for example, the visionaries Sir George Trevelyan and David Spangler, to mention only the best known, conceived their tireless work for the social realization of the New Age on the basis of such revelations. (In the case of other representatives of New Age vision, the source of their inspiration is less clear.)

It would lead away from our subject matter to pursue these histori-cal and cultural considerations any further, although in doing so we are really also working with the facts of our inner world. But even facts of the inner world, so soon as they are expressed, come to be-long strictly speaking to the facts of the outer world. They then con-tinue to interest us only to the extent that, as realities of our cultural environment and contents of our thinking, they influence the way we live. For our personal experience and realization of the New Age, it is techniques and methods that are of primary value, since they are helpful here and now for our strategies. Stories and myths, especially unusual and exotic ones, are profitable only when reflection on them makes us aware of hitherto unnoticed relationships. An overdose of knowledge of other times and other peoples distracts us from our own lives and experience and burdens our minds with extraneous material. As in nourishing the body, however, it is sometimes useful for our minds to take in extra ballast—for example, material from the fields of history or ethnography. Here, too (depending on one's di-gestive capacities), it is the less exotic materials that are most easily assimilated.

A great many good books are currently available that consider the spiritual history of our culture from the point of view of the New Age. An overview of developments over the last ten years is provided by *Unfinished Animal* by Theodore Roszak, an American historian of Hungarian origin, who was perhaps the first to see potential for the New Age in America's social problems of the sixties. Most impor-tant among popular-scientific publications is still *Le Matin des Magi-ciens* (The Dawn of the Magicians), a bestseller by Louis Pauwels, a French journalist, and Jacques Bergier, a leading chemist. This book became a milestone on the road to the New Age for a great many readers. Since by the sixties receptivity for these new ideas had passed beyond a certain critical threshold—which was not yet the case at the time of the publication of H. G. Wells's *The Open Conspir-acy*—Pauwels and Bergier's work has continued to exercise a major influence.

An impending "breakthrough into the new consciousness on the part of many people" is the central theme of Marilyn Ferguson, whose book *The Aquarian Conspiracy* provides numerous examples of social and personal transformation. Ferguson especially emphasizes the im-portance of bodily processes and interpersonal relationships and in this way creates a more favorable basis for the adoption of New Age strategies, which after all are primarily anchored in these two areas.

Many New Age books offer no more than food for thought—and that mainly for people who are merely looking for word games and feel no real desire to develop greater competence in the way they act and live. Since you, dear reader, have been made invulnerable to verbalism by the insight that what is complicated and remote from reality does not promote happiness, you are looking for practical pathways into the New Age. For that reason, you are not likely to find satisfaction in dilettantish anthologies or collections of speculative essays on "evolving cosmic consciousness" and other eclectic catchphrases of armchair psychology. In fact, some of the New Age books are no more than museums of ideas from East and West clumped together on the basis of conceptual similarity.

Equally questionable are those scholarly and scientific surveys that merely investigate propositions about propositions without giving consideration to the concrete methods that the primary propositions were based on in the first place. So-called interdisciplinary surveys, for the most part, do not concern themselves in the least with reality, but instead amass lists of propositions that various specialists, restricted by their individual disciplines, have subjectively worked up. Here we see the arrogant approach of representatives of the old established academic disciplines, which mainly consists in marketing as "objective truths" subjective statements by scientists concerning objective data. Those who belong to the science industry are generally capable neither of perceiving these facts nor of entirely forgetting them. The usual "solution" is to hide the scientist's subject behind various measuring devices. Complicated methodological and statistical procedures then draw attention away from reality and into the enchantment of pseudoexact statements comprising the "magic" of scientific quantification. There have always been scientists who have been aware of this situation, and some have also proposed epistemological methods that did not simply pass over their subject of study. Albert Einstein and Werner Heisenberg did this, for example, in the natural sciences. In the humanities and the social sciences the problem is somewhat more difficult, as we shall see.

The know-how embedded in psychotherapies and methods of spiritual development is only now beginning to be shaped into New Age strategies and thereby to become available to the public. Up to this point it has been mainly the convergence of the natural sciences and spiritual views of the world that has interested New Age–directed people. It is often forgotten that the teachings of the most ingenious scientists and the most influential founders of religions are very simple to apply practically (think, for example, of the Einsteinian relativity equations or the Four Noble Truths of Buddha). By contrast, pseudoprophets in either field attempt to exploit human gullibility by

marketing mysterious and complicated doctrines. The interdisciplin-
arily oriented work of Fritjof Capra,[10] who has attempted to organize
our thinking around a new scientific picture of the world, is a rare
exception in that it does not make the new outlook unnecessarily
complicated.

Although it is not my intention here to set up a debate with New
Age science, one related question cannot be set aside: What importance does scientific knowledge actually have for the New Age? As
Capra has shown us, our worldview and the thoughts we hold influence our perception and thus our action, not only on a psychological
level, but also, so to speak, on a parapsychological level. C. G. Jung,
together with the physicist Wolfgang Pauli, developed a theory of
synchronicity; Rupert Sheldrake developed a theory of morpho-
genetic fields. These theories make it possible for us to take a rational
approach to the fact that thoughts and events that are neither causally
nor spatially connected can mutually influence each other and simultaneously manifest in different places.

SELF-REALIZATION*

A New Age "conspirator" by no means relies on the notion that enlightenment or elevation of consciousness will automatically take
place just because these phenomena and methods related to them
exist in the universe. *Enlightenment Doesn't Care How You Attain It* is
the title of a humorous little book in German,[11] and although this
statement is in some sense accurate, it is also true that a person has to
do something in order to attain enlightenment, or rather, in order to
permit it to take place. Perhaps people who are not qualified to train
in Dhamma strategies aimed at liberational elevation of consciousness
can also become enlightened. However, those who fritter away their
mental capabilities on mere word games are hardly likely to become
enlightened, however scientific such games may be. Investment of
psychological energy in fantasies and visions and in filling the mind
with randomly accumulated knowledge leads to neither enlightenment nor liberation.

It is a common misconception that the New Age can be automatically realized through a change in thinking, through imaginative
ideas about new ways of looking at the world. Thought experiments,

---

*This is a translation of *Eigen-Verwirklichung*, which actually means "own-
realization," used by the author to convey the sense of "do-it-yourself."—
Trans.

meditation, fantasizing, wishful thinking, and visions lead neither to better understanding among people nor to harmonization of the state of affairs in the external world. For those ends, concrete, operable strategies are necessary. Fantasizing is necessary for the anticipation of goals, and without proper meditation, training the mind for liberation is impossible—but neither is enough. For a happy life, cultivation of concrete action and a suitable lifestyle are indispensable. Dependency on imaginary worlds of science, magic, and occultism and concomitant wishful thinking and invocation of higher intelligences bring about alienation from reality, a weakening of the ability to distinguish between different realities, and paralysis of the power of decision. We know how important these latter mental powers are for liberation. Someone who neglects them only seemingly participates in the New Age.

The following simile may serve to illustrate the state of affairs described above. Imagine a child who lives in difficult external circumstances, who has no systematic pedagogical guidance, but gets his "education" from television programs, the random consumption of which represents the sole joy of his sad existence. The child switches channels according to whim, but particularly enjoys entertainment programs. Out of these scraps he puts together a view of the world. This worldview must correspond to the popular view, otherwise the child will not be popular with his friends. In this simile, the creators of the television programs and the television station stand for the higher intelligences and prophets of the New Age; the child stands for a person who is open to the New Age, one who has some real sense of the situation in the world. Unfortunately, the child cannot tell which images come from whom, nor can it consistently use the broadcasts for its long-term benefit. If the broadcasts do not encounter a reliable subjective basis (as presented at the beginning of this chapter), or if they get jumbled up as a result of continuous switching from one to the other, then even though the messages are received they may bring about a condition bordering on psychosis. Even tremendous consideration on the part of the broadcaster does not help this situation. This simile could be taken even further. Let me restrict myself, however, to pointing out several *major misconceptions of the New Age movement*, which are relatively easy to remove if we are not relating with our own mental capabilities ignorantly, as the child was. First, it is not enough for new philosophical ideas and images of the world to be devised and broadcast; second, undiscriminating reception leads to no more than seeming participation; third, philosophical ideas are still by no means instructions for action; and fourth, even models and instructions for action increase happiness and promote liberation only when enacted resolutely, with subjective purposiveness, in the context of our own personally devised strategies.

Someone who relates so foolishly to his or her mind's potential as merely to await grace or help from the outside is bound to fall victim to fatalism, which in turn—insofar as it involves any intelligent thought at all—is connected with a kind of deterministic worldview that precisely characterizes the outmoded conventional sciences. Convinced that the future can be shaped but that it will be shaped by others—computers or supernatural beings—these fatalists live in scientific or religious thought-castles, into which they have fled from reality. They live not in what is, but rather in some vision of the future, which they eagerly seek to realize through so-called pragmatic views that ignore or distort truth and reality.

If we wish to reduce our own and others' suffering, then we must constantly keep in mind the boundary between thought-conceived goals (possible contents of the inner world) on the one hand, and the present, interpersonally experienceable reality of the outer world on the other. Only if we do this will our daily life be a satisfying journey on the razor's edge, in which we fall neither into the abyss of short-sighted materialistic pragmatism nor into that of optimistic fatalistic fantasies.

If science is neither our hobby nor our bread and butter, then scientific knowledge is personally useful only to the extent that we can apply it directly to solving the concrete problems of our lives. Historical knowledge and political awareness can create compassionate understanding and tolerant communication—toward both victims and perpetrators. Such a balanced attitude enables us, while perceiving the suffering of the world, to neither fall into apathy nor work up useless agitation. Equanimity preserves our competence, permitting us to contribute optimally to the solution of personal and social problems wherever possible. Precise perception of injustices and of senseless panic measures and all the suffering that results from them incites us to engage personally wherever we think our effort is most likely to have an effect. Political and social action can also provide practice situations for New Age strategies, if we do not let mindfulness and prudence turn into rabid activism.

Political, juridical, and economic measures do no more than palliate the suffering of the external world; they do not eliminate its causes. We can only tackle suffering-producing ignorance, aggression, and greed in our fellows after we have coped with our own ignorance (*avijjā, moha*), aggression, and greed. In short, putting our own inner world in order is a prerequisite for successful and effective action in the outer world. Though one individual's contribution is relatively slight, our action does have an effect in shaping history. The overall world situation is a framework we cannot escape. We cannot pretend that the facts of history do not exist. The breakthrough into the New Age cannot be an anonymous historical event—we have to bring it about personally. Our happiness is dependent on our own personal history, and a characteristic of the true New Age is that personal uniqueness does not get lost in the general flow of history. The general flow of history only creates the external context.

Dangers of Anomy Overcome by Sīla

The New Age path to liberation requires each one of us first to deal competently with the outside world; second, to come to grips with our inner world; and third, to practice a liberated lifestyle. Unfortunately, in our day and age, meaningful action in the outside world is becoming harder and harder. There is a lack of reliable reference points for action and for interpersonal relations, because traditional morality, based on obedience, is dissolving, and a new morality is just in the process of being produced. Consumption, business, and industrial production is governed by an all-out push for growth and by ruthless competition. Even in private life the majority of people submit to this dominant force. Only a few people with spiritual interests manage to stand outside it, at least part of the time. How many such people do you yourself know?

In persons and groups not capable of controlling their activity and of consciously choosing among motivations, the roots of suffering proliferate. Thus persons, groups, or even whole civilizations come to be at the mercy of accidental impulses and suffer the unwholesome effects of chaotic trains of events. Concerned social scientists explain this kind of state as social depression based on anomy, that is, a slackening or default of social and moral ideals, ethics, and spiritual values. Ethical responsibility is shifted off onto others, particularly onto the impersonal institutions of government and the law. It is forgotten that ultimately all institutions are composed of individuals. People who are politically and socially engaged are for the most part not familiar with Dhamma strategies. Thus they act without benefit of an overall view and get lost in illusory solutions to problems. Involvement in such illusory solutions usually comes about through one-sided implementation of basically well-intentioned approaches to action, which belong to one of the following three types:

The first is uncompromisingly strict stigmatization and suppression of external causes considered "bad." Behind this approach is the unillumined conviction that if only everything on the outside were in order, then everybody would be inwardly happy. This kind of approach reaches its worst point when, as a result of partial success, its perpetrator begins to believe he or she has hit on the one right way of doing things. (In fact, something like this has taken place on a vast scale with our entire civilization; we have become obsessed with dominating and exploiting nature through technology, to the point where we are now facing catastrophic results.) On the interpersonal level, campaigns to implement this type of illusory solution can take either a pseudorevolutionary, militant form or else petrify into authoritarian, conservative rigidity.

Extremists on the Left as well as the Right have a great deal of delusion and hate-filled intolerance in common. These two political orientations are also expressions of the personal psychological poverty of their adherents, who are incapable of openness and independent self-determination. They are negatively dependent upon the hostile images through whose negation they define their own identities. They are positively dependent on the authority of a leader or an inviolable ideology. These same mechanisms are also present in many "normal persons." Although they may seem at first glance to be less drastic and less obvious, they do not cause less suffering. We have only to think of the unanimity with which, for example, members of social fringe groups are stigmatized and mistreated. Unfortunately such degenerate behavior is to be found not only in the public at large but also in certain sectarian groups who like to make use of the New Age label in presenting themselves.

The second type of illusory solution arises from a passive stance on the part of people in positions of responsibility. Lack of interest and minimalism, fear of being exposed, perhaps also a myopic kind of pacifism, inhibit the execution of necessary measures. The ongoing cover-up of this kind of indifference is handled variously. Some shift the responsibility onto institutions and impersonal regulations, ordinances, and laws. In so doing, they increasingly reduce flexibility with regard to liberational possibilities, both for themselves and others. This is even praised as "loyalty." Others, whether well-known politicians or ordinary citizens of the Silent Majority, let themselves be pacified by a sense of the prevailing pseudofreedom and are seduced into a laissez-faire approach. When circumstances then become increasingly unsatisfactory, they interpret this as proof that it is futile to attempt to intervene in such complicated situations. People believe that everything will somehow work out after a while or that somehow someone will come along and solve the problems. If things get really bad, people hope for the advent of a savior—perhaps an impersonal one in the form of computer technology, or an actual messiah, or a powerful politician who will create order. One can also just fatalistically wait for retirement. Waiting is characteristic of this particular type of illusory solution. Indeed, it is a well-known fact that this kind of hoping for solutions or salvation takes place not only in the world of public bureaucracy but also in the realm of religion.

Individuals and groups who are interested in the New Age are particularly susceptible to the third type of illusory solution. This is escape into the magical or the mystical, or into a paradisiacal ideal world of the future, far from the suffering-ridden reality of here and now. The principles of the Dhamma strategies synopsized on page 13, to whose concrete, everyday application this entire book is devoted, protect us from drifting off into such an illusory solution. These principles are particularly significant as a kind of counterweight to the third type of illusory solution. We could even say that neglecting them causes the power of the third type of illusory solution to take over. The third type of illusory solution is the most insidious, because spiritually advanced individuals who possess powers and abilities generally unknown to the perpetrators (and the victims) of the other two types of illusory solution can also fall prey to it. Particularly those who have practiced and developed psychic skills and powers without first having established a reliable basis in themselves fall prey to the magical-mystical worlds.

The reliable subjective basis for wisely structuring one's life was characterized at the beginning of this chapter as trust in one's own competence. That it is possible to have recourse to our own competence and capability at every moment is an important principle of personal integrity. In the technical terminology of the Abhidhamma, a basis for developmental spiritual training that is founded on a sense of personal integrity and competence is called *sīla*. In the language of our conventional psychology, *sīla* could be defined as "personality integration resulting from harmonization of relationships to society and the environment by means of autochthonous regulation of behavior." Chapter 6 deals in greater detail with how to create a reliable basis for the development of further liberational strategies. If a person is completely firm in the saddle, borne up by tamed and orderly psychic energies, protected against accidental external influences, and undisturbed by feelings of guilt or bad conscience, such a person can, like a warrior, a genuine strategist, acquit himself well against any unexpected enemy—even if that enemy is an unsettling, uncanny, or even hostile magical phenomenon that unexpectedly penetrates the environment. Here too a reliable subjective basis is necessary.

Magical and mystical abilities, which can automatically arise as by-products of training in Dhamma strategies, are not bad or dangerous in themselves. It is only relating with them unintelligently that brings about unwholesome results and suffering. Actually everything that is ununderstandable—whose appearance and mode of functioning cannot be explained by ordinary rational means—is magical. In everyday life the abilities of an auto mechanic can be experienced as magical by someone who knows nothing about cars—as, for example, when by just listening to the motor the mechanic arrives at detailed knowledge about damaged parts. Sometimes a watchmaker can make a watch work again just by "taking a little look." Thus we call magical any happenings that we cannot fit into our picture of the world as limited by the conventional sciences. For shamans, spiritual healers, and yogis, magical phenomena have an orderly place in the world, and the process of working magic is quite familiar to them even though it remains impossible from the point of view of our technology. But mystical powers and the worldview they are based on have become more accessible to modern science. Interestingly, it is not the psychologists but rather the natural scientists, particularly the physicists, whose understanding of the universe has become closer to that of mystics of all times and cultures, as Lawrence Le Shan has shown.[12]

To make the magical and mystical accessible to persons of inadequate integrity, who have not developed a reliable subjective basis and who have not been trained to make distinctions within the inner world, is dangerous. A person who cannot distinguish between realities and choose appropriate ways of working with them is not suited for magical knowledge; it will throw his life into chaos and may result in clinically diagnosable psychosis. The life of a whole group can also become psychotic, as has happened with a number of sects. This can also happen to an entire civilization, as presently threatens to be the case with the armament-crazed developed countries. If one considers that the fascination with the "magical" game of war materiel cost 800 billion dollars in 1984, and that the tiny budgetary allotment for social welfare, feeding the starving, and projects promoting interpersonal and international understanding was cut back, then diagnosis of such a trend becomes easy. That our civilization as a whole is producing psychotic behavior in a number of areas and why this is so has been shown by the fine analyses of the English psychiatrist R. D. Laing.[13]

Even though the anatomy of human destructiveness will not be investigated more closely here, we can accept as valid the data of social scientists showing that fear of the outer world and the suffering (*dukkha*) experienced within are related to the phenomenon of ethical anomy that we have been discussing.

The continual increase in Western society of mental illness, aggression, suicide, brutality, sexual abuse of children, prostitution, degradation and suppression of "feminine" sensibilities on persons of both sexes through morbid educational methods, spiritual slaughter of future industrial workers in training institutions, animal torture in the name of science, abuse of pharmaceuticals, drug addiction, addiction to work, collective health damage resulting from unnecessary chemicals in food, poisoning of plants and animals by herbicides, insecticides, industrial waste, and exhaust fumes, destruction of the ecosystem through uncontrolled exploitation of resources, unnecessary public works, senseless creation of jobs even as automation is increased, political intrigues and scientific preparations for collective nuclear death (more than two-thirds of scientists work on military projects!)—these are the most obtrusive signs of the new era of our civilization. These are all symptoms manifesting in the external world; the causes, however, are to be found in the greed, aggression, and delusion that is rooted in the inner world of individuals. The anomy noted by social scientists manifests on the level of social symptoms but is ultimately an expression of the pathology of individual people. Greed, aggression, and delusion constitute the lowest common denominator of this pathology, known in the Abhidhamma as the three roots (*mūla*) of suffering.

It is illusory to hope for a solution through scientific and technological progress on the material level or to hope to force a change for the better through interventions in the external world. It is equally illusory to hope to liberate every individual from greed, aggression, and delusion. However, it is possible and makes sense to encourage the less deluded among us to dismantle our own greed and our own aggression. It is the purpose of the liberational strategies given in this book to show insightful people possible ways to free themseles from suffering (*dukkha*) by gradually eliminating all forms of violence in their own inner worlds.

Liberation is purification of the mind, freedom from everything that troubles our lives and distorts our perception. The less our inner world is soiled, the more we experience freedom within ourselves and the more competently we can function in the outer world. Competent functioning also requires ethical rules. Competent action guided by ethical rules leads to realization of higher values and opens up areas of happier living. Ethical rules and values that we develop on our own have a high degree of effectiveness and set standards for our fellow human beings who may not be equal to generating ethical rules themselves yet are intelligent and open enough to appreciate them independently. When we exemplify liberated activity that causes no suffering and is conducive to the welfare of ourselves and others, then we effect more in the world than we could through preaching, penalties, or tricks. Our own example of liberation and happiness in everyday life is more convincing than scientific and philosophical proofs. Concrete action and a liberated lifestyle are by far the most effective way to communicate the spiritual values and ethical rules through which social anomy can be overcome.

Our times have brought an increase of mental illness, aggressive behavior, and social fears, but on the other hand, the number of people aroused to greater mindfulness and awareness of these dangers has grown. The New Age can have no historical significance at all so long as the less obtuse among us are incapable of developing personal strategies for overcoming greed, aggression, and delusion. Our great chance lies precisely in the fact that the number of people who are receptive to and interested in training themselves in Dhamma strategies is on the increase. All of the above refers primarily to Western Europe and North America, because in the Third World—in totalitarian states and countries shattered by war (in which, by the way, the majority of the world's population lives)—other problems have first priority. The New Age requires a sense of solidarity or sympathy that is not only political and motivated by compassion (*karunā*) for those who live far away; more important is a sense of solidarity based on sympathetic joy (*muditā*) in the success of others who, near or far, no matter in what circumstances, are making progress in self-liberation. Authentic liberation (*vimutti*) is free from bias. It is not restricted to the elimination of the suffering of particular social classes or sex- and age-groups, races or nations. What we are talking about is as many people as possible, regardless of external group affiliation, freeing themselves from the unwholesome need to cause suffering to others out of greed, aggression, and delusion.

A liberational sense of solidarity or sympathy finds its most concrete expression in our acknowledgment, confirmation, and—to the extent possible—support of those people in whom we recognize a selfless (that is, free from greed), generous, aggressionless, compromise-ready, impartial, discerning state of mind. Every person at one time or another manifests such a state of mind and is thus able to act to reduce suffering. If a person is systematically reinforced in this, it can lead to a lasting change in his or her lifestyle. We can empathize with a person's good actions even if we are also aware of his or her bad side. We can relate with our fellow human beings in a realistic way, that is, a way corresponding to how they are actually behaving. We must not let ourselves be deluded by our derogatory concepts about people, which sum up a whole person on the basis of one mistake.

There are no good or bad people, only good or bad qualities or states of mind. In some people, the good comes to the fore more often. With such people, in whom we continually see liberational tendencies, we should try to arrange friendly meetings to have exchanges about our experiences in developing and applying Dhamma strategies. From such friendly encounters among people oriented toward inner progress, a network of relationships can form, a New Age conspiracy that is anchored in reality. The Abhidhamma calls such relationships "noble friendship" (*kalyāna mittatā*). In this way there could arise not only a "conspiracy" that is based on like convictions, not simply a "breathing together," but a situation in which people experience goodness together. If we do this, we are not merely relying on a belief that a New Age conspiracy is somehow in the air; we are actualizing it concretely in everyday life.

This is the deeper meaning behind the title of this chapter. Happiness and joy must be personally experienced; it cannot be thought up theoretically, scientifically ascertained, or technically contrived. Being happy is simple. The broader and clearer the vision we have in structuring our daily life, the more harmonious our inner world becomes, and the clearer and simpler the ethical governance of our action. Liberational rules are not commandments, not results of outside programming, not a matter of obedience. They grow out of our own experience, that is, they are autochthonous, they are a part of our personally experienced wisdom. This autochthonous ethical attunement, *sīla*, is not easily shaken by outside influences. Thus it shields us better from anomic depression than can heterochthonous—imposed-from-outside—ethics and morals composed of commandments and prohibitions.

Saddhā: Questioning Trust

How wonderful it is, dear reader, if you can arrange your own life in an increasingly simple way and to experience increasingly greater happiness. Definitely the most important thing is to tune in to ourselves so that our state of mind or attitude can remain as pure as possible. It is good to act guilelessly and simply, in a way that creates no suffering. From simplicity, clearly viewed, arises confidence, a form of trust, which in the Abhidhamma is called *saddhā*. Simplicity does not at all mean simplemindedness or gullibility. Even though cultivating a noble attitude and advancing in mindfulness and freedom will increasingly protect you from the dangers of the world, you will never be entirely proof against them. We all are occasionally the victims of actions of others that cause us suffering. Even if you can accept such suffering-producing actions of others as karmically[14] caused, that does not mean that you should heedlessly expose yourself to them. It is definitely helpful to rely on friends and trust other New Age "conspirators." However, trust is not blind faith and therefore includes questioning or testing. Trust grows through experiential testing. But questioning trust must not become doubt or inquisition. It is enough if we continue to maintain an overall perception of how the people we trust behave—in particular, whether they are keeping something back or are being open. Trust follows our own experience and the "inner voice" of intuition, which lets us organically sense what is good and trustworthy. In addition to this direct-experience orientation, certain rational criteria by which the integrity of persons and institutions can be tested are also valid in determining our sense of trust. Mere outer affiliation with the New Age movement is no guarantee. So, before I sum up the point of this chapter, I would like to sound a warning.

Interpersonal events in daily life are composed mainly of transactions motivated either by a need to get "more of something" (greed) or by a need to fend off something that has been perceived as a threat (aggression). It is relatively rare to find ourselves in a situation that is characterized by goodwill. For that reason we appreciate all the more the pleasing atmosphere of most New Age programs, groups, and societies, which try to realize a vision of cosmic harmony. However, a sharp either-or separation between the "always-good New Age alternative" on the one hand and the "dangerous situations with people in everyday life" on the other does not exist. In every person we find two kinds of behavior: struggle for survival based on the model "every man for himself" and the liberational mode of behavior of altruism, which expresses the outlook "I am only a part of the cosmos" and "the happier all participants in the cosmic happening are, the better my prospects for happiness are." Weak, unsure, and suffering people are necessarily primarily concerned with questions of survival. By contrast, strong, liberated people contribute voluntarily through their actions to the welfare of the community. The material and social status of these people is not of prime importance.

The conventional rules and regulations for juridical, business, and political processes are based on the survival approach. They were originally developed to protect the needy, the threatened, the weak. In actual practice, however, these rules and regulations are usually

used against the weak by the powerful, who possess knowledge of
these rules and regulations and pretend that they are the ones who
are threatened. Although these rules and regulations and the agreements derived from them are so often abused, they can continue to
have value in the New Age if they are properly applied. For the orga-
nizers of New Age programs and administrators of alternative institutions, to the extent that they are not fully purified beings, also sometimes become weak and are in need of "something more."

At that point agreements and clear regulations are useful for all
concerned. So we should not rid ourselves altogether of the survival
principles that protect need and weakness; rather what we must do is
assign them the right priority. Instead of maximizing, we should try
to optimize. That means that we should not place supreme value on
these principles of survival but use them only to the extent that they
contribute to the clear regulation of concrete situations. This is valid
for all relationships with institutions, groups, and individuals—even
for the intimate relationships of friendship, marriage, and the partnership between teacher and student.

It may well be, dear reader, that your own relationships are proceeding flawlessly. Your investments of work, money, mental effort,
and respect are well thought out, and you feel that they are nowhere
being misused, let alone exploited. It is an important principle of liberational strategy to keep in mind situations and relationships that are
free of problems. We should not ignore the good in our own psychosocial household. How about entering a *stop* at this point and drawing
up a short balance sheet of your material and spiritual investments?

Surely you have already thought over what goals and persons and
institutions you would like to promote and have considered what you
do get or will get out of this activity subjectively. Ultimately it is entirely a matter of your own personal choice and responsibility how
you go ahead and whether or not you would like to restructure your
investments. In this regard, the trustworthiness of people and groups
you may wish to support can be weighed according to certain criteria,
which can be formulated in the following questions:

1. Does the person (institution) provide clear information
   concerning goals and methods? Does this information
   correspond to my own perception? How are "heretical"
   questions responded to? Does the information consist of
   more than just promises? Is what is happening freely
   spoken about, without circumlocution or concealment?
2. Do the methods correspond to the goals? Is the process
   free from articles of belief that imply that one "achieves

freedom through obedience," "lies one's way to the
truth," "fights one's way to freedom," "attains knowledge through belief"?
3. Is the process free from secret-mongering? Are agreements understandable and clearly formulated? Are agreements kept to? Can one acknowledge publicly what is
going on?
4. Are the liberational efforts and methods of others not
ridiculed or otherwise impugned? Does one continue to
have a free choice of methods?
5. Are derogatory images unnecessary? Is there no bad-
mouthing of persons and groups? Does the possibility
remain open of seeing something positive in every living being?
6. Is each person regarded as responsible for his or her
own deeds? Is the authority of a guru ultimately superfluous? Can one experience one's own well-being without a middleman? Is abandonment of one's own understanding unnecessary?
7. Do the teacher, aides, or guides respect the freedom and
needs of those they are working with? Is there respect for
one's personal autonomy and dignity? Do the advanced
students or higher-ups respect the limitations and right
to self-determination of the others? Does the recipient of
gifts initiate an end to such giving in order to avoid exploitation or exhaustion of the givers?

Relationships for which you can answer all the above questions
with a "yes" might well be beneficial for your further development.
For it would by no means be helpful in the long run to cultivate a relationship that does not meet the above criteria. Trust leading to confidence—designated in Abhidhamma psychology by the technical term
saddhā[15]—cannot be based merely on belief; rather it must arise out of
critical testing of persons, institutions, and their methods. In the psychological and spiritual supermarket, there are enough offerings so
that each person can choose one that will further his or her personal
happiness and development while taking into account the above
seven criteria.

THE BOTTOM LINE

The purpose of this chapter was to order the whole range of New Age
phenomena so that all aspects could be related meaningfully to our

own experience on the appropriate levels. Only a subjectively relevant connection to us personally has any meaning for a happier way of life leading to greater freedom, upliftedness, enlightenment, and liberation.

The analysis proposed in this chapter need not correspond in all details to how you yourself would interpret this range of phenomena. You have now, however, gained enough of an overview to enable you to make your own analysis. Two steps are necessary for this: first, to acquire a personal connection to all the facts; second, to take into account all aspects of your life so that nothing is overemphasized and nothing is neglected. For many it will be enough just to know that they want to learn more about some things and actively cultivate others and occasionally translate some aspects of them into action. Also, we should not pretend that there are not things we would like to avoid. There is no compelling obligation for all of us to devote our mental energies in the same degree to social life, politics, science, art, self-analysis, meditation, or training in interpersonal relations. Each person must select the areas that correspond to his or her personal makeup. For the most part we find happiness in areas of life in which we are able to accomplish something ourselves, through our own means. However, clarity about everything that exists in the world altogether, or better, openness toward whatever is conducive to liberation and development of our personal potential in all areas of life will make our life richer. With this kind of approach, we will not be robbed of our spiritual freedom either because of complicated entanglements or because of exclusive concentration on one thing. When we have our own bird's-eye view, it becomes easier to be happy.

3

Threefold Knowledge and the Economy of the Mind

To find our place in the inconceivable manifoldness of life is not an easy task. However, if we do not achieve this, we have little prospect of living a pleasant life. Even if we are presently living a comparatively pleasant life, we have not necessarily achieved much, since things may change for the worse at any time. Assuring or even improving our psychosocial standard of living requires more. In order to get on with our personal development and liberation, we must continually create free space in which to try new things. This requires competence in dealing with our own mental energies. Such competence consists primarily in economical deployment of these energies toward three different ends: first, finding our place; second, creating mental and spiritual free space; third, experimenting with new things. Many people are incapable of attaining these three. They expend all their energy on merely keeping above water, on simply not losing themselves in the manifoldness of life.

The inconceivable manifoldness of life is called *papañca*[1] in Abhidhamma terminology. We are all drawn into the net of *papañca*, and yet it makes a great difference whether we clearly define this net as the context of our life and see in it mainly fruitful relationships, or whether we are simply hopelessly entangled in it. In chapter 1 we began to train our attention and mindfulness to distinguish four aspects of experience—or, to put it another way, to tame the manifoldness through the four foundations of mindfulness (*satipatthāna*):

1. bodily experience, which gives us a reliable, intersubjective reference to reality
2. feelings, emotional reactions, which exercise a directional influence on our action
3. the state of mind or level of consciousness, in which we orient ourselves according to various criteria
4. programs for thinking and acting that seek to control life situations

In chapter 2, we looked at the manifoldness of facts and methods that we encounter under the general heading "New Age." This selection from other people's wisdom was ordered in such a way as to enable each reader to develop his or her own personal relationship to this multiplicity of facts. Out of this manifoldness only such knowledge was offered as could be of significance for a person's own personal program of development and liberational strategy. The reader was encouraged to organize subjective knowledge concerning the various aspects of his or her life so that he or she could discern what was essential to work on in everyday life. Reading this book thus became a spiritual or psychological exercise with the goal of finding a reliable subjective basis.

Relating with this subjective basis, we continued our investigation according to Abhidhamma criteria and encountered the liberational principle *sīla*. We understood *sīla* as a principle of self-regulation based on insight. *Sīla* constitutes a reliable subjective basis for relating to the world.

We also looked for principles of New Age politics that do not complicate life but make it simpler and happier. Now we are going to go a step further and try to gain a clear view of the manifoldness of life from the standpoint of mental economics. We will continue to relate to external facts only in terms of their subjective impact, that is, only to the degree to which, as knowledge and motivation, they influence the way we arrange our lives. We will reserve our discussion of joy, which is the strongest motivation for liberation, for the next chapter.

POWERS OF MIND

Most people expend all their energies trying to maintain the status quo, regardless of how unprofitable that status quo might be. This is very uneconomical. Nonetheless, people lacking the ability to achieve a clear overview tend to prefer to go along with their habitual confusion, since any new free space they might create would anyhow immediately get filled up with fresh chaos. If we possess neither an overview nor a reliable subjective basis, experimentation can only be dangerous. In this case fear that the challenge is too great is justified. We might also be afraid of going mad. And in fact, for most people any broadening, change, or reorganization is dangerous. In case you are not at all familiar from personal experience with the emotional threat of possibly going mad, then everything to do with alterations of consciousness, uncovering of hidden potentialities, and unleashing of psychic powers will seem to you playfully easy or even familiar and homey. However, this still does not lessen the importance of the fact that both the support of *sīla* and free space are necessary for the cultivation of new abilities. Actually, we already know how to create free space—by entering a "Stop" in habitual programs, through pausing, through meditation and strategic action. Meditative pausing and mindful conduct—both are necessary in order not to lose ourselves in the manifoldness of *papañca*.

In order to fulfill the immeasurable possibilities of human existence, we must elaborate them concretely in the course of a happy life. Happiness is something we have to want very deeply, very personally. No one can provide a happy life for someone else. When we really want something, then we are willing to invest more than when we are merely acting out of a sense of obligation or when we are being pushed by others. Happiness-producing spiritual investments are voluntary energy expenditures that bring greater freedom and greater capacity for happiness. Thus they make possible growth in the economy of the mind. Knowledge, confidence, willpower, concentration, and mindfulness are the powers—as it were, the currency—of the mind, that which, mentally, we have to invest.

Knowledge in the specific sense in which we are using the word is called *paññā* in Abhidhamma psychology. It is knowledge concerning liberational strategies and insight into the laws of interdependence governing the manifoldness of life (*papañca*). This knowledge is one of the five mental or psychic powers that must be developed on the path of liberation. The powers of knowledge, confidence, willpower, concentration, and mindfulness are present in every person as potentialities or faculties. However, only after they are well developed and consciously available can they properly be called spiritual powers (*bala*). These five powers are perfected on the Path of Power (*bala magga;* see chapter 8, "Strategies of Power"). Together with a flawless realization of *sīla*, they are part of the necessary equipment of yogis with supernatural abilities. Such high spiritual accomplishment requires long training, and the New Age strategies include only the basic principles of such training. Higher training requires precise self-knowledge, deep insight into and perception of reality as it is. Entry upon the Abhidhamma path of seeing (*dassana magga*) already requires major progress on the path of liberation.

What is important at this point is primarily the insight that not just knowledge alone, but also the other four powers of mind must be cultivated. How to prepare the ground for liberational confidence (*saddhā*) was discussed in the last chapter. Practical instruction for training willpower, concentration, and mindfulness will be given in later chapters. For harmonious progress, mindfulness (*sati*) plays a crucial role, because it suppresses nothing and registers everything as it is. Mindfulness notices without interfering. *Sati* consists of continual *noticing*, of nonselective *apprehension* of real processes, and of *recollection* of what has taken place. Mindfulness is more than attention and perception; it is the extended maintenance of presence of mind. This is valid for all four realms of experiencing, as we saw in chapter 1. Mindfulness training always goes hand in hand with development of the wisdom that can make essential distinctions and knows the way to liberation. Mindfulness simply notes when a distinction is made, without altering anything. In this way it conveys an unbiased picture of the mental situation, and on that basis effective adjustments are possible.

The mental power *paññā* has a central function in other respects. It is the knowledge composing the metaprograms that steer the individual programs of our biocomputer in the course of developing liberational strategies. *Paññā* illuminates things and recognizes their characteristic features, properties, functions, and relations. It is like a tree whose roots reach down to the individual basic principles of reality, whose trunk is knowledge of truth, and whose branches represent transitions to the different states of consciousness. This simile could be taken further to show, for example, how different fruits grow on each branch in the same way that different specific skills and ways of seeing are inherent in the various states of consciousness. So *paññā* knows all this, and it orders and divides. But it neither moves nor binds—these are tasks for the other powers of mind.

For the growth and cultivation of *paññā* in our inner landscape, the same ecological principle is applicable as in farming—the principle that monoculture (in this case, exclusive cultivation of higher knowledge) cannot bring good results in the long run. To use a medical metaphor, we could say that the higher knowledge of *paññā* means about as much for a happy life as knowledge of the composition and preparation of a medicine means for healing. If through lack of trust we do not have the willpower to ensure that we take the medicine properly, without distraction or interruption (i.e., with concentration), the desired results will not ensue.

Keeping in mind that knowledge in the sense of *paññā* becomes a liberating power only in combination with confidence, willpower, concentration, and mindfulness, let us now consider this knowledge more closely but in a broader sense.

THE MENTAL HOUSEHOLD

Even with the greatest effort of will and concentration of mind, we would not be able to put our psychological house in order all at once. So long as we are not completely enlightened, there will always remain some dirty smudges in the dark corners of the psyche.[2] It is part of the art of housekeeping to get rid of the dirt that accumulates by means of economically responsible expenditures of effort. In the psychic economy (the word originally meant "housekeeping"), this involves mindful stocktaking and willing utilization of mental capacities, faculties, dispositions, energies, and skills. Dealing with mental waste and dirt, proper disposition of eliminated material, and selection of mental food play an important role in the psychic economy. Not less important is psycho-ecological knowledge concerning access to, and interactions of, inner-world contents. This inner ecology must go hand in hand with economic organization, which initially may be limited to appraisal of contents as "unprofitable waste material" or "material helpful toward liberation."

Perhaps, dear reader, you could make use of this opportunity for a "*Stop*" and a switch from the program "Taking In Information by Reading" to another program, one that starts from the question: "What contents of my inner world are presently helpful toward liberation?" Mindfully recall which themes occupied your inner world today and which daily-life situations were particularly significant or burdensome for you. What programs did you employ that were directed toward mastery of your situation? What strategies did you come up with? Briefly take stock of the day.

When you have finished with that, switch to mindful noting of your emotional reactions. In connection with what contents and contexts did you have a bad feeling? You can depend on your feelings! An unpleasant feeling-evaluation indicates the presence of nonproductive defilements. Simply register these obstacles[3] without getting further involved with them. Then mindfully note what material is associated with good feelings—what are you content with, what seems to you beneficial and liberational? In this way, use your feelings as criteria in an organic process of evaluation. Now you can make use of the reliable subjective basis of *sīla* to gauge the extent to which your conduct was independent of outer and inner forms of greed, aggression, and delusion. To what extent did you take your own sense of self-determination and ethical value judgment as your reference point and basis? Were you able, on the basis of the sure ground of your *sīla*, to distance yourself from situational compulsions, to create some free space and consciously try out something new? Leave yourself enough time to think about these things before you continue reading! What we are working with here is the treasure-store of your own experience, your own wisdom!

We feel good when we see that something has succeeded. Experiences of success bring joy and increase our trust in ourself, trust in our own capabilities, and trust also in the methods that have proven successful. Trust and joy cause our interest in penetrating further into liberational teachings to deepen. *Saddhā* is trust that is based on critical testing, not gullible compliance, not exaggerated self-esteem resulting from intoxication with success, and not blind faith either. We cannot create trust in ourselves by giving ourselves a pep talk, and it makes no sense to pretend our power of trust is greater than it is. Only truthful mindful noticing of what is really there produces the kind of knowledge that is useful for liberation.

What makes up the power of knowledge—or better, what knowledge is useful for what purposes? For the sake of a clearer view of our inner household, we could distinguish the following three types of knowledge:

1. Information about external facts. This also includes communications from others about their inner experiences, observations, and opinions.
2. Direct impressions from our own experience. This is not just accumulated information; it is material that is present and available as part of the treasure-store of our inner world. Included here is immediately experienced knowledge about the state of our inner world, our inclinations, faculties, powers, skills, and capabilities.
3. Wisdom or *paññā*, which enables us to see a broader context, to experience ourselves as part of the cosmic harmony. Such wisdom is liberational, because it leads to the elimination of suffering caused by suppression and rejection. Here strategic knowledge about the path of liberational mind-training is included.

All three types of knowledge help to shape the state of our mental world, the psychological ecology that produces our conception of the external world. Thus the culture we have created as well as nature as changed by us are expressions of our mental ecology. The world is, in this sense, a product of the mind—just to the extent that the raw material of the external world is shaped by our activity. If I understand and accept this, I take two further steps as a result:

1. I acknowledge myself to be the creator of my own world and
2. I assume responsibility for my own creation.

In these steps the fundamental principle of the liberational ethics on which Dhamma strategies are always based becomes clear. Responsibility is not shifted off onto a guru, god, or leader. This means that we do not work ourselves up into an addictive dependency on any kind of external authority. And it has a further important consequence for our development: neither childish hope for the saving grace of an authority nor fear of the disfavor of an authority befogs our perception of situations. This does not mean we need utterly reject the benevolent help of a powerful being—whether it be a teacher or a god—as long as we ultimately rely on our own efforts toward liberation and take refuge in our own capabilities. Seeking help and self-reliance are not mutually exclusive. Meaningful help improves our chances of fulfilling our potential within our own sphere of power.

All three—*sīla*, the state that is a reliable subjective starting point; *saddhā*, confidence; and the process of actualizing happiness in accordance with *paññā*—are rooted in the fundamental principle of taking responsibility for oneself. Through this, we become master in our own mental household.

In the few sentences above, I have summarized the most important aspects of an idea that now requires more detailed explanation. In an earlier work, *Psychische Interaktion, intrapsychische Struktur und individuelles Wertsystem* (Berne, 1975), I presented an epistemological and a social-psychological analysis of the interaction between the facts of the inner world and those of the outer world. The present elucidations are based on that analysis. Confirmation and deepening of my understanding of the processes through which we structure our world came from conversations with Gregory Bateson; readers with further theoretical interest are referred to his books *Steps to an Ecology of Mind* and *Mind and Nature*. With the intention of encouraging you to form your own picture, I will now indicate some of the correspondences between the outer and inner systems of ecology and economy, primarily by means of similes and metaphors. Draw your own practical conclusions, applicable in everyday life, as you did in taking stock of your material and spiritual investments at the end of chapter 2.

Every child, in the course of growing up, internalizes the culture into which it has been born. Cultures differ according to country, social class, and so on. But whatever their differences, cultures shape our inner world by communicating the roles, modes of behavior, outlooks, and mental structures that are present in the child's living space, in its home. To the extent that this primary ecosystem of the child is harmonious and healthy, the basic structures of its inner household will be harmonious and healthy. We may note here in passing how close to each other the meanings of "home," "household," and "ecosystem" are. Language has stored the knowledge of this commonness of meaning: the Greek word *oikos* originally referred to the dwelling place, the house, the living environment. The further Latin development of the word brought out the sense of thrift-minded distribution and management that was already latent in the Greek *oikonomos*, "householder."

In learning a language, every child acquires the multifaceted knowledge contained in that language. This knowledge divides the unified world of the small child into the individual facts of *papañca* (manifoldness of life). Coherent contexts within the world are determined only by the structure of language. If everything goes well, the child later also gains know-how for working with individual things. The maturing young person then also internalizes the economic skills and ecological knowledge of other members of the household. Various types of knowledge are accessible to different persons to different degrees, depending on what culture they are part of and on their individual talent and level of development. For the most part unconsciously, the individual continues to apply repetitively what he has learned, as part of the continual process of structuring the world. Only rarely does someone win through to insight concerning this cycle and come to an understanding of the ceaseless unconscious repetition involved. Only rarely does someone succeed in recognizing the suffering that is caused by this repetition. However, as soon as someone does see through the repeating cycle of suffering,[4] then he also becomes aware of the causes of the suffering. At that point, he is not far from finding possible ways out of it. He leaves the home that is the cradle of suffering and by adopting homelessness becomes part of the cosmic ecosystem. If, developing beyond all attachment, he also frees himself from cosmic yearnings, then he has fulfilled the path of liberation and establishes his home beyond suffering.

However, insight into suffering and the wish to be free from it are not sufficient for attaining liberation. Without the technical know-how contained in concrete strategies, liberation is not possible. And of course, we must also know what it is we need to liberate ourselves from in order to utilize the appropriate strategies to progress along the path. Thus the wisdom of liberation has two dimensions that go beyond ordinary knowledge: first, it takes freedom as an ethical value; and second, it takes liberation as a guideline for action. Such liberating, holistic wisdom, as already mentioned, rarely arises. In the Abhidhamma, we find it precisely elaborated under the name of *paññā*. The liberational paradigm of the Abhidhamma consists of the Four Noble Truths, which, taken as an inseparable unity, represent the highest wisdom:

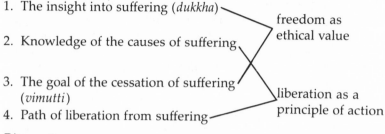

1. The insight into suffering (*dukkha*)

   freedom as
   ethical value

2. Knowledge of the causes of suffering

3. The goal of the cessation of suffering
   (*vimutti*)

   liberation as a
   principle of action

4. Path of liberation from suffering

Diagram 3

In our search for the causes of suffering in the previous chapter, we recognized greed, aggression, and delusion as the roots of it. In our present considerations, we are working toward wisdom, *paññā*, that will provide a comprehensive overall view dispelling delusion. We see that two basic discoveries are crucial: first, we must find a place in the cycle of suffering from which it is possible to undertake changes; and second, we have to find a method for recognizing the causes of suffering and replacing them with causes of wholesomeness. This is accomplished through the technique of *wise apprehension* or *wise reflection*, which translates *paññā* into action and is the basis of all Dhamma strategies.

The wise and comprehensive view of *paññā* is not derived from fragments of knowledge composed of isolated data and experiences; rather it is based on global cognition of interactions and relationships integrated into a multidimensional matrix of knowledge. The aforementioned Four Noble Truths, for example, constitute an indivisible matrix of knowledge. Thus if suffering and its causes are understood as a cycle of suffering that arises in dependence on conditions, then it is not only the first two truths that are implied. The third truth, the possibility of liberation, and the fourth truth, the strategy for attaining liberation, are also contained in this fundamental paradigm of the Abhidhamma.

The point at which it is possible for any person in any situation to halt the cycle of constant repetition of suffering and arouse the seed of happiness lies in the inner household. This is where strategy can be applied—if we are able to create space for it. Then we can overcome the set of conditions that produces suffering. More precisely, we can break out of the cycle by noticing automatically running, unwholesome programs of perception and action, stopping them, and replacing them with others that are realistic and beneficial. The freer a perception is from distortions due to greed and aggression and the more clarity of vision it allows, the closer to reality it is. Actions are beneficial that are not deluded and that, as a result of generosity without greed and sympathy without aggression, are conducive to harmonization of all ecosystems. Here we have in clear outline the basic principles of wise action leading to a liberational, happiness-furthering way of life. Out of this arises the concrete task of developing sympathetic strategies, generosity, and clear vision.

In one sentence: Practically speaking, what we have to do is set our inner household in order and develop the tools that are present there in such a way that, like a wise *oikonomos*, we can feel at home in an ever broader area of our external environment.

MATRICES OF KNOWLEDGE

A matrix takes in something, encompasses it, accommodates it as a vessel accommodates its contents. A matrix contains a basic form that can be developed further. Examples of matrices that contain something incomplete and transform it into something complete are casting molds and wombs. In the seed or embryo is the nucleus with its chromosomes—the matrix that determines how the mature animal or plant will look. The Abhidhamma term for matrix is *yoni*, which in Pali means "womb," "origin," and "ground." *Yoni* is the origin from which something differentiated, something fully developed, evolves. It is a matrix that lays a groundwork within the seed or embryo; it is thus fundamental for the fully developed result. The adjective *yoniso*, which we shall use frequently, means "in the manner of a womb," "fundamental," "reality-related," and "wise, because taking into account the totality of conditions." *Ayoniso*, by contrast, means "alien to reality," "false," and "unwise." *Yoni* and *ayoni* are indices for all states of consciousness and matrices for all true or false knowledge. You can well imagine, dear reader, how important it is for effective alteration of consciousness and for the evolution of wisdom for us to relate properly to *yoni*.

Yoni are matrices for knowledge that leads to wisdom. Concepts of everyday language are also matrices of knowledge. These concepts could be made precise by integrating them into the technical vocabulary of the sciences and scientifically organized disciplines. In this way they would take their place within clearly defined systems and attain a more unequivocal meaning. They would be rationally defined in terms of individual, unique points of reference. But reality is not unequivocal in this way, because facts are not related to each other only rationally. The more unequivocal concepts become, the less they correspond to the manifoldness of life. Thus their validity is reduced. Particularly sciences that deal with the inner world and processes within living beings must come to terms with this and admit that their concepts have only a limited validity. Scientists try to compensate for this by introducing large numbers of concepts and justifying them with huge quantities of computer-generated data. Nonquantifiable factors are barely considered. In any case, concepts are not particularly good matrices for dealing with knowledge in a realistic fashion and causing wisdom to arise from it.

Psychoanalysis made a valuable contribution when it introduced to the psychological disciplines the possibility of using myths and fairy tales as matrices of knowledge. This led to a general reevaluation of myths and fairy tales, which before that, owing to the mindless rationalism of the scientific age, had been all but totally expunged from popular consciousness. In attempting to understand the inner world with the help of myths and fairy tales, depth psychologists are coming nearer to a view of its manifold contents. They are beginning to find order in *papañca*. Still it is hard to find myths that contain the liberational wisdom of the Four Noble Truths. Myths and fairy tales are useful tools for tidying, organizing, and harmonizing the inner household. They are not, however, matrices of liberational wisdom.

Liberation involves not only the contents of the mind. Wisdom matrices must take into account the structures of the mind and its way of functioning as well as contain a dynamic of liberation. No science or myth is capable of transmitting more than knowledge. And without a technique for its practical application, without a method, such knowledge is powerless to change our lives. Modern psychological disciplines lack such applicability to a large extent. Their concepts and theories do bring knowledge but do not develop it into wisdom.

Psychotherapeutic psychologies constitute an exception to the extent that their paradigms comprise matrices in the sense of *yoni;* they transform apprehended knowledge into applicable guidelines for action. But they are concerned only with the treatment of the mentally ill. They have not gone so far as to consider liberation.

Stanislav Grof gives an overview of the latest achievements in this area in his *Beyond the Brain: Birth, Death, and Transcendence in Psychotherapy,* a book that considers most of the important contributions of New Age science. As the main spokesman of transpersonal psychology, Grof names Ken Wilber, "who produced a successful synthesis of seemingly incompatible data from the most diverse domains." He laments, however, the fact that Wilber's model is "not of greater pragmatic value." Characteristically, such purely conceptual syntheses are difficult to apply practically. And of an ethical orientation toward freedom—which is indispensable, for example, in the matrix of the Four Noble Truths—we cannot speak here at all. All these latest theories and models are deterministic; that is, their authors believe fatalistically in a certain evolution and see no necessity to apply knowledge in a practical effort for liberation. In short, myths as interpreted by depth psychology, transpersonal syntheses, and system-theory models do not necessarily make possible the kind of processing of knowledge that matrices in the Abhidhamma sense do.

As you have surely noted, the image of the biocomputer has been prominently employed in this book. Actually it is cybernetics, the science of regulatory processes in intelligent systems, that is closest to the wisdom of the Abhidhamma. But the New Age can no more reduce the mind to a computer than previous disciplines could banish it into a hologram or the works of a clock. In point of fact, the language of myths and of cybernetics both prove inadequate in helping us to understand the strategy of liberation. We will also have to abandon the metaphor of the biocomputer and attune ourselves increasingly to the Abhidhamma matrices that we have elucidated under the names *saddhā, sīla, paññā,* and so forth. These represent concrete procedures of liberation. Therefore, we must practice restructuring our experience and activity with the help of liberational matrices.

Conditioned Arising

Let us now turn our attention to a concrete matrix of liberational wisdom. In the Abhidhamma terminology it is called *paticca-samuppāda,* or conditioned arising. It is a matrix that makes it possible for us to view the cycle of suffering analytically and to see it in the context of the Four Noble Truths as something that can be overcome. *Paticca-samuppāda* is a circular paradigm comprised of twelve links of generation or arising. For the sake of clarity, we will not immediately consider all of them. We will analyze the interdependence only of those elements that are most important for creating free space, for making liberational decisions, and for getting out of the cycle of suffering. In any case, the matrix of conditioned arising in its completeness and perfection can be penetrated only through very advanced meditation. This generally requires a thorough study of Abhidhamma. Meditative penetration and complete knowledge in themselves also imply a process of transcendence that makes possible a letting go of the whole. When wisdom penetrates the cycle of conditioned arising and the tendency toward liberation focuses on the unconditioned, that which is beyond suffering, then any choice is possible. The liberated will is free; it goes beyond conditioned arising.

Any situation I find myself in is conditioned to a certain extent by my previous actions. Even the aspects of the situation that I myself have not brought about take on a form in my perception that is conditioned by my previous activities and perceptions. I choose, so to speak, how I apprehend situations, what situations I create, and what situations I get involved in. This is a more detailed explanation of the insight mentioned earlier that I am the creator of my own world. From this it is also evident how important the choice is of what perceptual habits I cultivate, what matrices structure my life. Through mindful action, stopping and pausing, I can indeed prevent unwholesome developments or interrupt ones that are already under way. But in order to bring about happiness-furthering, wholesome developments I have to be able to do more. I have to be able to view each situation in terms of a liberational matrix and direct available energies toward the unfolding of well-being (see Diagram 14, pages 280–81). The energy or the "material" out of which life situations are created is already present, but the frame of reference or "form" in which they are cast is a matter of choice. The frame of reference is determined by the matrix (*yoni*). The technique of choosing and applying a particular *yoni*, which is called *yoniso manasikāra*, or wise apprehension, is the foundation of all liberational strategies. It will be presented at the end of this chapter.

The nature of my contact with the outer world is conditioned by the various matrices of my inner world. There are to be found the *yoni* that are the breeding grounds of my happiness or unhappiness. In other words, whether my interactions with the world develop into weal or woe depends on what is embraced by the matrix, what it is that breeds in it. Expressed in still another way, according to Abhidhamma, we can choose what comes into being (*bhava*) in *yoni* and what kind of creation of it becomes, through the process of birth (*jāti*), a being separate from the outer world. Diagram 4 (page 55) illustrates this process of conditionality.[5]

It can be seen from the diagram that purified experiencing, the full experience of life, not reduced by greed, aggression, and delusion, leads to the reality-related path of liberation (*vimutti*). Any intelligent person can cultivate his mode of experiencing in such a way as to leave behind the repetitions of the cycle of suffering. What *vedanā*, the full experience of feeling, means will be seen in greater detail in the next chapter. For now, let us concern ourselves just with the matrix that encompasses the repetitive mechanism for an experience of suffering brought about by greed and so forth, divided into its component parts. As a whole, the experience of suffering is overwhelming. However, when it is divided into its separate parts, then we can more readily eliminate the causes of suffering. The most important task here is to determine the points of connection between the parts. These are points at which we can best cope with suffering. How contact between the inner and outer worlds functions (points 2, 3, and 4 in Diagram 4) is shown in detail in Diagrams 1 and 2 on pages 10 and 11. The process at points 5, 6, and 7 is pretty much fixed, and an analysis of this part of the matrix would be fairly meaningless for our work with the liberational strategies. Of interest for us is the transition between 2 and 3 and particularly that between 4 and 5, since at that point it is possible for us to influence the process of consciousness (see Diagram 6 on page 64).

Let us see now in terms of examples how the liberational matrix illustrated in Diagram 4 can be utilized in concrete situations. The following account is that of a young woman, who, without knowing anything about the paradigm of conditioned arising, discovered by herself certain processes of repetition in her experience, saw through them, and rejected them (numbers of points in Diagram 4 are given in parentheses):

> Whenever I let myself get emotionally and socially involved with a man beyond the normal, everyday, superficial level of getting together (3), our expectations (6) would soon turn out to be incompatible, which led to suffering (1). So as a solution I tried to avoid getting involved altogether (2) or, when I couldn't stand it alone anymore (1), allowed for only superficial contact (3) . . . Then I met a nice man and it seemed as though we had found together the right style for our relationship. We could talk about anything, but eventually I had to go through (4) the same thing again. Even though we had made clear the nature and extent of our wishes and desires (5), had openly discussed (7) our expectations (6) of each other, and had come to clear agreements, nevertheless we got into conflict (1) again and again. Obviously, we had harbored expectations (6) based

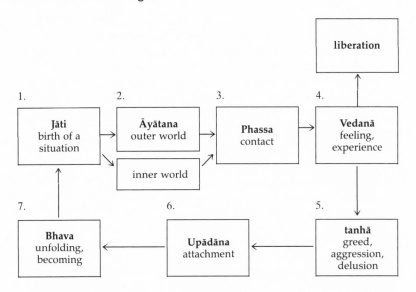

Diagram 4. The Cycle of Suffering

on unadmitted motives (5), and tried to manipulate each
other (7). In heated arguments we then tried to force each
other to change, but this only destroyed our relationship.
For months I suffered from having lost this man (6). For
more than a year now I have been trying to get clear about
the causes and how they work. I don't want to have to go
through a repeat performance.

It is impressive to what extent the author of this account was able to
express some of the most important aspects of the situation in words
and how close to the paradigm of conditioned arising she came. (For
reasons of space and privacy her account has been somewhat short-
ened. The description of the subjects of conflict and of her adventures
with superficial relationships have been left out.) The author is today
in a totally different situation and would now compose her account
differently. Nevertheless, she agreed to publication and to the abridge-
ments, for which I thank her.

Another woman, who has been working with liberational strategies
for a number of years, also kindly gave her permission for publication
of the following account, which involves conscious application of
the matrix of conditioned arising. The theme is similar to that of the
previous account. Please try to identify the points in the matrix on
your own:

A friend toward whom I felt a deep emotional love had
pulled out of our relationship little by little without ever
letting me know what his motives were. It took me two
years to be able to let go of my disappointed love for him
completely. During this time I made a point of speaking
openly about my feelings and expectations in all my relationships. I even learned to accept the superficiality of a relationship if, in spite of mutual attraction, openness was
missing. Nevertheless, I did not succeed in developing a
harmonious, equal partnership with a man. Recently, I had
a friendship with a man to whom I didn't want to commit
myself even after a year of intense relationship. We both
did have a desire for marriage and we had openly admitted
this to each other, but my emotions remained strangely
untouched. Although this surprised me, I did not hide it
from my friend. Coincidence would have it that he was
evicted from his apartment. We were more or less forced to
have him move in with me temporarily. I found it very important to insist on his looking for a new apartment, because I wanted to continue living alone. My friend was in
fact soon able to rent another apartment, but found that he
was not at all inclined to move into it.

In this situation his pronounced affection and my cold-
ness became all too clear. Continuing the relationship became unbearable and impossible. We separated from each
other with a great deal of suffering. In spite of my openness, he had obviously begun to hope that I would change
my mind. And I saw too late my unwillingness to be tied
down. Probably his affection did me good. When I think
this over now in connection with conditioned arising (I
have the diagram in front of me), I can see that in spite of
his positive and my negative feelings, which were irrecon-
cilable, our relationship was able to continue as long as I
was able to impose some sense of meaningfulness on it
(delusion) and he continued simply to demand it (greed).
Exposing our emotions had the effect of dissolving our
connection, a reality-true outcome.

The two accounts have much in common (and in fact were chosen
for that reason). Subsequently, both authors went on similar quests
for solutions. They got involved in political work, the feminist movement, encounter groups, and meditation. Neither of the two is a psychologist or social worker. I am of the opinion that these accounts
could also have been written by men, although it is unlikely that
many men in our culture would ordinarily reflect in this way about

personal relationships. (However, it is doubtful on the other hand, that, for example, psychologists, psychiatrists, clergypersons, or social workers, despite their professional "education," could think in such a wise and realistic way about their relationships, without "psychoanalyzing" their partners and branding them with "diagnoses.") In any case, experience teaches us that it is futile to try to develop human understanding on the basis of categories like sex, profession, race, generation, or social status.

These considerations should not create the impression that the matrix of conditioned arising applies only to interpersonal matters. All situations arise in dependence on a number of conditions and thus can be changed. All relationships, not only those with people, but also relationships to things in the external world and attitudes toward realities of the inner world—all arise dependent on conditions. All relationships, attitudes, and situations can keep us prisoner in a cycle of suffering if we apprehend them unwisely (*ayoniso manasikāra*). On the other hand, any situation can also act as a springboard toward liberation if it is considered wisely. Thus it is not the people, things, and situations that we get involved with that are responsible for whether we suffer or make progress on the path of liberation. Rather it is the *way we deal with them*, the way we apprehend them that is responsible. However, for the methodical practice of *yoniso manasikāra* (wise apprehension), certain things and mental objects are more advantageous than others, as we shall see later in considering concrete strategies. Liberational strategies cannot be learned all at once. Wise apprehension is also something that we approach step by step, getting closer with each new insight, until finally our matrix of knowledge becomes a reality-true *yoni*. The same is true for assimilating the matrix of conditioned arising. In Abhidhamma books, over a hundred variations of the matrix of conditioned arising are described, all of which are *yoniso*, reality-true. In Diagram 5, the fundamental matrix, which encompasses all possible cycles of suffering, is shown.

Before I describe some examples of how my clients and students gradually discovered the matrix of conditioned arising, some explanation concerning the significance of *karma* is in order. As can be seen from Diagram 5, we distinguish between the causes and effects of *karma*.

Karmic cause (*kamma*) is actively executed volition, intentional action, deliberate speech, and purposeful thinking and planning—that is, everything we can decide to either refrain from or execute. Here and now karma is represented only by three points on the circle of conditioned arising—8, 9, 10. Eight is craving, which manifests on

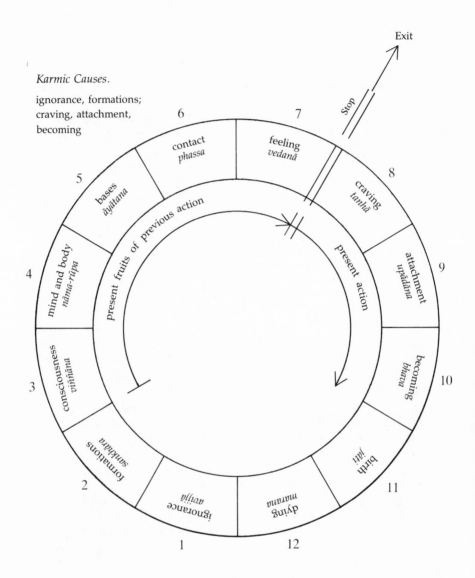

Karmic Causes.

ignorance, formations;
craving, attachment,
becoming

Exit

Stop

6 contact *phassa*

7 feeling *vedanā*

8 craving *tanhā*

5 bases *āyātana*

9 attachment *upādāna*

previous action

present action

present fruits of

4 mind and body *nāma-rūpa*

3 consciousness *viññāna*

10 becoming *bhava*

2 formations *sankhāra*

11 birth *jāti*

1 ignorance *avijjā*

12 dying *marana*

Diagram 5. Fundamental Matrix of Conditioned Arising

the emotional level as greed and aggression and on the cognitive level as ignorance. Nine, attachment, consists of expectations, fixed views, and indulgence in sensuality, that is, attachment to programs that are based on greed, aggression, and delusion and, when carried out, bring suffering. Ten, becoming, is the preparation and development of programs that bring about the rebirth of a situation or consciousness. Craving and attachment are always karmically unwholesome, because they bring suffering, cause frustration and disappointment, and thus constrict our experience of life. Becoming, on the other hand, can produce unpleasantness but also pleasant experiences—for instance, when it is a meditative unfolding (*bhāvanā*) of consciousness or a structuring and cultivating of liberational programs. In that case, becoming is not conditioned by craving.[6]

Karmic effects (*vipāka*) are the outcome of previous intentions, craving, attachment, and becoming. These effects are results that can no longer be changed in any way. Such an effect is an unpleasant experience (*vedanā*) if the karmic cause was tainted by greed or aggression (*akusala*, unwholesome). Greedless and aggressionless intentions result in effects that are either pleasant or neutral. The effects are fruits of karmic causes, which, arising from the past, perpetuate themselves as formations (*sankhāra*) of body and mind and as delusion and ignorance (*avijjā*).

We cannot alter the past, because past is past. As banal as this sounds, most social scientists and psychologists, psychiatrists and educators show by what they do that they have never grasped this simple truth. We also cannot alter the future, for it does not yet exist. All that we can change is the present, because we can create conditions that bring about well-being and happiness and eliminate karmic causes that lead to the conditioned arising of suffering. This amounts to overcoming delusion and ignorance through *paññā* (wisdom); eliminating greed through renunciation and generosity (*dāna*); dispelling aggression through sympathy and nonviolence (*ahimsa*).

Though insights and knowledge that we acquire with our everyday consciousness are related to what we experience directly, they are made up mostly of ideas thought out in words. Verbal knowledge has far less effect than knowledge gained in relating with concrete facts. Thus knowledge concerning conditioned arising will be far more effective once you yourself have uncovered facts corresponding to it in your everyday life. Perhaps the following descriptions, which come from friends, analysands, and students will encourage you in this undertaking.

In the nonjudgmental receptive atmosphere of the psychoanalytic situation, heed is paid not only to experiences out of earlier times but also to current problems involving psychological factors. Generally we find it unpleasant to look within ourselves when we find we are becoming aware of something that we wish we had forgotten forever—especially when we have no idea how to deal with it. Thus the tendency might appear in an analysand to justify actions of his about which he feels shame and embarrassment by explaining them deterministically as inevitable "responses" to external "stimuli." Just like the experimental psychologists, he is ready to attribute to his emotional life, which is objectified as his "nature" or "organism,"[7] at most a statistical intervening function. The causes for all action and suffering as well as those for happiness are sought externally. If the therapist (unlike most parents, teachers, and supervisors) does not exploit the guilt feelings of the analysand in order to get him to do something, then the fear of seeking out the conditions of suffering within disappears. With growing trust in the therapeutic process and in one's own liberational tendencies (critically questioning trust, saddhā, has an important guiding function in psychotherapy as well), there comes a point in the process where there is a change of paradigms, that is, other criteria are adopted.

As soon as a person notices that the outer as well as the inner bases (āyatana, point 5 in Diagram 5) are necessary as conditions for the arising of a conscious impression (phassa) and that his negative feeling (vedanā) need not turn into an aggressive demand (tanhā) for the destruction of the bases of suffering, then he is no longer a patient. A person who can adopt this kind of approach has done away with the greater part of delusion (avijjā). Now it is possible, instead of feeling "This medicine is so unreliable it's driving me crazy. I'm throwing it out!" or "If I could just get that one appliance, I'd be completely satisfied with the house!" to experience similar situations in a more subtle way: "The effect of this medicine does not correspond to my expectations. The desired relief takes place only under certain circumstances." Or: "Trying to achieve contentment with my house only increases my craving for more and more gadgets."

We also notice that the inner bases (āyatana)—consisting of expectations, prejudices, and views—condition contact (phassa) and thereby also feelings (vedanā). Later we perhaps notice that the craving (tanhā) for what is pleasurable leads to attachment (upādāna) and so forth, as was clear from the reports by the two young women I quoted earlier. Then we notice that attachment conditions a continuing process of becoming (bhava), which gives birth (jāti) to states of experience with karmically corresponding features. And whatever is born must

eventually die (*marana*). If this process of "re-death" is not overcome through wisdom, then death simply conditions further ignorance (*avijjā*), which makes possible further development of suffering-
ridden formations (*sankhāra*). Borne by the formations, consciousness
(*viññāna*) arises, which results in the split between word and reality,
mind and body (*nāma-rūpa*), through which in turn regeneration of
the sense bases (*āyatana*) is perpetuated. In turn the sense bases make
possible further contact (*phassa*), and this leads to the conditioned
arising of similar experiences.

This is a very brief and simplified sketch of the cyclical process of
paticca-samuppāda. Once again, the point of this paradigm is not a supposedly nonevaluational scientific view of the type often presented in
psychological theories. Rather it is a view that definitely expresses
value. Liberation is the openly confessed value orientation of this
paradigm, the purpose of which is to gain a view of the laws of experience that shows that pathological conditioning and conditionality
can be shattered by mindfulness and insight and that they can be voluntarily replaced by liberational directive formations (*abhisankhāra*).

In a repetitive cycle of suffering, all twelve factors do not have to be
present, and all of them need not always be perceived. What is crucial
is whether or not a person recognizes the repetitiousness, is able to
apprehend it as arising conditionally and break out of it. The following short accounts of how patients discovered on their own the conditionality of the process will be more illuminating than further theoretical explanations. What we are dealing with here are microanalytic
observations of short sequences characterized by suffering. Characteristically, these could be wisely apprehended by the patients only
when they were able to replace them by liberating sequences. I cannot
rid myself of the impression that people simply need programs, because both in therapy sessions and in everyday life I see again and
again how they repeat suffering-producing sequences, to which they
are shackled by controlling programs that make them even more complicated—unless somehow, sometime, they have managed to work
out a liberational program for a similar situation and are thus able
to replace the repetitive suffering-ridden program with a liberating one.

In the course of a marriage therapy case, I had noticed for some
time that the husband repeatedly treated the wife condescendingly,
patronizingly, particularly when she was acting independently; and
that she repeatedly made him into a culprit, particularly when he was
being attentive to her or she had caught his attention. Since both were
familiar with psychoanalysis and were concerned to obtain a good re-

sult from the therapy, they readily described events from their child-hood, especially their relationships to the parent of the opposite sex. In this way it became clear that the husband had a deep motivation that had come about through his mother's exaggeratedly demanding approach to social relations, as a result of which she had raised him to be "a gentleman under all circumstances, but especially in circum-stances where it was particularly difficult." In the case of the wife, it was discovered that every expression of affection toward her on the part of her father had had the effect of making her feel obligated, all the more so because he could never openly admit his desire for a re-sponse to his affectionate behavior. She was in fact respected by her parents as an independent person only when she ignored them. Such constellations are not rare in our culture.

The view that everything in a human being that is not brought about chemically is the consequence of his evolution or upbringing is typical not only of psychiatrists. This view was also an object of fixed attachment for the married couple in the case under discussion. More-over, they were deluded by the psychoanalytic belief that all pa-thologies have their roots in our childhood. Nevertheless, with time it became possible for them to relate increasingly to present events. Thorough and painstaking (*yoniso!*) attention was given mainly to those interactions that were suspect because they happened either be-fore a major confrontation or before a breaking off of communication.

One such interaction took place whenever she said: "I have the feeling that you . . ." and then expressed some presumption about him. Subsequently he would either be silent or get angry. Another such interaction came about when he asked her some question or other, and she, instead of answering, shouted at him: "You're trying to manipulate me!" She was probably sometimes right, and he often admitted it. Nonetheless, it remained a riddle for a long time how it was that in spite of all their mutual love and consideration, they re-peatedly caused each other to suffer. It took a long time for them to notice that they were not only harming each other, but even more, harming themselves as a result of an unwise apprehension of the situation. Each saw the cause of his or her own experience in the nature of the other, in accordance with the pattern: "I'm happy (or suffering), because you are thus-and-so (and not as I'd like you to be)."

It is remarkable that even during repeated viewings of videotapes, generally each of them observed the other with increasing intensity. They did, however, succeed by themselves in opening their percep-tion to the manifoldness of the conditions of their own experience. Thus they transcended the S-R (stimulus-response) paradigm, which not only appears in psychology but in our culture is also deeply implanted in most people. My clients succeeded in reaching an insight that encompassed several discoveries:

1. They stopped shifting the causes of their own experience onto the other person. The pattern of mutual blaming subsided. Only thereby did perception of conditioned arising become possible at all.

2. They began to distinguish between feelings and presumptions. The wife stopped saying: "I have the feeling that you . . ." Instead of that, she asked: "Is my assumption correct that you . . . ?" She realized that her unpleasant feeling arose through her attachment to her presumptions and had nothing to do with her husband. And he stopped asking questions when he had the unpleasant feeling (actually conditioned by contact [*phassa*] with his own worrisome projections) that his wife, left to herself, might fail in what she was doing. Instead of trying to protect his wife by means of preventive questioning, he now explicitly expressed his concerns.

3. She made the very important discovery that we can better enjoy pleasant feelings when we do not drift off into craving, that is, when our capacity for experience is not vitiated by greed. She was also gradually able (first in the therapy sessions, then in everyday life) to confirm through her own experience that unpleasant feelings subside faster when we do not permit aggression-motivated impulses to develop (*bhava*).

4. They grasped the paradigm of conditioned arising and were afterward able to use it as a matrix for concrete situations. They commented on their experience of conditionality with phrases such as "Yes, that's true, I saw it that way at the time and it had the effect on me of . . . ," and "Do you remember, that was when I was so stuck on my version of the situation that you . . . , and as a result it conditionally arose again and again that . . ."

5. They learned through the use of Diagram 4 (page 55) to analyze the cycle of suffering, to distinguish between feeling, craving, attachment, and the process of becoming, and to make use of their opportunities for choice. In one of their last therapy sessions the two of them worked out Diagram 6, which they named "The Crucial Point."

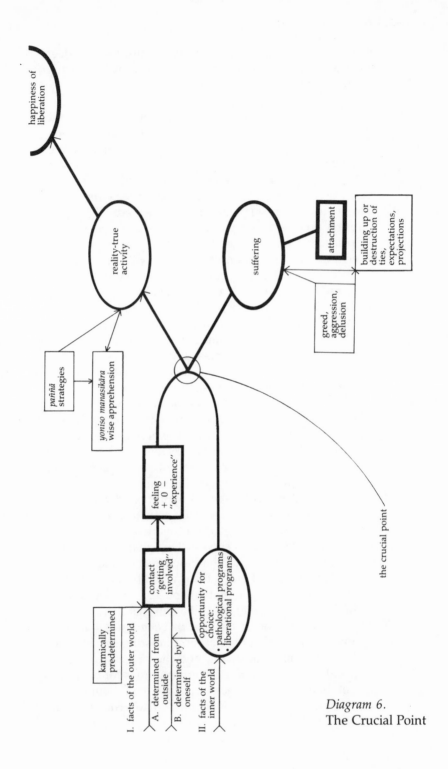

Diagram 6.
The Crucial Point

The therapy session at the end of which Diagram 6 was designed was full of insights and discoveries, yet there was no sudden enlightenment. All the insights were only possible because of many hours of previous work; they had matured slowly. Both marriage partners had already several times discovered various conditionalities of the arising of suffering by themselves and had them confirmed by me. They also had been long familiar with Diagram 4. In this session, after a remarkable sequence of therapeutic insights, I explained to them in greater detail the classical fundamental matrix of conditioned arising. Immediately afterward I received Diagram 6 as a confirmation of their understanding. Nevertheless, the couple required a considerable time, after they were no longer patients, to become proficient in the technique of wise apprehension connected with the matrix of conditioned arising, which they had discovered on their own. What took place easily and without problems in the presence of a marriage therapist was not so easy to apply outside the therapy situation. As I learned recently, four years after the conclusion of therapy, the couple succeeded in developing a number of their own strategies. In fact, the two are continuing to train in these strategies and report that they are very much enjoying going through such an adventure of the mind together.

With grins, the two recall the historical session of "the crucial point." It is interesting that at that time they both became aware of what had happened without a videotape and without repeated consideration. It was an exceptional sequence: she expressed one of her presumptions about his experience, introduced by the words "I have the feeling that you're embarrassed and don't want to talk any more about . . . ," and noticed at that instant that she was trying to impose one of her views on him by passing it off as a "feeling." She paused. She knew that he accorded a great deal of respect to her feelings, which he then showed again by trying to verify her version of his intentions experientially on his own. Then he actually did become embarrassed when he did not find in himself either the imputed embarrassment or an intention "not to want to talk any more about it." He sat there uneasily. She remained silent, then continued on in her sedate way about how she wanted (on her own, naturally) to furnish their holiday cottage, made a few more long pauses, in order, as she herself discovered soon afterward, to provoke one of his "attacks." And in point of fact, in one of the pauses he did come forward, very mildly, with a protective, patronizing question, whereupon she shouted: "You always interrupt me! You just want to manipulate me with your questions!" His concerned question as well as her accusation sounded strangely hollow; both sensed that experience and expression were not in agreement. In that moment he already knew that he would have to behave differently if he wanted to set boundaries for her and that behind his protective questions were other things—his anger over her insinuation of embarrassment, his hurt feelings about her independent approach to the decorating plans, and finally his fear of the bill.

This entire sequence took place in less than a minute and was followed by about a minute of silence. Thereafter, without any intervention from me, both partners nodded to each other with smiles of understanding and began to recount to each other what they had each seen in themselves. Their sudden enlightenment was obviously conditioned by long preparatory work.

WISE APPREHENSION

How difficult it is to grasp the situation of another person accurately can be observed in group conversations, for example, in a circle of friends, in a self-realization group, or at the family table. When such a conversation takes place, it always makes a strong impression on me how differently the various participants see the situation, even when they have the same information. Take, for example, group consideration of arguments for or against something in the external situation of one or more of the people. It could be about making changes in the living room, installing electric or oil heating, where to go on vacation, or something else of the sort. In order to see the situation accurately and make wise decisions, we make an effort to be thorough in noting all the critical factors and then to think over what effect they might have and what conditions have to be met in order to achieve the desired result. However, we might also declare from the start that figuring the whole thing out is too much for us and settle for a superficial understanding of the situation in the hope that "somehow things will work out." Then we just blindly go along with whatever happens.

What is under debate is an external situation, the facts of which are easily seen and grasped. The calculations are simple; grocery-store arithmetic, so to speak, is sufficient: If a melon costs 99 cents, a cucumber 39 cents, and a pound of tomatoes $1.49, how much do I have to pay for two-thirds of a pound of tomatoes, three cucumbers, and two melons? Right at the beginning we could give up on multiplication and calculations with fractions, just put a bill in the vegetable man's hand, and hope that "somehow" we will get back some change. This might be how somebody from a Third World country would act who had only had four years of school. We, however, who know how to do algebra, proportions, interest calculations, and . . .

Dear reader, have you ever considered the fact that illiterates, who seldom learn more than counting or addition, are sometimes better able to deal with psychological and emotional matters than mechanical engineers? By the way, how did you fare with the passage about the algebra of the fundamental matrix of conditioned arising?

Would this be a good place to enter a "Stop," to try an adventure in experimenting with your own mind? Why not read the explanation of the *paticca-samuppāda* one more time, beginning on page 60 with the words "As soon as a person notices . . ." Now find out how confident you are when it comes to sorting out a concrete situation in terms of the algebra of conditioned arising. Thus far you have read a few pages on the topic. How many pages does one have to read to develop any confidence at all about four times five, four times six, four times seven, and so on? And how much practice is necessary to really be able to use two times two when shopping?

Allow yourself enough time for comparative reflection.

We may note that repetition develops a great power of inertia, and not only in the cycle of the conditioned arising of suffering. Repetition of liberational efforts also has a strong effect. Repeated thorough apprehension of situations, repeated direction of the attention onto the pathways that lead out of unpleasant experience, and repeated attentiveness to the good—these are important principles of liberational mind-training in general and of wise apprehension (*yoniso manasikāra*) in particular. Through repetition we make ourselves familiar with what is worthy of attention and make ourselves better able to penetrate the important aspects of reality. Repetition increases the joy of penetration. Our attention naturally inclines toward that with which we have repeatedly occupied ourselves.

In Abhidhamma psychology, the term *manasikāra* refers to the act of attention, the turning of the mind toward its object. *Manasikāra* is the mental factor present in every consciousness that unites all other mental factors present and directs them toward the object of consciousness. On a higher intellectual level, *manasikāra* is reflective apprehension and consideration. Thus *yoniso manasikāra* is sometimes translated as "wise reflection," by which is meant the repeated thorough and painstaking kind of reflection. *Manasikāra* is the first orientation of the mind with regard to its object and its first spontaneous evaluation. And this is exactly where the difficulty lies: The *how* of the apprehension happens spontaneously and can hardly be influenced directly. Our mind is in possession of matrices that are spontaneously invoked in accordance with habitual programming at the moment of first orientation of the attention. In order to prevent deployment of an unwisely (*ayoniso*) apprehending matrix and to replace it with better *yoni*, the systematic practice of wise apprehension is necessary.

To a certain extent, your progress through the pages of this book up to this point has already been—without naming it—an exercise in wise apprehension, and thus you are already aware of the essential requirements for a systematic assimilation of *yoniso manasikāra*. Let us review these requirements:

1. *Mental powers:* knowledge, confidence, willpower (exertion), concentration, and mindfulness are embryonically present in every person. However, only the one who perceives them in himself or herself, cultivates them, and—most important—harmonizes them, can develop them into veritable powers. For daily-life application of *yoniso manasikāra*, mindfulness and the powers of willpower and concentration (which hitherto have only been mentioned) are especially important.

2. *Criteria for ethical evaluation*, which enable us to distinguish that which produces suffering from that which furthers happiness. Actions motivated by greed, aggression, and delusion we already know to lead to suffering. By contrast, those based on generosity, sympathy, wisdom, the liberated trust of *saddhā*, and the protection of *sīla* are wholesome causes that have felicitous effects. Taking suffering on oneself or seeking it out—the beliefs of certain religions notwithstanding—has no ethical or spiritual advantage. Enjoyment of what is pleasing is ethically unobjectionable; only greed for it brings suffering.

3. *Matrices of liberational knowledge*, which enable us to see concrete situations holistically and—in the ideal case—as conditioned, so that the self-perpetuation of the causes of suffering can be interrupted. The matrix for distinguishing bodily experience, feeling, state of mind, mental contents, which we initially practiced in chapter 1; the trust-building questioning of *saddhā* (p. 38); the three pairs of opposites representing the roots of motivation: greed-generosity, aggression-sympathy, delusion-wisdom; and the cycle of conditioned arising explained above—all these are examples of such matrices.

4. *Metaprograms*, which direct the process of choice and the practice and application of liberational matrices and coordinate the utilization of available programs into a strat-

egy. The seven main principles of Dhamma strategies (page 13) or the Four Noble Truths (page 49) are frameworks for such metaprograms. For each strategy, the reader will find in the following chapters metaprograms for systematic practice and application in everyday life.

Let us take a closer look at the plan for practicing *yoniso manasikāra:* First, the four requirements must be present; second, the plan should make possible determination of methodical steps and rules (thus a kind of algebra); and third, it should prepare daily-life application of this algebra in terms of concrete strategies. Thus we conclude that a special algebraic system for the organization of wise apprehension is necessary.

AKKHEYYA: THE ALGEBRA OF WISE APPREHENSION

Akkheyya are technical terms of the Abhidhamma that designate clearly defined units of experience and techniques. They are symbols of a canonical psycho-logic and names of operations in which alterations of experience are accomplished. Wise apprehension of a concrete situation of life and adoption of a matrix as well as the devising and weighing of a strategy take place in the simplest and most beneficial way by means of *akkheyya*. However, no one expects you before beginning to practice Dhamma strategies to memorize a compendium of the Abhidhamma or to sign up for an Abhidhamma course[8] in order to master the entire algebra of *akkheyya* so that you can devise formats for the exercises. You will find in this book detailed and proven exercise schemes that will prepare you to carry out the Dhamma strategies described. The exercises could be compared to a vehicle that helps you to advance on the road to a fulfilled, happy life. Like the driver of a vehicle, you require only a rudimentary knowledge of the functioning of your vehicle. Such knowledge is basically contained in the present chapter. In the next chapter, you will learn a bit more about the nature of your vehicle and how to drive it. But we are already about to embark on our first test drive, the basic exercise in wise apprehension.

Before we systematically execute the exercise, we should clearly recognize its goal. It should enable us to apprehend the real events of our lives in such a way that we can deal with them in a happiness-furthering way. We want to learn to see daily reality in a wise and thorough fashion, so that we can recognize its deeper laws and on the basis of this knowledge devise a better way to work with the practical setup of our lives. Basically, you have already successfully carried out such a demanding enterprise by learning to apply the highly complex (twelve-link!) universal formula of conditioned arising as a matrix for everyday life. The basic exercise for wise apprehension is concerned with recognition of a much simpler matrix. This matrix also encompasses the conditioned arising of suffering, but is composed of only the following three links, which repeat cyclically:

Beginning of an unpleasant incident.
Attachment, that is, disregarding the possibility for a "Stop."
End, that is, completion of the unaltered process. This completion conditions repetition of the same beginning.

Although such processes are repeated countless times in the course of daily life, you will probably notice at the beginning how difficult it is for someone with no practice to connect what occurs to this three-link paradigm. This difficulty is due to the fact that we are conditioned to see the things of manifoldness (*papañca*) in a fragmented, isolated way, outside the context of conditioned arising, and to order them in terms of superficial features. In accordance with habit we take things in terms of an unconsidered system of language, which is indeed helpful for ordinary information but is insufficient for a unit of liberational know-how, of *paññā*. In order to gain a better understanding of the difference between ordinary superficial apprehension and apprehension by means of *akkheyya*, let us consider different possibilities for expressing the units of experience of the following incident:

1. a. Jack and Jim go mushroom gathering
    b. Jack sees a mushroom
    c. Jim picks the mushroom
    d. But Jack was the first to see it and starts a fight
    e. Jim does not want to give Jack the mushroom and as a result gets punched
    f. Jack celebrates his victory
    g. Jim is bitter and plans his revenge
    a. Jack and Jim go mushroom gathering

2. A. Conflicting views
    B. Conflict
    C. A fight
    D. Savoring victory
    E. Revenge

3. A. Conflicting views
    B. Development of the conflict
    C. Completion of the fight
    A. Conflicting views

Before you read any further, please take the time to determine how these three modes of apprehension differ.

Obviously, we could also consider this incident through application of the twelve-link paradigm of conditioned arising, but this is not necessary for formulating a Dhamma strategy. From the point of view of its content, the incident described above belongs in the categories of strategies of sympathy and strategies of power. But we will not begin by concerning ourselves with the content. Moreover, "in greater detail" does not always amount to "more thoroughly and to the point," as we will see in connection with the strategies of ecstasy. Let us stay with the question of how superficial apprehension and wise apprehension differ. Or asked in a way that is more to the point: What are the essential requirements for apprehending an incident by means of Abhidhammic algebra in terms of units of experience (*akkheyya*) that make possible liberation from the repetition of suffering?

We recall the four requirements for systematic assimilation of *yoniso manasikāra*, enumerated on page 68:

1. The mental powers mindfulness, knowledge, confidence, willpower (exertion), concentration
2. Criteria for ethical evaluation
3. Matrices of apprehension
4. Metaprograms for planning exercises and for application of the practiced skills in everyday life

Adopting the one-sided emphasis of scientific-rationalistic approach, we could say that the matrices are the most important requirement, because they apprehend the mental powers and the rest as *akkheyya*. This is an example of the one-sided approach that overvalues perception and knowledge, impugns the act of ethical evaluation, and would destroy the balance of our mental powers. All four requirements must be fulfilled in order for us to be able to work with the algebra. In computer terminology, we would say that the mental powers represent the parameters of the hardware, the criteria are the system by which the data are calculated, the matrices are the data-processing programs, and the metaprograms are the computation procedures. The criteria, matrices, and metaprograms are thus part of software, and the algebra of the *akkheyya* is the programming language. As soon as, through practice, we have fulfilled the four requirements to a certain degree, we recognize and understand the language in which we ourselves can write new programs for our biocomputer. In this language, using personal programs, we will compose our own strategies.

The basic principles of the algebra of *yoniso manasikāra* are as fundamental for our mental data-processing as the rule of three or the equation $(a + b)^2 = a^2 + 2ab + b^2$ are for outer data-processing. Some of these principles are already familiar to us from our reading thus far; the rest can be conveyed through a brief explanation. They tell us that (1) attachment, (2) distortion, (3) repression, (4) abuse, and (5) simplemindedness bring suffering and that the conscious exercise of their opposites characterizes wise apprehension:

1. Apprehension of current happiness or suffering as momentary and changing is wise and does not lead to attachment. Such wise apprehension makes possible a flowing experience of feeling, cramped and narrowed by neither greed nor aggression and not dammed up by attachment. By contrast, experience marred by attachment arises through unwise apprehension of reality. "I want to hold onto this experience, possess its continuation, do it again" is unwise reflection (*ayoniso manasikāra*); its tendencies to hold on, to possess, and to do are connected with attachment. To know that "all feelings are impermanent" and "attachment causes suffering" while experiencing either happiness or pain is wise apprehension. We have, in fact, already discussed this principle in detail earlier on.

2. It is wise to apprehend things in a manner that is free from ego-identification, mania for permanence, and masochism, and without glossing over anything unpleasant. Unwise apprehension and reflection, on the other hand, are distorted by just these perversions. Unwise distortions are defined in Abhidhamma (*Visuddhi Magga*) in the following manner: "The perversions are the three, namely perversions of perception, of consciousness, and of view, which occur as apprehending objects that are impermanent (*anicca*), painful (*dukkha*), not self (*anattā*), and foul (ugly) as permanent, pleasant, self, and beautiful." Overcoming the perversions leads to annihilation of attachment: this is the main theme of the "strategies of power" discussed in chapter 8.

3. While wise apprehension does make use of concepts, it is essentially directed toward reality. From the moment that apprehension and reflection are based itself only on conceptually itemized *akkheyya*, it is unwise and leads to suffering.[9] When apprehension is based only on concepts, those aspects of reality are suppressed that are not conceptually graspable. Such apprehension is defective and causes distortions to arise by perceiving for the most part only concepts and becoming attached to them. The theme "word and reality" plays a major role in the strategies of power.

4. In order not to lose our overview in dealing with objects that we

need and that we enjoy, in the framework of *yoniso manasikāra*, these objects are traditionally divided into the following categories.

a. nourishment ⎫
b. clothing ⎪ objects of need
c. shelter ⎬
d. health care ⎭

e. other objects related to purposes of education, transport, profession, recreation, religion, culture, etc.

This classification makes possible a wise apprehension of our own commitments and needs in such a way that their satisfaction through purposive action can be assured. It is wise to be watchful of the four areas of need so that exaggerations do not develop in any of them— say, in the form of gluttony or dependence on medication—that might result in neglect of the other areas. Thus at a banquet we might reflect as follows: "If these tasty dishes are consumed in a manner not corresponding to their purpose, suffering will result." In this way health is maintained. The same goes for drinking. We thereby find measure in drinking, and our reputation remains intact.

But also going beyond a given moment, it is useful to consider to what extent our interest is distributed over all five areas in a balanced way. Do I buy clothes to clothe myself or to compensate myself for frustrations in other areas (for example, in the area of personal relations)? At this point you might find it amusing to undertake the "algebra exercise" of thinking of ways in which these areas can be combined that do not reflect their essential purpose. For many people, for example, eating is the only culture; for others, modes of transport are objects of religious devotion. (What about your own case?) A use of objects not properly corresponding to their purpose only seems to satisfy our needs; fundamentally it stimulates them further and thus tends to lead to the addictive demand for more. This results in increased abuse, which always causes further suffering. Wise apprehension of the five categories of useful objects prevents frustration of needs and harmonizes the network of relationships to things of the outer world. Conditioned arising pertains here, just as it does to relationships with people.

5. It is not only relationships to persons and things that can be wisely or unwisely apprehended. The same goes for ideas, feelings, and mental objects, as well as alterations and blockages. Happiness and suffering are dependent on how we apprehend positive things

or problematic things, and particularly how we apprehend solving problems and cultivating positive situations. Simplemindedness, which manifests in superficiality, impatience, and in the violence of so-called radical solutions, is a characteristic of unwise apprehension. Wise apprehension (*yoniso manasikāra*), then, is basic proficiency (*kosalla*) in dealing skillfully with real things (*sabhāva-dhammā*) in the case of gain (*āya*) as well as loss (*apāya*) of the good. *Yoniso manasikāra* makes possible the subtle and nonviolent action that characterizes "proficiency in right means" (*upāya-kosalla*). The second book of the Abhidhamma canon[10] gives a beautiful description of the kinds of proficiency that also determine the nature of apprehension and reflection:

> Therein what is proficiency (in knowing) gain? In one paying attention to these states, bad states which have not arisen do not arise; also bad states which have arisen are abandoned; moreover, in one paying attention to these states, good states which have not arisen arise; also good states which have arisen exist for increase, for maturity, for development, for completion. That which therein is wisdom, understanding, discernment, noticing, insight, comprehension, goad . . . absence of dullness, truth investigation, right view, this is called proficiency (in knowing) gain. [Proficiency in right means (*upāya-kosalla*), however, is considered to be the understanding, which is everywhere effective at the right moment and arises on the spot, of right means and the path of development of this thing or that thing.] All knowledge of method is proficiency in right means.

So much, then, for systematic presentation of the algebra of *yoniso manasikāra*. We may note that the principles of this algebra can be applied to all the themes dealt with so far. We could easily have presented this entire book in the language of this algebra and have discovered all the possibilities inherent in this system. However, our goal is practical application of this algebra with a view to attaining a happier daily life.

BASIC EXERCISE IN WISE APPREHENSION

Let us now practice wise apprehension with regard to an unpleasant, painful event that has actually happened to you and about which you have an intuition that it could have come out entirely differently if you had known beforehand what was about to take place. This intuition is an indication that even as the event was taking place you could have apprehended it differently. Let us not take too difficult a situation for the exercise. Also for the first try, do not choose a personal-relationship problem, but rather some annoyance with a machine, an animal, with a place or the way to it—a completely ordinary nuisance to which you were exposed not too long ago. Bring to mind the beginning and the end of the event.

Take a comfortable position so that you will not be distracted by physical discomfort, but hold the book in such a way that you can read the step-by-step instructions on page 76. When you have read an instruction, carry it out with your eyes closed and do not open your eyes until you are ready to read the next instruction.

Did another development spontaneously unreel as a result of a different way of apprehending the situation? If we had gone through these seven steps in a workshop, a discussion would now follow. There are so many interesting questions: Did you effortlessly make use of any of the algebra we have discussed in the process of "constructing" a new view? Did you note anything in the way of a matrix? Recount the annoying incident you chose! Did the fist in which you held the motives against interrupting tense up? In what way was the "constructed" apprehension more thorough and to the point or otherwise different?

You can do all this without a group discussion and can even penetrate more deeply by yourself if you are patient with yourself and refrain from doing yourself violence. In a light and easygoing way, go through the seven steps of *yoniso manasikāra* once more before reading further.

Manasikāra is the first orientation of the mind with regard to an object that has just cropped up in the stream of awareness. This encounter with an object of consciousness involves a spontaneous apprehension of the object connected with a habitually activated matrix. This apprehension can be either unwise (*ayoniso*) and thus suffering-producing or wise (*yoniso*) and thus liberationally happiness-producing, depending on what kind of a matrix is brought into play. The exercise for *yoniso manasikāra* divides the mental process into steps that make possible an interruption of the unwholesome development and the construction and practicing of a wholesome, happiness-furthering one. The steps themselves are a constructed apprehension of the mental process; in a self-conditioned perpetuation of a repeating cycle, they happen with lightning speed. Division of the stream of experience into steps is purely for the sake of exercise, and there should be no attempt to force free-flowing liberated experience into a fixed mold. *Yoniso manasikāra* opens awareness to freedom.

1. Let the beginning, development, and end of the annoying event unreel before your inner eyes and ears. *Go ahead!*
   (Close your eyes!)
2. Repeat the first step!
   (Close your eyes!)
3. Were there any opportunities at the time to interrupt the development of the event temporally? Let the development unreel again from the point of view of this question. *Go ahead!*
   (Close your eyes!)
4. Why didn't I interrupt? In the course of the development, was I in the grips of inner compulsions and designs? Which ones?
   Reflect on the context of the incident and enumerate the motives on your fingers—count them off and, as it were, store them on your fingers. *Go ahead!*
   (Close your eyes!)
5. I now have my motives for not interrupting in my hand (if I curl my fingers into a fist), and thus I can easily halt the development and fill the gap with the idea of a pleasant break (sitting down, meditating, lying down, enjoying a cup of coffee, and so on) before continuing with the unreeling of the development.
   Let the events unreel, interrupt, fill the gap with something pleasant, continue to the end!
   (Close your eyes!)
6. The pleasant interlude gives me the possibility to gain more remove from the inner or situational compulsion. From this distance I can more clearly perceive the events unreeled up to the interruption and evolve a wiser apprehension, which will be primarily characterized by the fact that it speaks against continuing the development. Let the events unreel from the beginning up to the interruption! From the pleasant distance construct a wiser apprehension!
   (Close your eyes!)
7. From the beginning and without an interruption, let an alternative development unreel!
   (Close your eyes!)

4

Intelligence of the Body and Joy

Our reality, fragmented by language, becomes a continuum once again in our bodily experience, if we cultivate our body-consciousness. This is the great opportunity for body-oriented psychotherapy and meditation methods. By organically ordering and unifying experience, they also make possible a restructuring and transformation of the world. The exercises for mindfulness of body that will be introduced in chapter 5 present the key to this. The more mindfully our awareness of our body flows, the more refined and coherent becomes the continuum, the seamless connectedness of all reality.[1] Even when the relations and boundaries between the things in this continuum are perceived differently by different persons, the world as bound into a whole by bodily experience is the best basis for communication and interpersonal agreement. The bodily reference to reality is the best guarantee of impartiality in knowledge and action, as we noted in chapter 1. That which has been bodily experienced, known, explored, and executed is unequivocal. In bodily reality, there are no lies. Though we can pretend something, what is pretended becomes true as soon as it is carried out, since no lie in this sense is possible. It really is what it is. Only the interpretations, and to a certain extent also the motivations, of bodily action can be falsified.

Earnest attention to the body and bodily related aspects of our experience brings many benefits on the path of liberation and happiness. We will recognize them directly as soon as we practice some of the concrete techniques of mindfulness of body. They are already evoked when we talk about the intelligence of the body. The word "intelligence" is used here in a literal, so to speak fundamentalistic sense. Intelligence fundamentally refers to comprehension of relationships and meanings. It is composed of two Latin words: the first, *inter*, means "between," and the second derives from *legere*, which means "to read." Here we are really talking about an *intel-legere*, reading what is taking place between really existing things. With more precise observation, however, we find that there are no discrete, immutable things per se; all things stand in relationship to each other, and all real things change. Reality-true experience apprehends the relationships between things and knows what happens when something changes. The previous chapter stressed that knowledge must relate to connections and conditioned relationships between things if it is to be considered wisdom (*paññā*) and be of help in bringing about a happy way of life. Now, wisdom is based on intelligent observation of bodily reality. As paradoxical as it may sound, the intelligence of the body has a value for the liberation of the mind that cannot be supplanted by anything else. The author of the Abhidhamma expresses this in a concise and pithy manner:

> There is one thing, monks, that, cultivated and regularly practised, leads to a deep sense of urgency, . . . to the Supreme Peace, . . . to mindfulness and clear comprehension, . . . to the attainment of the right vision and knowledge, . . . to happiness here and now, . . . to realizing deliverance by wisdom and the fruition of Holiness. What is this one thing? It is the mindfulness of the body.[2]

The way in which happiness and a sense of urgency are related with the experience of the body and represent sources of energy will be thoroughly discussed below in the section "Joy and the Sense of Urgency" (page 100). Let us attempt to see clearly how intelligent and indispensable this relatedness to the body is.

BETRAYING THE BODY DRIVES US CRAZY

Respect for bodily anchoring in reality has been cast into oblivion in our culture in the name of scientific enlightenment. For a long time we only looked upwards to the *logos*. Only at the beginning of this century did Sigmund Freud and Ivan P. Pavlov draw our attention again to the importance of the body. Freud made clear that we can only understand that part of a total experience that relates to the message from our own body.[3] Pavlov showed in his experiments that not only men but also dogs can be driven crazy when they lose their bodily anchoring in reality. Because Pavlov's experiments are very instructive, I would like to give a short account of them here.

A dog usually goes to its feeding place as soon as it sees or smells food there and begins to eat. If, however, shortly before feeding, a circle of light is projected on the wall, the dog learns to go to the feeding place as soon as the light appears. Its digestive system even learns to react to the light with peristaltic activity and salivation before the food itself is seen or smelled. Once this point has been reached, the scientist begins a new little game with the dog: every time the dog starts to move upon the appearance of an ellipse-shaped light, he receives an electric shock. The hungry dog soon learns to made distinctions: (A) The light circle is an "invitation to dinner," which permits stomach movements and salivation. (B) The light ellipse is a warning of pain; in other words, it is better not to move when it appears. Now, in the name of science, something nasty is done. A so-called experimental neurosis is evoked. The hunger-crazed dog is also given food after the appearance of a light circle that is not entirely round, on the one hand; on the other hand, after the appearance of a slightly rounder light ellipse, it is given a shock. In addition, the difference between the two kinds of light signals is continually diminished. At first, the dog prefers to abandon eating. As its hunger increases, however, it begins to risk shocks and pain in order to get relief. The scientist continues to make the "nasty" ellipses rounder and rounder and to make the "nice" circles flatter and flatter. The dog is now completely at the mercy of this contrived situation and dependent upon the grace and power of the experimenter. The only choice left to it is death by starvation or madness. According to the scientific reports, Pavlov's dogs chose madness.

It is highly probable that Pavlov was so captivated and blinded by his discoveries regarding reflex mechanisms that, unlike Freud, he failed to think either about the ethical aspects of his work or about the significance of conscious experience. You, however, might pause at this point and give your thoughts and associations a chance to unfold. How does the relationship between power-possessors and those dependent on them appear in your own environment? Do you know of examples of authoritarian, master-type male personalities who are or have been dependent on the grace and favor of a spoiled daughter or lover? What means of power do the weak have? Arousing guilt feelings? Driving the partner crazy? Blackmail? Withdrawal of affection? These are all frequent themes in our society. Have you ever known a pampered man who acts completely awkward and helpless and yet gets practically everything he wants?—not only from women whose maternal instinct he knows how to exploit, but also from men to whom he pretends to subordinate himself. This is also a recurrent theme. What do we know about the unclear and equivocal relationship between consolidation of power and abuse of power? Who is making a victim of whom, and who is making whom the victimizer, the culprit? When we apprehend such concrete situations clearly (*yoniso manasikāra*), we find once again the same old causes—alienation from reality, aggression, and greed.

Many other questions come up in relation to the Pavlovian experiments, which can only be answered unequivocally from the certainty of one's own anchoring in reality. What does "crazy" or "deranged" mean? De-ranged in relation to what? To what extent did Pavlov's dogs betray their bodies? The smell of food, the circle of light, hunger, and the actual experience of food are all bodily realities—where among them does intelligence lie and where madness? Where is the lie? Is the relationship between bodily experienced things always equally certain? Is it comparable to that between thing and word? Such questions cannot be answered by words of explanation. Clear comprehension (*sampajañña*) concerning these matters is nevertheless conveyed in the chapters that follow, with the help of exercises in mindfulness of body.

Here is a question related to experimentation on animals, perhaps the most important, but one that unfortunately is almost always ignored: What happens inwardly to the scientist who systematically practices torment of other living beings? What kind of changes in consciousness and deep structures of personality does a person experience who, for tactical reasons, always presents himself as subordinate and helpless? This behavior stays with him. His success in getting what he wants is only one side of the coin. Similarly, the inner world of a person who believes he has saved many situations and won many struggles by lying does not remain without traces of this approach. And the scientist? With time he becomes a specialist in treating everybody—including himself—by the same means and methods in which he has had so much practice. He can't help himself? Yes, it is true; his supposed power is limited. Attainment of insight and penetrating knowledge concerning this kind of relationship is a sine qua non, an essential condition, for the cultivation of the higher stages of *sīla*, the reliable subjective basis for liberation.

It is easy to understand that the intelligence of the body is so important for joy and self-confidence, for impartiality and clear comprehension. On the other hand, seeing its interpersonal and ethical implications requires still further observation. But for the moment, let us stick with the benefits of bodily anchoring in reality that are already familiar to you. What do we actually gain by communicating with others unambiguously and truthfully? What is nonambiguity? What is anchoring in reality? Take a little time to reconnoiter your own life situation and check back to page 38. What do you discover in retrospect? Before reading further, note what occurs to you concerning your own communication skills and potential.

CHEERFUL DETACHMENT FROM THE BODY

Bodily anchoring in reality and clear unambiguous communication not only prevent madness, derangement, exploitation, and fraud; they can also lead us out of a personal aberration or a derangement on the level of society as a whole. Gregory Bateson, whom I have already mentioned several times, concerned himself intensively with such issues. The results of his research make it possible to see the further consequences of the discoveries of Freud, Pavlov, and others. Bateson brought together the findings of several disciplines—not in the manner of the systematizers mentioned in chapter 2, by compiling fragments of conceptual knowledge, but by unifying the ordering principles of various ways to knowledge into a universal epistemology. This epistemology investigates the process of knowing of the scientist and the dog, the mentally disturbed person and the therapist, and compares the results of this process—the worlds, so to speak, created by the process of knowing. Thus it is closer to Abhidhamma than conventional psychology or theory of knowledge, which often consist of theories about theories. Batesonian epistemology should enable the psychological disciplines, and especially psychotherapy, to profit more completely from the layered, multidimensional, interactional, and holistic mode of apprehension of the Abhidhamma than they could at the time of the first Abhidhamma translations at the beginning of the twentieth century.

Although Bateson himself, as he told me personally, came in contact with Abhidhamma only briefly during his stay in Peradeniya, Sri Lanka, the service he has performed in making Abhidhamma understandable is comparable to that performed by the French psychoanalyst Jacques Lacan in making Freudian thought understandable. Lacan showed that during the first half of this century, the biological determinism, the mechanistic approach to identity, and the principles of economy of energy were all that were understood of Freud's work.[4] The principles of interpretation of modern semantics and cybernetics were not as yet at hand. Thanks to the work of Bateson and the Palo Alto School, we are able today to benefit much more from Abhidhamma. Thus our situation corresponds to the situation of contemporary psychoanalysts, whom Lacan enabled to understand the discoveries of Freud much more deeply, more completely, and in a way far closer to Freud's original intention.

Before I explain how bodily anchoring in reality can lead us out of deplorable states of affairs of the inner world (madness, mendacity, etc.) as well as of the outer world (exploitation, manipulation, etc.), and before I deal with Bateson's contribution to the understanding of the way out or solution in greater detail, I must call attention to three important themes. They play an important role in Abhidhamma and also in the work of Bateson: distinguishing levels of communication, integrative overcoming of opposites, and the processing of conflict through humor.

The smile of the Buddha is proverbial. In Pali it is called *hasita*. The "consciousness that produces mirth" (*hasituppāda-citta*) is what the Abhidhamma calls the cheerful joy of an enlightened one, who in "remembering certain curious contrasts is caused to smile."[5] This smile is a bodily expression (*kāya-viññatti*) of joy, which arises after a conflict has been overcome (*uppāda* means "arising, generating"—recall *paticca-samuppāda*, with which we are now quite familiar) and which may possibly be followed by a verbal expression (*vacī-viññatti*). In other words, as a result of liberational overcoming of conflict, the afflicting element appears vestigially only as a curious and amusing contrast. Such a liberational step brings relief and also creates an upliftedness that in turn makes possible an objective solution of the problem—if that is still at all necessary. This relieving sense of distance at first brings about a bodily expression of joy, which in the next step permits a joyful reflection on the verbal level. Free from affliction, excitement, and compulsion to act, the meditative smile is radiant. This is only a very brief account of the Abhidhamma view on the arising of the many kinds of laughter and smiles and other expressions of joy. We will have occasion again later to discuss the various kinds of joy in greater detail.

Bateson approaches the theme of humor through an analysis of play in animals. How the joy arises that animals express in play is something that cannot be discovered without asking about their introspective activity. Animals manifest the same behavior in playing that they do in fighting. The difference lies in the fact that in playing they do not harm each other, because they know that "this is a game." How do they know this? Thoroughly apprehending observation uncovers the fact that with animals there is an invitation to play, a kind of provocative nudging, which on another, more global metalevel conveys the message "This is a game!" This global, all-encompassing communication is saying that the whole situation—the network of relations, the procedure, the mutually complementary actions—is meant to be analogous to another, similar global situation that is known to both playing animals. Thus reference is made to another whole that is structured in accordance with the same paradigm, just as is done by the analogically modeling computer. This analog communication conveys a complete message, a self-contained whole. The series of un-self-contained exchanges of actions and messages during the course of play is itself digital, like the sequence of fingers (Lat., *digitus*) in a pair of hands folded together. The entire course of the game can be divided by thoroughly apprehending observation into a sequence of parts that fit together for which only a digital matrix is applicable. However, the bodily reality of an experiencing being remains a continuum the whole time, throughout the various changes in the situation. The division into digital and analog is artificial, a product of thought. Every communication between sentient beings is always both digital and analog as long as it is healthy, bodily anchored, and natural. This is forgotten by scientists and writers who write about art, the life of groups, or the co-evolution of persons and affirm that one of the two modes of communication is more fundamental, more precise, or more important than the other.

Only when a person or group of persons becomes alienated from bodily reality does the split between analog and digital take place in the realm of ideas, and consciousness rejects one or the other of the two categories. Only at this point can the madness, de-rangement, exploitation, and manipulation conditioned by this state of affairs arise. Thus default or unclear communication of one of the two types of messages, or in other words, nonthorough apprehension (*ayoniso manasikāra*) of the situation, leads to suffering. Now, with the help of the Batesonian double-bind matrix,[6] let us see how something of this nature takes place in concrete situations and how one can break out of such a cycle of conditioned arising.

Let us note once more with emphasis that both the thorough apprehension of the double-bind situation (i.e., the Second Noble Truth of "knowledge of the cause of suffering") as well as knowledge of the way out (the Fourth Noble Truth of the "path of liberation from suffering") must be at the conscious disposal of the person wishing to free him- or herself. The insight concerning suffering (the First Noble Truth) and cessation of suffering as the goal (the Third Noble Truth) are not enough by themselves. Bateson, Jackson, Haley, and Weakland, in their pioneering article "Toward a Theory of Schizophrenia" (1956), listed the following five elements of the double-bind matrix. (The remaining three come from the Abhidhamma.)

1. A "victim" is chosen by those who have the power to do so or by those to whom power is allocated (think of the

case of a spoiled, "weak" daughter who chooses her guilt-laden father as a victim).

2. The victim must be exposed to repeated experiences of painful uncertainty (like Pavlov's dog).

3. The victim learns on the "primary" level—so the authors say—to decipher digital signals and to behave in such a way that punishments and pain can be avoided (obediently following the instructions of parents in order to avoid withdrawal of affection; in the case of Pavlov's dog, not going to the feeding place when the light takes the form of an ellipse, and so on).

4. On another, secondary level, something conflicting is analogically perceived in which gratification is promised. ("Only when you ignore your parents do they respect you," as in the example I cited earlier from the marriage-counseling case; in the case of the dog, "Light signals food and punishment.")

5. The whole situation must be accepted as inescapable— and be defined as such on a "higher," tertiary level (the child believes that she can find love and respect only in her immediate family; the dog can appease its hunger only within the framework of the experiment).

6. Once all these five conditions have been programmed into the victim, they no longer have to actually manifest in his or her external world. It is enough for any one of the five conditions to appear and the crazy dog or the schizophrenic child develops fear, anger, or panic. The triggering signals can from this point on also be hallucinated and the missing details of the afflictive situation continue to appear, conditioned by the repetition of voices and visions in the inner world.

7. If the victim is freed from the continuously repeating situation by a savior, yet without having gained insight into it, then conditions of victimhood continue to exist. The victim continues to seek out new dependencies in the suffering-free situation; for example, now he or she prays to the grace-giving savior. The double-bind programming has not been erased; it is only that the victim's fear, anger, and panic have been transposed into dependency, submissiveness, and obedience. The victim's will and ability to live remain reduced. The experimentally impaired dog has overadapted to his new master; the

"crazy" child develops in another relationship into a completely devoted and submissive sexual partner or into a fanatic devotee of some sect.

8. Liberation can come about only if the victim penetrates with understanding into all five conditions, is able to relegate them to primary, secondary, and tertiary levels and then find the way out on a still higher level of meta-communication.

What is this "still higher level"? What is the "highest level," the level on which the way out is to be found?

After explaining the conditions of the double-bind, Bateson and his colleagues show the way out of the double-bind by means of the following story: A Zen master holds a stick over the head of his student and says: "If you say that the stick is real, I'll hit you. If you say it isn't real, I'll hit you. If you say nothing at all,'I'll hit you." The Zen master is a person of authority. The student has the instruction just to sit and meditate. Both know that the highest definition of the whole situation is "the path to liberation." That is the major difference. The way out consists in the student's taking hold of the stick and putting it aside.

The Zen master is benevolent in the highest sense; he is without aggression, without greed, and is not attached to words, which constitute the conditions of the double-bind. The student is unobstructed in realizing the way on the physical level. Thus he is liberated.

A young psychologist who collaborated with me years ago on liberational workshops expressed her leap into liberation in a poem, which represents at once her matrix and her metaprogram for the way out of painful conflict:

> Do you see
> the bead-wet net of the spider is
> a miracle of beauty
> the meaning
> so hard to understand
>
> Ungatherable
> the years lived through
> Much fallen into deep depths
> Much left behind
> forever lost
>
> Without understanding
> trust in now
> Boldly be senseless
> Overthrow rules and

declare them exceptions
Switch principles on the fly
Let the absurd
hit the bull's-eye
[JESSICA WILKER, 1982]

The poem speaks for itself. It points to bodily anchoring in the now, shakes off social and conceptual double-binds, lets all of life (including the absurd) become conscious. It is a powerful leap into freedom, freedom from limitations, freedom for meaningful life. An awakening to meaning can be an awakening to the will and energy to live. Only at this point is the danger overcome (see point 7 in the above double-bind matrix) that the liberated person might once again subordinate him- or herself to an authority or a belief—even a belief in the absurd, in chaos, or in gaily abandoning oneself to the unconscious. Breaking out, escaping into cosmic homelessness, only liberates and transcends if we have already put our own inner household in order. Only after elimination of the inner defilements (*kilesa*) can the outer ecology be harmonized, can perception become free from obscuration and distortion. Then you see: nature is a miracle of beauty . . .

Dear reader, I know that it would give you great pleasure to be with me here in this meadow in the midst of the Sri Lankan jungle where I sit and write these lines—far from the city, at rest in the lap of nature, surrounded by the voices of birds and all the other sounds—actually, there's quite a lot of noise, for the jungle is anything but still. A few minutes ago, some cheeky monkeys swiped the pastry my wife served me with tea. Why don't I throw a stone? Why don't I use a stick or maybe an air rifle to scare the monkeys away? Why do I choose to live here with the monkeys? If you were sitting here with me now under this tree, we could share many situations with each other that could serve as building blocks for life's double-bind. Certainly this situation in the primeval tropical forest would provide us with enough time and space so that we could transcend them all within a few moments. In that way, any sense of affliction would become a "cheerful recollection of certain curious contrasts"—the enlightened smile.

Dear reader, if you can momentarily drop the programming you have received based on the conventions of Western painting and do *not* perceive the following picture as a representation of a rectangular rod bent into a triangle, and if you do not make your survival dependent on deciphering this image, then you won't go crazy over it; you will experience neither affliction nor anger. You will laugh cheerfully over the "curious contrasts" of the visual double-bind. You will not let yourself be caught by the visual double-bind. You have had a look at it and composedly turned away. Is nothing left now but a "cheerful recollection of certain curious contrasts"—*hasita*, the enlightened smile?

LEVELS OF EXPERIENCING

The experiment presented in chapter 1 has already shown us that there are modes of experiencing that are devoid of thinking. As banal as this may sound, there are many people for whom it is not a proven thing. Time and again I have been confronted with the fact that many participants in workshops on New Age strategies, though they have indeed understood that there is experiencing outside of thinking and are even able to carry on learned discussions on this point, have never actually themselves clearly undergone such a nonthought experiencing.

Although it is essential for an understanding of Abhidhamma to be familiar with thought-free experiencing, we are not at all talking about getting rid of thinking altogether, as some schools of meditation preach we should. Being like a child who has not yet learned to think has nothing to do with liberation and enlightenment. Liberated experiencing, it is true, will never fall back into certain unpleasant areas (for example, depression or psychosis);[7] nevertheless, fundamentally, all levels of experiencing are accessible to it. No level of experiencing is left unconsidered in liberational mind-training, but none of them is the object of clinging. Every level of experiencing is essential for something in life. Nonconceptual experiencing of the body is necessary for learning a dance or a sports movement, and the unfeeling calculation experience is necessary for errorless addition when shopping, doing accounts, or constructing a bridge. In fact, for liberational mind-training all experiencing types are required and must therefore be cultivated.

So in particular spheres of life, certain types of experiencing are beneficial. For developing, practicing, and applying New Age strategies, it is particularly important that we are capable of recognizing which life-sphere we are in at a given moment and of determining which type of experiencing to adopt. In everyday life, such adaptation of our mode of experiencing to given circumstances happens automatically, that is, without conscious control. Advanced Dhamma-strategy practices work primarily with the transitions between various realities and the modes of experiencing corresponding to them. We have already touched on this theme; thus the following consideration of differences in types of experiencing will be familiar. Nonetheless, you may perhaps find it refreshing to bring to mind once more the spheres and types of experiencing you went through as you were reading the various discussions on overcoming conflict. Investigate yourself, using the preceding chapter sections as a manifold of bases for several types of experiencing. Thus, how did you experience

- The system-theory analysis following Bateson?
- The Abhidhamma explanation of transcendence through humor?
- The communication through a poem?
- How about the passage on Pavlov?
- What effect did the Zen story have?
- What about the invitation to participate emotionally in the amusing, conflict-laden writing situation of the author?
- Finally, what about the graphic presentation of the double-bind situation, which called into question our culture-conditioned program for perceiving visual representations?

What levels of experience were activated in you by the various presentations? You are now in a position to carry out a self-diagnosis indicating which levels you are particularly talented at. It would be worthwhile to reread the section entitled "Cheerful Detachment from the Body" (page 81) with this in mind.

For the development of Dhamma strategies, it will be sufficient at present to be able to distinguish the following four levels.:

1. Immediate experiencing of real events, processes, and states (and the feelings and sensations associated with them) bodily taking place in the present moment.
2. The bodily experienced meaning of represented (remem-

bered) events, relations, constellations, situations, and scenes (and the feelings and sensations associated with them) that have lead to current states of feeling and alterations of consciousness.

3. Conceptual thinking related to the flow of immediate experiencing or to the felt meaning of entire situations, which are presently happening.[8] From this thinking are derived matrixes and programs for apprehension and action (to the extent that they are consciously accessible and thus also "thinkable").

4. Conceptual thinking whose content has no relationship to the current state of the thinker and thus which has no conscious relationship to experiential reality. This could be a kind of non-reality-related babbling that is unconsciously motivated and directed, or mechanical data-processing (for example, calculation), or it could also be wise reflection on rules and programs with the help of the metalanguage of Abhidhammic algebra—in other words, planning and coordinating of liberational strategies. The key point here is that this level of experience has no present bodily anchoring in reality.

In the real sense, only the immediate experiencing of the first type is anchored in a reality accessible to any person who might happen to be present. Thus we call it intersubjective. On this level of sensual existence (*kāma-bhava*) the strategically weighed actions take place that comprise the shared world of New Age conspirators. Only on this level is it possible really to breathe together (*conspirare*), to work together, to change the world and bring about harmony between sentient beings and the cosmos.

Discussions and lectures, the writing and reading of books—all conceptual thinking—structure and present contents that are less real than immediately experienced events. While reading, listening to a talk, reflecting, dreaming, or discussing, we can indeed also experience bodily meanings and feel changes in our state of mind. This, however, is a secondhand experience of reality—it is derivative rather than original and thus less real than immediate experiencing of the first type. Feelings and sensations, experiences of meaning, and emotional states connected with secondhand experience are subjectively real, since they take place in the body of the experiencer. They do not belong, however, to the reality of the world that we share with each other intersubjectively. Even when a group of people, during a lecture or sermon or a group meditation, develops similar experiences of meaning and emotion and these parallel experiences elicit the same bodily expressions (*viññatti*) of bliss or anger from the various individuals—even then we do not have a case of participating in a shared reality. To put it in terms of an image, this no more creates a shared reality than twenty-two goalies jumping into the air and making the gesture of catching a ball create a soccer game. Or another image: If two people are aroused to sexual excitement at the same time in the same room, that hardly means that they are taking part in a sexual act of physical union that will result in offspring. Equally without fruit, unfortunately, are the many "group projects" offered today under the New Age label that are connected with lovely ideas and views of the world but have no immediate shared anchoring in reality.

Group meditation is an activity that has proved helpful for many. Not only is it more economical for the group leader to give instruction to ten people instead of giving individual instruction ten times; it is also easier for the meditator to keep to the outer aspects of the discipline, to limit distraction and fulfill the time requirement, when ten other people are also physically there in the same place. But that is all there is to it. There is no further "shared activity" in the meditation hall, for each person must meditate for him- or herself. However, mention should be made of exceptional situations, which very rarely come up in meditation, in which the group can be of further help—for example, if a meditator is unable properly to distinguish the spheres and levels of experiencing or is lacking clear comprehension concerning the meditative domain (*gocara-sampajañña*). (I shall discuss this point in detail in chapter 5.) In addition, in connection with misguided meditation the same thing can happen that so often takes place in psychotherapeutic and other groups—emotions arising in one sphere of experience (group fantasy, daydream, role-playing, etc.) motivate ill-conceived actions in another sphere of experience (the intersubjective reality of political or family life, etc.). It can then unfortunately happen that inadequate clarity of comprehension appears together with an inability for thorough apprehension, and inadvertently a catastrophe is caused.

Distinguishing and testing of levels and spheres of experiencing, which is entirely ignored by conventional psychological sciences, is extremely important for working with Dhamma strategies and receives major attention in the Abhidhamma under the headings of *sampajañña* (clear comprehension) and *vīmamsā* (investigation), depending on the context of application, as we will see in the following chapters.

In all our strategy practices, we will distinguish the four levels of experiencing introduced on page 88:

1. That which is perceived by the senses and felt with the body
2. Feelings and bodily anchored meanings
3. Thinking with reference to present experience
4. Thinking without any immediate reference

The sequence in which these types of experiencing might appear in practicing a strategy is shown in Diagram 7. Note that two kinds of feelings arise: that of body awareness (time point A') and that connected with bodily experienced meaning (time point B"). The unfolding of a strategy begins (time point 0) with the conscious recollection of a past situation considered from the point of view of a possible strategy (time point A). Then, under certain circumstances, the past action could be repeated imitatively on a bodily real or quasi-real level (for example, in a psychodrama or imaginarily):

A. In consciously recollecting situations that are either problematic or promising for further liberation, we have recourse to relevant knowledge (in Diagram 7, the diamond labeled "K"), coming from past apprehension of the actions in question. This knowledge is concretized into experiencing of the first type.

B. In thorough apprehension of the consciously recollected situations the main role is played by bodily experienced meanings (time point B') and the feelings associated with them (A' and B", second type). However, conceptual thinking (third type) is also necessary.

C. For analysis and consideration of possible matrices and programs, thinking that is independent of current experience (fourth type) is utilized.

D. Preliminary acting out of the chosen strategy is accomplished either mentally by means of bodily experienced meanings and the feelings associated with them (second type) or tried out in the clearly defined, enclosed, and protected context of a psychodrama or therapy situation as immediately bodily experienced (first type) theatrical actions.

Application of a strategy takes place in a concrete life situation and requires skillful utilization of all levels and types of experiencing. Well-practiced strategies are spontaneously applied at the appropriate moment in accordance with the situation. Even when they are executed playfully without any effort, the characteristic mark of Abhidhamma strategies is always consciously thorough apprehension of

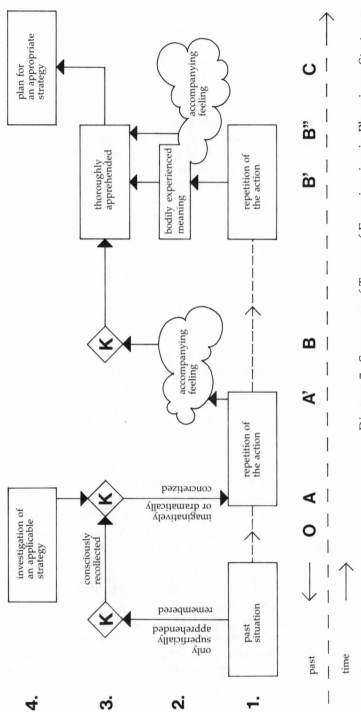

Diagram 7. Sequence of Types of Experiencing in Planning a Strategy

reality and mindfully clear comprehension of the purpose and suitability of what is to be done. Clear comprehension (*sampajañña*) will be examined in detail in the next chapter; an understanding of thorough apprehension (*yoniso manasikāra*) was the objective of the previous chapter. Here the object of our interest is the four levels of experiencing, which we have learned to distinguish in our foregoing discussions, the strategic relevance of which is illustrated in Diagram 7, and whose further relations to one another are illustrated in Diagram 8. Diagram 8 portrays certain unwholesome developments that

These empty diamonds refer to apprehension that can be with or without reference to concrete situations and thorough or superficial. A diamond labeled "K" refers to apprehension of reality-anchored knowledge (of situations, feelings, etc.); a diamond labeled "A" refers to apprehension of abstract knowledge.

These solid diamonds refer to things of the external world to be apprehended.

Chains of information-processing by means of reflection, planning, and so on, are represented by boxes labeled "thinking."

Feelings are indicated, as in the previous diagram, by clouds. In connection with this, note that the oval-shaped box that stands for a decision concerning action also belongs to the level of feelings, sensations, and emotions and not to that of thinking. (Cf. in this connection the presentation on intentions for action on p. 000f. and Diagram 9.)

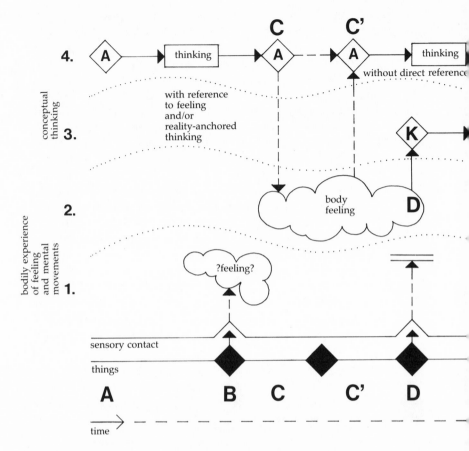

Diagram 8. Levels of Experiencing and Concrete Reference

can crop up in the absence of clear comprehension, as well as possibilities for overcoming them through mindful attending. We are already familiar with most of the symbols in this diagram.

In Diagram 8, several experiential scenarios are illustrated in which the levels of experiencing change. These changes are represented by vertical arrows. The solid arrows show conscious concrete reference to a reality-anchored experience; the broken arrows indicate unconscious effects that go unperceived. Thus we see in Diagram 8 that at Time Point A a process of abstract thinking (fourth type) begins, which, at Time Point C, triggers a mentally related feeling. Extremely critical here is the distinction between the following two possibilities.

One possibility is that we do not notice at all that a feeling has been

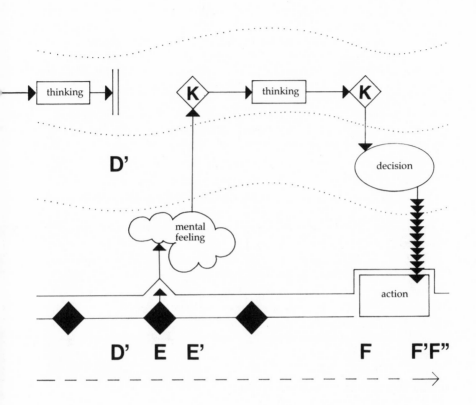

triggered and continue unmindfully with abstract thinking. We do not perceive that knowledge C' is not identical with knowledge C because C' includes the distortion resulting from the unheeded feeling. This abstract thinking is not only devoid of concrete reference but from C' on is also invalid.

The second possibility would be to heed the triggered feeling, to apprehend it (Time Point D), and, to the extent necessary, to work on it by thinking about it. When we have resolved the problem of the feeling in this manner, the thinking related to it is interrupted (Time Point D'). Later we could resume the abstract thinking and continue with it without error. The exercise leading to this is referred to by Nyanaponika Thera as "obtaining the bare object." This exercise makes us capable of dealing competently with distractions, as will be described in the next chapter.

For the present, let us turn back to Diagram 8. We see that at the same time as abstract thinking is running from Time Point A to C, a feeling arises at Time Point B, triggered by sensory contact with things in the external world. This sensory contact is uncontrolled (neither consciously screened out nor mindfully apprehended), and the mental movement triggered by it remains unconscious; thus it can hardly be called a feeling. Nonetheless, this mental movement constitutes a distraction, which has an unfavorable effect on the thinking that is taking place at the same time. We will deal with this theme in detail in connection with exercises in concentration.

The idea here is not that for someone who is well versed in Dhamma strategies, the mistakes and distractions portrayed above never happen. The purpose of the exercise is rather to train our attention so that we are able to notice these obstacles and overcome them. Diagram 8 shows this kind of competent way of dealing with the obstacles at Time Point D. Mental movements triggered by unintentional sensory contact are intentionally screened out (horizontal double line) and feelings triggered by thoughts are mindfully worked on. As a result, at Time Point E a reality-anchored experiencing becomes possible. This leads to thinking that is pertinent to the actual state of affairs (Time Point E′) and thus makes it possible to plan an action (Time Point F). The experiences from E to F have been presented to a more detailed sequence in Diagram 7. Here in Diagram 8, the emphasis is on the question of concrete reference, which can be directed toward feelings as well as toward external reality.

STREAM OF FEELINGS

Through apprehension (*manasikāra*) all things are created . . .
Feeling (*vedanā*) combines all things . . .
Through mindfulness (*sati*) all things are mastered . . .[9]

Our body is the only thing that each of us can perceive from the outside as well as feel from the inside. Count Dürckheim, who has contributed so much to the introduction of Zen Buddhism to Europe, coined the distinction between "the body [*Körper*] that I have and the body [*Leib*] that I am." In the Abhidhamma a number of concepts are used for body, which, however, on a more subtle level of analysis, cannot be reduced to a twofold division of physical body [*Körper*] and lived body [*Leib*]—for I am not the lived body that I feel from the inside. When thoroughly apprehended, this lived body too is only an egoless husk, as each one of us can prove beyond doubt to himself or herself with a little patience through systematic contemplation of the body.

The body, whether felt from within or perceived from without, is ultimately a conceptual construct, a reification of processes. External perception of it can be almost endlessly augmented by extending and refining our senses through prostheses such as microscopes, space cameras, light meters, scales, thermometers, acoustical-analysis equipment, measuring devices for waves and radiation, and so forth. All these prostheses of perception permit us a better apprehension of the world by enabling us to perceive or invent smaller or more all-embracing things. Even if we were able to penetrate into superstellar and subatomic realms in this way and there—distinguishing and enumerating things in new and unforseeable ways—perceive reality much more precisely and reliably than we can with our naked senses, we would still find only processes that we make into things by means of conceptual labels. And this goes as well for all things related to our bodies, whether we see these things created by perception—even on microscopic and subatomic levels—from the outside or feel them from the inside. That it would be illusory to look among perceivable things for an "I" or ego is obvious.

But what about the process of perception itself? Is there perhaps a perceiver, an "I" that experiences and—this is a crucial point—that can itself be experienced, felt, or somehow otherwise known? The answer of those who are fully enlightened is: There is no "I," no self, no core identity of the person, no ongoing authority that experiences. The Abhidhammikas go further and say: No assumption of an "I" or self is necessary to understand the way the mind functions, to know the inner world, to master life. And even more important: Belief in an ego leads inevitably to frustrations and depressions—to suffering.[10] For us, it is certainly interesting to know these answers. However, personal conviction as to whether or not there is an ego has no particular importance in liberational mind-training and in developing New Age strategies. For us it is important to learn methods and techniques that make us able to lead a happier life, that increase our capacity for happiness. A person committed to liberation wants to realize the way him- or herself and therefore does not cling to views concerning the existence or nonexistence of an ego or self (*anattā*). He or she is far more interested in knowledge about what to do and what the result of doing it will be. It is reality as we experience it that counts.

For a healthy person who feels at home in his or her own body, sensual experiencing (*kāma*), the inner feeling of the body, is more real than views, images, or other perceptions from the outside. Here there are many interesting and amusing experiments that could be conducted: Touch with your palm a corner of the edge of this book; then touch your palm to the top of your nose. When do you feel something from outside and when from inside?

If we carry out this experiment with various parts of the body, we obtain some interesting insights. What do you feel if you now touch the same spot on your palm with the index finger of the other hand? Then with the little finger? Which finger do you feel more from the inside and which more from the outside? Can you feel the spot on your palm without touching it with the corner of the book? Take the time to pursue each question through bodily sensation.

Do you feel your body in those places where you are touching your seat or the back of your chair? You could also perceive these places from the outside, with the help of a mirror, for example. For the average Western person, there are many parts of the body that are only perceived from the outside—for instance, the toes. My students tell me they find it enjoyable while bathing in the tub to sit with their eyes closed and train themselves to feel their individual toes by pressing them against the faucet. In the tub, one can also conduct instructive experiments related to the feeling and perception of temperature and cohesion, which are very useful for shamanistic mastery of the fire and water elements.[11]

There are many places, especially inside our bodies, that we feel only when they are injured or when we are sick. Pains are the only thing some people can feel in their bodies; even warmth, pressure, twitching, stretching, and so on are experienced by them from the inside only as unpleasant. It is amazing how great is the number of people who, though they are not considered psychiatrically ill, experience no pleasant bodily feelings—perhaps with the single, questionable exception of sexual contacts. And these are questionable because for the most part they are not experienced in direct relation to bodily experience but lost in fantasies of images and concepts.

In the previous section, as we clarified the distinctions between levels of experiencing, we noted that even feelings that are connected with imagined events take place really, bodily in the present. Abhidhamma distinguishes clearly between such bodily expressions of mental feelings (which also include any physiological changes that take place) and actual bodily feelings or sensations, which we will discuss shortly. The mental feelings (*ceto-sam-phassa-jam-vedanā;* literally, "mind-contact-born") are our positive, negative, or neutral reactions to mental representations of things desired, not desired, or to which we are indifferent. They are always related to our view about what is good, beautiful, and true; they indicate whether the perception at hand is in conflict with our views. Only fully enlightened arhats or buddhas are free from mental feelings, because they do not cling to any views that could contrast with what is experienced. It is completely fine for us, who are not yet fully enlightened, to orient ourselves on the basis of mental feelings, as long as we do not sink into a swirl of emotions as a result.

It can, however, happen that strong mental feelings cause loss of bodily anchoring (remember the example of the double-bind) and at the same time elicit strong physiological side-effects. These sometimes lead to irreversible pathological changes in the body, which express themselves as muscle tension, stiffness, growths (cancer), disorders of metabolism (depression) and digestion (stomach ulcers), or collapse of the immune system (AIDS), if the person in question does not manage, by means of some healing method (therapy, meditation, liberational mind-training) to free himself or herself from them and achieve a healthy emotional life.

Systematically trained and developed mindfulness enables us, through a reality-true way of life and wise inner economy, to keep our feelings flowing. This means heeding good feelings as pathfinders and painful feelings as warning signals and considering them both as indicators of corrections that may need to be made. This will keep them from resulting in bodily or mental blockages. The conditioned arising of suffering was introduced in chapter 3; here we need only repeat: A mindful, full experience of feeling (*vedanā*), not constricted by greed, aggression, and delusion, leads to the reality-true way of liberation. It is only through unmindful craving (*tanhā*) and attachment (*upādāna*)—see Diagrams 5 and 6, pages 58 and 64—that the free flow of feelings is dammed up and rigidification sets in, resulting in a thing that is subject to the suffering of sickness, old age, and death.

A stream of free-flowing feelings, on the other hand, has a vivifying effect. Feeling not only has the hedonistic qualities of pleasant and unpleasant; it also feels vibrations, currents, pressures, and warmth. These are vital impulses inherent in all that is living. Karmically conditioned, they perpetuate themselves as life formations (*āyu-sankhāra*). As long as clinging to views and the mental feeling-reactions conditioned by this clinging do not interfere, no suffering is generated. Pain remains only a signal that pressure, warmth, vibration, or current are too strong or that there is an imbalance of these four elements (four *dhātu*: pressure = the earth element, warmth = the fire element, current = the water element, vibration = the air element) in the contact between the outer and inner sense bases (*āyatana*) or in the body itself. These four *dhātu,* which according to Abhidhamma are the smallest perceptible constituents of the body, are thus not material entities but rather energy waves or impulses. So if you are harmoniously established in your mental as well as your bodily ecosystem, your developmental potential will be enlivened by the finely pulsating feeling of bliss. If this is not the case, but you persevere in experiencing your painful feelings with composure and mindfulness, then your liberational tendencies will be concentrated and aroused (*samvega,* sam = together, *vega* = impulse, speed). Here we are jumping ahead to the next topic, for *samvega* means a sense of urgency, and *ubbega* (*ub-vega*) is an important property of joy.

JOY AND THE SENSE OF URGENCY

A real sense of meaning comes from the innermost feelings. When such a sense of meaning manifests as inclination, desire, and exertion, then it is energetically nourished by our physical and mental vitality (*jīvita*). Joy and the sense of urgency give the inclination toward freedom impetus and direction and connect it to the frame of reference of *paññā,* wisdom, because both the energy of bliss and the knowledge of interest, the pleasant as well as the goal-oriented, are present in joy. Such connections can be directly experienced through meditative investigation of the inner household. At the same time, this is a clearer statement of what was meant at the beginning of chapter 3— namely, that the immeasurable potentialities of human existence can be fulfilled only if we ourselves live them in a completely concrete way. Happiness—we ourselves have to want it urgently. We have seen this again and again. Nobody can command someone else to lead a happy life. Ordering ourselves to be happy, whether because we can afford it materially or because we have reflected and decided in favor of it, does not work either. We must first know the strategic way to proceed; we must permit feelings to flow freely and mindfully guard them from blockages resulting from greed and aggression. Only then can the uplifting energy of joy or a sincere sense of urgency well up in us.

True interest requires knowledge of the matter at hand. This is true also for the strategies of happiness, which become interesting and rewarding only when they are put into practice.

You have only to remember how you learned football, tennis, dancing, or how to drive a car. Remember how many times you had to try again and how much time you devoted to learning and practice.

When we really want something, then we invest more in it than if we were imposing a duty on ourselves or were being obliged to do it by somebody else. Happiness-promoting mental investments are voluntary expenditures of energy, which create greater freedom and capacity for happiness and thus make possible growth in the economy of the mind. Knowledge, confidence, willpower, concentration, and mindfulness are the powers to be applied, the currency of the mind that must be invested. Mindfulness of bodily processes and feelings, from which urgency and joy arise, is also the means by which the intelligence of the body can be brought into play.

Happiness and joy can only be lived. They cannot be theoretically thought up or technically produced. Real, lasting happiness requires joy, but above all also clarity. Clarity cannot be obtained by shutting our eyes to everything that conflicts with happiness, contentment, and well-being. Therefore an essential strategy is dealing properly and skillfully with the facts of life that are not conducive to mental comfort and using them as an incentive to spur us on to liberation. Actually, there is a great deal of suffering in the world. This was considered in connection with personally relevant facts in chapter 2, and the subjective significance of it made clear. Adversity, trouble, frustration, grief, and pain are not empty words. We are all familiar with the distressing nonverbal reality of suffering to which these words refer. We also know the causes of suffering: greed, aggression, and delusion. All this is familiar to us and need not be repeated here.

With all this suffering around us, how can we experience joy? The answer is straightforward: through our choice of a way of seeing, through wise apprehension, *yoniso manasikāra*, as already explained in chapter 3. It is of crucial importance to have a way of looking at things that is not static but process-oriented, like the knowledge that all things are impermanent (*anicca*). This experiential wisdom makes it possible for us also to perceive the subsiding of suffering and to be joyful about it. To focus our interest in this joy and to direct our capacity for knowledge on overcoming suffering would be a wiser apprehension of the same reality. Therefore we are joyful about our abilities and the progress we make on the path of liberation. Nevertheless, we do not shut our eyes to suffering and its causes. If we feel at home in our own bodies, protect our well-being through mindfulness, and wisely apprehend the nature of reality as characterized by suffering, then, although suffering continues to pain and upset us, at the same time it awakens in us a sincere sense of urgency (*samvega*), which arouses energy.

Mindfulness meditation (*satipatthāna-vipassanā*) and the other mind-training methods of the Abhidhamma work a great deal with joy, as we shall see from the exercises. It would be too much here to go into all the technical terms for joy, rapture, enthusiasm, delight, bliss, and cheerfulness. *Ānanda* is perhaps the most common term for the joyful results of yoga and meditation techniques in the Pali and Sanskrit traditions. The Abhidhamma, however, explains *ānanda* and *pīti* (Skt., *prīti*) as synonyms. *Pīti*, even in the modern colloquial languages of most Indian peoples, refers to sexual rapture as well as to the joy of religious ecstasy and the trances of shamanistic healers. But also the quite mild joy without excitement (*pāmujja, pā-mud-ja*) and the kinds of interpersonal joy indicated by terms derived from the same root, *mud* (e.g., *muditā;* see chapter 6), are considered to be forms of *pīti*. We shall thus limit ourselves to the notion of *pīti*, which combines joy, rapture, and interest and plays an important role in all Buddhist meditation techniques as well as in all everyday Dhamma strategies.

The *Visuddhi Magga*,[12] the practical Abhidhamma training manual, gives instructions for development from everyday experiences of joy (*pāmujja = tarunā-pīti*) up to *pīti*, higher states of consciousness, in the following five stages:

1. *Khuddikā-pīti*, "minor happiness," which is able "only" to raise the hairs on the body, fills one with awe.
2. *Khanikā-pīti*, "momentary happiness," is like a flash of lightning. It is significantly more intense, but does not last even though it may arise frequently.
3. *Okkantikā-pīti*, "showering happiness," is enrapturing and lasts longer. As waves flow over the shore and then break on it, so it breaks after flowing over the body again and again.
4. *Ubbega-pīti*, "uplifting happiness," is powerful enough to lift the body in the air. It can bring about a leap or outright levitation. The impulses (*vega*) of energy released are evener, calmer, and more sustained and can last a very long time.
5. *Pharanā-pīti*, "pervading happiness," fills the whole body with composed serenity, calm and free from all movement, as air completely fills a balloon or the sea an abyss.

One of the joys brought about by the five stages of happiness is a total tranquillity (*passaddhi*) of body and mind. This takes place in the highest meditative absorption, *jhāna*, which is the basis for the exercise of magical powers (cf. chapters 7 and 8, "Strategies of Ecstasy and Power"). However, during the first years of learning and executing

Dhamma strategies, we will more sensibly consider it sufficient to note mindfully, at the appropriate moment, what causes us to get gooseflesh during experiences of awe and fright in everyday life. Externally well-organized situations of systematic meditation will permit us to be more open toward the other side effects of joy.

Experience shows that it is wise simply to be open toward extraordinary experiences without striving for them. It might be mentioned incidentally that certain talented participants in meditation courses and shamanism workshops manage through willful resolve to achieve some enraptured hair-raising after only a few days. Such unusual abilities are, however, only the inconsequential by-products of training in Dhamma strategies. Nevertheless, it is good to know that people who, after an intensive meditation course, continue to practice *satipatthāna* meditation for three-quarters of an hour once or twice a day, experience a joy pervading their whole body that they often compare with the bliss of sexual fulfillment. Through the instruction received in the course, however, they are aware of the dangers of developing greedy dependency on joyful experiences. They also know that the support of *sīla* (cf. page 32) and the cultivation of Dhamma strategies provide them with protection and security. Thus some of them report, without being uneasy about it, that they sometimes experience lightning- and wavelike upwellings of joy of a sensual (*sāmisa*, lit., "fleshly") or supersensual (*nirāmisa*) nature even arising spontaneously in everyday-life situations.

SEX WITHOUT SENSUALITY?

A chapter about the body would be incomplete by modern standards if it did not include a discussion devoted exclusively to sex. Recently an edition of the Colombo (Sri Lanka) *Daily News* printed that old standby joke about the prospective secretary who was filling out an application form and after the question "Sex?," wrote "Occasionally," and then added in parentheses, "Mainly with top executives." In fact, the staying power of this joke (which can easily be updated by changing the occupation and/or gender of the applicant) says a great deal about the post-1960 Western view of sex, a view that mocks its own lack of sensuality, meaning, feeling, joy, concern, consideration, openness, and sympathy—not to mention love.

What is wrong with sex at the office (which supposedly helps one get ahead), with the obligatory sex of the marriage bed, with the liberal, "no-strings-attached" sex of student tours and business and vacation trips, with group sex, or with deadly serious sex, viewed as a mission? What is sexual freedom? Or is renunciation of sex the answer? In fact, all these questions are meaningless because wrongly formulated.

False questions and misleadingly defined themes for discussion—not only concerning sex—are a major feature of today's conversations. The ideas that are suggested almost always result from culture-specific and historically conditioned overcompensations for past injustices. When it comes to sexual matters, though, these distorted formulations take on particularly grotesque forms. We only have to think of the flood of literature concerning "feminine sexuality," followed by another wave on "masculine sexuality"—all in the name of "sexual intercourse for those incapable of relationship" or "exchange of lovemaking services." Another opinion is that the answer lies in masturbation or at best in the perennially reviled realm of homosexuality. Only the bold dare take their chances in the arena of the "battle of the sexes." So-called healthy aggressiveness is supposed to be a characteristic of manliness, while feminine sexuality is supposed to consist of "surrender" to the male (and hopefully women know how dangerous he can be). What is actually wrong with such ways of looking at the problem?

A suitable treatment of this theme would fill a large volume; I must therefore content myself here with a brief discussion of those aspects of erotic life that are of immediate importance for the development of New Age strategies. Please note that I have decided in favor of the word "erotic," which perverts the healthy, holistic, interpersonal character of life less than do other terms. "Sex" in current usage means the rubbing together of mucus membranes (with or without a layer of rubber in between), or perhaps it may also include images, illusions, vague situations, seductive stimulations, and everything that is prohibited by educators. Yet everyone who has sex knows vaguely that there is also "something more" connected with it. This "something more" can usually be legally regulated: then everything is clean and we have our work time and our leisure time under control. That interhuman relations consist of mucus-membrane rubbing, joint filling-out of tax returns, and (not) keeping promises—this is true for established citizens. For young people and those less well established, the situation is entirely different: what matters most here may be job hunting and then "sex, drugs, and rock 'n' roll" (all listed in the same tone of voice). But probably the following expatiations on the theme will be no more than a summary of the knowledge that you yourself already possess.

The sexual vices of our civilization are not the only results of false perceptions of problems that have led to the present impotence of Western spirituality and—as Erich Fromm has put it—to its "necrophilic orientation."[13] Necrophilia, partiality toward an impotent deadly, is visible in false apprehension (*ayoniso manasikāra*), which

- divides and reduces life, particularly as manifested in bodily reality, into dead, static concepts
- because of envy and so on, attempts to level everything to the point of uniformity by destroying whatever is better or different
- stamps out everything nonuniform, establishes it as taboo, as extraordinary and shameful
- recognizes as valid motivation only need, lack, poverty, necessity, struggle, compulsion, guilt, and retribution

The illusory solutions for the suffering thereby conditioned accept the false apprehension as valid and simply strive to overthrow the present state of affairs. Thus the sex organs, set apart and hidden from the realm of the "acceptable," and the embarrassing rubbing of mucus membranes—still set apart, without feeling-based anchoring in conscious sensuality, excised from the context of human encounter—have today been declared shame-free, freely available and exchangable goods. Moreover, their value is independent of any relationship, and they are a market item as well as a means of marketing. Sex is on the title page; the rest of the human being has been torn off and pushed aside, since it is an impediment and embarrassment to business.

Less visible, but equally productive of suffering, are the misleading problematizations of abreaction, orgasm, trance, social class, and the struggle of the sexes. Only those who are disturbed and threatened in their relationships to members of another class or the other sex perceive all encounters in terms of struggle. Only for those who are frozen in a particular state of consciousness do all other states represent either trance or an extraordinary religious condition. Pathological dissociations—as in the case of sex—are accepted as the norm, and what was hitherto taboo has become the mode. The exchange and consumption of fashionable goods, of physical and social externals, is in supply; inwardly felt sensuality and religious experience cannot be marketed.

How relieved many western women would be if they knew that millions of women—Asians, for example—cannot have an orgasm, because they have no word for it in their language, and because the inhibitions and blockages that are broken through in orgasm do not exist there in the required form. In cultures that do not hold the body to be evil, people more readily dare to feel their bodies from the inside, to let themselves pulsate, to be aroused to rapture and experience joy sensually, even if the friction of mucus membranes is not always involved. Not that Asians, especially those living in cities, do not have sexual problems; not that there is no sexual inhibitedness or cruelty, particularly in the strict patriarchal structure of the Hindu and Islamic cultures. Greed, aggression, and delusion, dammed-up violence and lust, blockages of the stream of feeling, and mental illness are present in people of all civilizations. Everywhere there are also stupid, simpleminded, and nasty people—as long as we do not restrict ourselves to distinguishing good and bad qualities from a microanalytic point of view. A solution cannot be achieved by changes in culture and civilization. Historical evolution will by no means produce a New Age by itself—the prophecies of some scientists and writers notwithstanding. Overcoming historically conditioned false apprehensions and their suffering-laden results is the task of liberational mind-training.

Sensual joy (*sāmisa pīti*) is, according to Abhidhamma, the present pleasant effect (*vipāka*) of wholesome intentional action in a past sensual existence (*kāma bhava*), motivated by greedless generosity (*dāna*) and aggressionless nonviolence (*ahimsa*). How could the fruits of wholesome action be bad? Only a deluded, greedy, or aggressive way of relating to sensuality brings unpleasant results. In the chapter section entitled "Conditioned Arising," this mechanism was elucidated in detail on several levels of outlook and action. Sensuality (*kāma*) does have to do with the senses and thus with bodily anchoring in reality. The sexual vices of our civilization are the result of abuse and repression of healthy sensuality, caused by a longing for body-alien ideas and concepts, which are then imposed on the "sex partner." Thus "sex partners" make each other into utilitarian objects; they take the "evil body" as a possession, make deals concerning it, and exploit it.

In cultures that do not consider the body evil, people dare to feel their bodies—without entirely focusing on external sense perception, but also without shutting it out—from the inside and thus to enjoy sensual bliss. However, it is not a matter of geographically pinpointing the cultures that make this possible; it is much more a case of a culture of the mind and heart that we can realize through liberational effort for ourselves and our neighbors. In the culture of loving encounter, which makes room for the whole person, there is certainly also enough room for sensuality and emancipated erotic life.

Catharsis: More than Knowledge

The dissociations, tensions, and blockages we have discussed require abreaction, a disburdening unloading, and many modern healers would like to understand therapeutic catharsis on this level of simplification. There are treatments offered by fashionable psychotherapists in which the patient is asked to take punches at a pillow while shouting "Bad mother! Bad mother!" These simplistic scenes appear spectacular and seem to have a powerful effect, at least on the surface. Characteristically, one never hears of such psychotherapeutic dramas relating to the father. Probably the therapists who encourage these scenes set themselves up as untouchable father figures, even if they are women. They pretend to know the inner world of their patients better than the patients do themselves. If a patient, after serious introspection, dares to express the view that this theme is of no personal importance, he or she is further manipulated anyway. Phrases like "It would be better for you to relate to this seriously" (as though the patient's manner of relating with it so far had not been serious) or "Your body language relays the message—you just need to overcome your psychological resistance!" are the usual means of pressuring the patient into a choice.

Also prevalent on the modern psychotherapy scene are various abuses of pseudoprofessional half-knowledge concerning the intelligence of the body. These come into play, naturally, in connection with such methods as biofeedback, rolfing, primal scream, and Gestalt therapy, because these few are the only methods that take the intelligence of the body into account at all. Lack of clear comprehension relative to Abhidhammic distinctions—for example, of what is inwardly felt and externally perceived in relation to the body in the theories of biofeedback and similar approaches—encourages such abuses. Graver, however, is the fact that psychologists and psychiatrists who work with abreaction techniques usually have one-sided therapeutic outlooks based on medical science's view of the person. So when in these pages we place a high value on the intelligence of the body, let us avoid falling into the trap of such oversimplifications.

The paradigms of Abhidhamma make possible thorough, wise apprehension, *yoniso manasikāra:* Bodily perception is important, bodily feeling is more important, more important still is the reality-true knowledge and the solutions available through it, and yet more important than that is catharsis and the liberational creativity that comes in its wake—all without any disqualification of what is important by what is more important. This is one of the fundamental principles of

Abhidhamma that is very difficult to understand—especially for us who have grown up in an "either-or" culture and who had antagonism between mind and body instilled in us in earliest childhood.

In the liberational approach of Abhidhamma, feeling, knowledge, catharsis, and action are not successive tasks; rather they are facets of one and the same liberational process. In relation to discovering, learning, and developing Dhamma strategies, it is only for reasons of presentation that feeling, knowing, and catharsis are dealt with separately. Before we go on to clarify in greater detail what catharsis means, let us take a brief look at still another frequent aberration of modern psychotherapy and psychiatry, namely, the misunderstanding of catharsis as acting-out and getting rid of something, whether by word, deed, or result, in the course of therapy.

A young doctor who was continuing his training in group psychotherapy and psychodrama with me was visibly impressed as he recounted the following example of a "catharsis" that had been described by the leader of a training group as a psychodrama and Gestalt-therapy technique. This group leader, a politically radical psychiatrist, had, however, been trained neither in psychodrama nor in Gestalt therapy. The supposed catharsis consisted in a female psychologist's squatting on a table and evacuating her bowels to the applause of the chorus of other group members, who called out: "That's the way, momma! Way to go!" This voiding did indeed get rid of some blocks, but it was no catharsis in the sense presented by Jacob Levy Moreno, the originator of group psychotherapy and psychodrama. Hopefully, one or another of the group members—at least in the course of cleaning up the results of the session—will have come by a little understanding of the role reversal between mother and daughter. In Gestalt therapy or psychodrama, such understanding would have had to take place, if indeed there was a severe enough disturbance in the patient to justify such a scenario at all.

Catharsis is more than an externalization of affects having their root in greed and aggression. Catharsis is more than an elimination and thingification of material that does not fit in with our development of well-being and happiness. Proper processing of eliminated material through the application of suitable programs is the inseparable flipside of the liberational purification process. In fact we have already encountered this holistic style of apprehension in the list of principles of Dhamma strategies (page 13). Wise apprehension (*yoniso manasikāra*), which is the basis for proper processing, is a component of our inner economy with which you became familiar with in chapter 3. How to apply suitable programs in properly processing eliminated material is one of the most important themes of the next chapter. What we are dealing with in these chapters is more than knowledge or cognition. We are concerned with guidelines for dealing with the facts of our own inner economy and for turning the results into happiness-furthering actions—concrete actions in the outer world and in our inner household.

Catharsis is more than cognition, which notices, apprehends, and distinguishes, and which applies personally assimilated paradigms of knowledge to the processing of eliminated material. That catharsis is more than cognition or knowledge is something that was clear to Josef Breuer and Freud when they made it part of their psychotherapeutic method. They based themselves on Aristotle's view, which defined catharsis in tragedy as purification of affects from the mind of the onlooker: "Tragedy is an imitation of an action that is serious, complete, and of a certain magnitude; in language embellished with each kind of artistic ornament, the several kinds being found in separate parts of the play; in the form of action, not of narrative; through pity and fear effecting the proper purgation of these same emotions." [14] Since the time of Freud, psychotherapists have made patients into the onlookers of their own tragedies, which they report to the therapists. Modern therapy *research* has produced theories that fragment the whole represented by the Freudian *art* of therapy in order to produce progress in particular specialized areas. Thus today there are techniques of therapy that focus only affectively on abreaction or only cognitively on knowledge.

The fact that this book treats body and joy in one chapter and mind and knowledge in another is logical and scientific. But the fact that mind and knowledge are dealt with primarily in connection with apprehension of bodily reality, while body and joy are dealt with primarily in connection with their intelligent application in the context of liberational wisdom—this leads to organic integration, to holistic harmony. In this harmony, the dichotomy between mind and body and knowledge and joy is resolved, unified in a simple "middle way." Because being happy is simple. However, it is not so simple to sort out the inconceivable manifoldness of *papañca*, even when we have the means—as we saw in chapter 3—at our disposal. For to do this, to actually travel the "middle way," is the concrete practice that leads to liberation, to freedom and happiness. We should try not to lose sight of this while reading the following chapters.

Moreno blazed the trail from the vicarious catharsis of the onlooker to the active catharsis of the actor without taking away the first type of catharsis from the onlookers of the psychodrama. It would be too

great a digression to give even a brief account of the liberational consequences of this development.[15] Therefore I shall note here only
Moreno's three crucial discoveries: the catharsis of the performer himself, integrative catharsis, and creative spontaneity as a principle
common to both. These concepts introduced into psychotherapy by
Moreno (one would almost like to call them "simplifications," since
they actually bind the linguistically fragmented world of psychotherapy into a simple continuum of healing action) are close to the
Abhidhammic apprehension of catharsis. In Abhidhamma, integrative
purification is signified by the technical term *visuddhi*, which is practiced in seven stages. (These stages constitute the framework of the
Visuddhi Magga, which I have already cited a number of times.) The
first stage, *sīla-visuddhi*, comprises clarification of the reliable subjective basis. Only with the protection of *sīla* can purification of the mind
(*citta-visuddhi*) be undertaken. In looking at the principles of "self-
realization," we focused on understanding the requirements for integrative purification. The deeper significance of what is meant by catharsis through integration will be appreciated in its full scope only at
the end of this book, when we have become familiar with the richness
of specific strategies.

Happiness, freedom, liberation, competence, and integration are
both guiding values and at the same time fruits of the purified way of
life that, with the help of Dhamma strategies, can be realized in ordinary everyday life. Liberation is purification (*visuddhi*) of body and
mind. It is being free from everything that obscures our experiencing,
that distorts our perception and hinders our action. The less our inner
world is disintegrated and soiled, the more we experience ourselves
as liberated and the more competently we can act in the external
world. Such competent action also includes generation and application of ethical rules. *Sīla* is an ethics of freedom that is supported by
competence and joy. Liberational ethics of this kind have a high degree of social effectiveness and therefore become a standard for those
of our peers who, although they are not able to develop their own
ethical principles, are open and intelligent enough to recognize what
is good on their own and to try to emulate it. When we set an example
that is liberated, causes no suffering, and is conducive to our own
welfare and that of others, then we accomplish more in the world
than we could by means of any lessons, penalties, or tricks. Our own
example of liberation and happiness in the down-to-earth situations
of everyday life is more convincing than scientific, religious, and philosophical treatises. In liberated, purified experience and action, the
high values of personal integrity and freedom are realized.

5

Strategies of Reality Anchoring

Effective action is possible only on the basis of reality-true perception that is extended in accurate thinking, reflection, and planning. True statements about real events are results of thorough, wise apprehension, *yoniso manasikāra*, which, as the most elementary technique of wisdom, we practiced at the end of chapter 3. Wise apprehension connects our mind with the given circumstances at hand. In the chapter section entitled "Levels of Experiencing" (page 87) we worked through to the understanding that what is bodily experienced is the most reliable reference point for reality. We have also repeatedly seen that mindfulness of body provides the key to the anchoring in reality. Four exercises in mindfulness of body are therefore the central focus of the present chapter. These exercises equip us with skills that permit us to gain a sure rootedness in the situation at hand, and on the basis of this anchoring, to carry out realistic and effective action.

The strategies for reality anchoring are connected with noticing, feeling, and experiencing. They are not actually strategies for action, concerned with execution of procedures and maneuvering of objects. They are much more strategies of perception that are meant to strengthen us in a mode of experiencing characterized by truthfulness and capacity for happiness. The purpose of the exercises is to enable us to make competent use of our thought, speech, and action in everyday life. For this it is important what we use and how we use it. Truthful speech, truthful thought, and clearly comprehended action can be better used than speech, thought, and action that is not anchored in reality. Let us take a closer look at the quality of truth. Clear comprehension, already mentioned a number of times, is a theme in itself, which will be treated in more detail at the end of the chapter.

Anchoring in reality (*yathā-bhūta*) is characterized by direct relatedness (*yathā*) of awareness to concrete events (*bhūta*) that are actually taking place. Reality is made up of processes and conditions that are present as real things (*sabhāva-dhammā*). Anchoring is not determined by concepts, but is something that is experienced as a purified and accurate awareness.

TRUTHFULNESS IN THINKING AND SPEAKING

Without truthful speech and thought, no purification of experiencing is possible. Speaking and thinking is true when it relates to real, not "thought-up," events and when it thoroughly apprehends these without distortion and places them in relationship. In this sense, truthfulness is an aspect of intelligence,[1] and lying is an expression of stupidity. We lie out of fear of facing the truth or out of inability to apprehend reality as it is. How unwise and dangerous every distortion of the truth is always becomes clear to us when we get into trouble over some action based on a false statement. Lying is a betrayal of the reality that is physically experienceable and therefore found in intersubjectively shared realms. In the chapter section "Betraying the Body Drives Us Crazy" (page 78), examples were given of the effects of losing our bodily anchoring in reality. Then we saw how returning to bodily reality—thus to truth—leads away from delusion and suffering.

In looking at overcoming suffering by means of catharsis, *visuddhi*, it became clear that only true, practical knowledge—completely leaving aside exclusively logical knowledge, that derived only from concepts—is necessary for purification of the mind. Bodily experiencing the truth is a requisite of catharsis. In such an experience of what is true and what is really possible, distortions and psychologenic hardening caused by lying and alienation from reality will be resolved. Distortions and hardenings in our mind and in our body, which supports the mind, are the inner counterpart of the lies, half-truths, and external distortions of reality to which we have adapted ourselves. The ignorance, fixed ideas, illusions, obscurations, and delusions that derange our thinking can only subsist so long as our mental activities run on without a bodily relationship to reality. Conversely, restoration of the relationship to reality has the effect of resolving these pathological hardenings and distortions. Knowledge, thought, and speech become true, and experiencing becomes anchored in bodily reality.

Knowing, thinking, reflecting, planning, and speaking have been dealt with as a series based on their similarity—their distinctiveness has been left aside. This has been done intentionally, for here we are primarily concerned with truthfulness, which is an important aspect of *sīla*. Without truthfulness, our subjective basis would slip away from us, our *sīla* would no longer be reliable. Once again we see that the ethics of *sīla* is anchored in mindfulness of the body. Liberational and happiness-furthering speech, thought, and experience is ethical because it takes bodily reality into account. In itself, experiencing is neither true nor false, because experiencing is just taking in what is noticed at the moment. Experiencing is always real, and what is experienced has its effect on our mind and body. As has been shown, a bodily anchored mode of experiencing has a wholesome effect.

Though thinking cannot simply be understood as a quiet conversation with oneself, it is sufficient for our purposes to define both thinking and speaking as processes of communication that convey relationships between signs in the form of statements. If these relationships are fully conveyed, then the communication is correct, even if the communicated contents are signs that relay no experiential reality or are absurd. "Childless mother," "castles in the air," "energy crisis," or even "jobless employees" are examples of frivolous combinations of signs, which, without true relationship to reality, hold together entire systems of thought. As much as such designations distort reality, we nevertheless understand that, for example, a person who works for others and gives his work in exchange for money is called an employee. We also understand entire systems based on lies, which are built upon alienation from reality but which have taken on the character of reality through extended repetition, which has its effect on all levels of experience. The following joke makes this clear: What is the difference between an neurotic, a psychotic, and a psychiatrist? The neurotic builds castles in the air, the psychotic lives in them, and the psychiatrist gets the rent.

Speech as well as all forms of thinking (reflecting, planning, remembering, designing, classifying, comparing, counting, etc.) can be either true or untrue. The more distorted or superficial the relationship of the thinking or speech to reality, the more deficient its truthfulness. Truthfulness is thus a fundamental relatedness to reality, in which things and events are seen in their right relationship to their temporal, spatial, and ethical contexts. This is all possible thanks to the power of mind that we have been calling mindfulness (*sati*). Mindfulness takes note of things as they are without distorting or altering the way in which they are interrelated. Supported by the other four mental powers (wisdom, confidence, concentration, and willpower), right mindfulness apprehends reality wisely. This is called apprehension by means of thought, or *vitakka*,[2] which plays a central role in the strategies of ecstasy, where mindfulness establishes anchoring to the object of meditation. The principles of reality anchoring are the same as the principles of the algebra of *yoniso manasikāra*, which were described in detail on pages 71ff. They tell us that (1) attachment, (2) distortion, (3) repression, (4) abuse, and (5) simplemindedness produce suffering, and that truthfulness is characterized by the absence of these five faults.

In practicing wise apprehension, *yoniso manasikāra*, working from the mind's side we brought the mind and body (*nāma-rūpa*) together. In moving on now to practice the exercises of mindfulness of body, we will be bringing the mind and body together working from the side of the body.

Exercises in Mindfulness of Body

The instructions for the exercises in mindfulness of body require no preliminary explanation, since the instructions indicate directly the body facts to be attended to. Also, the importance for liberation and the high level of usefulness of mindfulness of body will already be clear to you from chapter 4. Now it is a question of actually trying out, first, mindfulness of breathing; second, apprehending the elements; third, noting bodily postures; and finally, walking meditation.

It is important not to forget that we are working here with *mindfulness* exercises, not body exercises. The body processes that we are learning to be aware of in the reality anchoring exercises should not be disturbed by any unnecessary intrusions.

1. ĀNĀPĀNA-SATI: MINDFULNESS OF BREATHING

You should practice in a well-ventilated room, where you will not be disturbed by other people, telephone calls, or anything else of that sort. If you are not accustomed to sitting cross-legged on the floor, you should sit on a comfortable but firm chair.

1. Sit up straight, but as comfortably as possible. The soles of both feet should be touching the floor and you should feel the pressure of that contact. The hands are relaxed, resting one upon the other (not folded) in your lap. The shoulders hang loose.
2. Speaking quietly to yourself, make the following resolution: "Now for three minutes I will do nothing but observe my inhalation and exhalation."
3. Breathe out with some emphasis.
4. Now feel the natural, uncontrolled inhalation, and say to yourself mentally: "Breathing in, breathing in."
5. Feel the exhalation and as long as it lasts, accompany it with the inner commentary: "Breathing out, breathing out."

6. Note inwardly when inhaling starts again: "Breathing in, breathing in."
7. If a pause in the breathing happens, say mentally: "Pause, pause," as long as it lasts.
8. Continue with observation and labeling: "Breathing in, breathing in" and "Breathing out, breathing out," for the remaining two and a half minutes. While practicing, breathe only through your nose.

After you have read and assimilated these instructions, practice with eyes closed.

As soon as you finish the exercise, retain your impressions and insights by formulating them into concise phrases, which could also be written down. In order to practice clear comprehension (*sati-sampajañña*) at the same time, respond to the following questions:

• Did I approximately fulfill the three-minute time requirement for the exercise?
• What was enjoyable about the exercise?
• What was unpleasant?
• Did feeling the inhalation and exhalation and labeling not get mixed up?
• Did I move my body? Did I have to move? Did I want to move?
• Were there distractions? How did I deal with them?
• In which parts of my body did I experience the breathing best, most clearly, most intensely?

The last question about parts of the body is very important for your further progress in this exercise. Basically, there are two ways to do advanced practice in mindfulness of body. Some people tend to experience most clearly the sensation of contact caused by the inflowing and outflowing air at the rims of the nostrils. If this is the case with you, it will be most beneficial for you to focus your attention here and after every distraction to return to the body sensation in your nostrils. Thus you will be making the orifices in your nose the gate and focus of your bodily anchoring in reality and will use them as a kind of refuge in later exercises. From this focal point, later in advanced practice, energy-giving joy, *pīti*, will spread out through the whole body.

Some people tend to experience most clearly the feeling of internal expansion and contraction, that is, the rising and falling of the belly that is connected with inhalation and exhalation. If this is the case with you, you should choose the region of the belly as the focus of your bodily anchoring in reality. You will focus your mindfulness on the processes of rising and falling, and after each distraction, you will return to the body sensation of your belly.

It is important for you, after trying both ways of practicing for a few minutes, to decide in favor of one of them and stick to it. Switching back and forth between the two options will continually cancel out your progress. It is as though during the building of a tunnel you were to direct traffic to an otherwise inaccessible place in the tunnel. Yet, once the tunnel is completed, the traffic can pass right through. In another simile, the two ways of practicing are like providing drinking water to a city reservoir from a mountain river while widening the riverbed. If the reservoir is full, then the construction work on the riverbed will in no way impair the water supply. Experience shows that the two ways of practicing are similar: if the purpose of one is fulfilled, then the goal of the other is also realized, but they may impede each other during the initial stages of work.

Rarely, there is someone who can feel neither the movement of the belly nor the sensation of the air in the nostrils. In that case, I recommend the following preliminary exercise; try this out, too, and see what happens:

- Sit down comfortably, preferably in a chair with a back, so that you can lean back at a forty-five-degree angle.
- Put your left palm (or, if you are left-handed, your right palm) on your belly and observe whether or not you can now perceive the rising and falling from the outside with your palm. Then try to feel the rising and falling without your hand, that is, from the inside.
- Using your finger, moisten the rims of your nostrils with a fair amount of saliva. Breathe in and out a few times, taking long and somewhat emphasized breaths, and observe your sensations. Do you still feel something in your nostrils even after the moisture has evaporated?

If no aid to sensation helps, then do not torment yourself trying to force a result. Perhaps you will have more luck with exercises 3 and 4, in which change of posture and walking are mindfully apprehended.

How to Deal with Distractions

The Abhidhamma principles for dealing with factors of distraction, which cause suffering and hinder happiness, are the same on all levels, from the large-scale level of politics—as explained in chapter 2— to the concrete apprehension of the body during mindfulness meditation. We do not repress such factors, but nor do we let them shape the flow of experience.

In the concrete terms of the mindfulness exercise, this means that one should note the distraction and label it for what it is, then return gently, but immediately and definitely, to the focus of mindfulness. Only when mindfulness has become securely anchored in bodily reality can we, in a very advanced form of mindfulness meditation, permit ourselves to use disturbances as secondary objects of analysis (see the *satipatthāna-vipassanā* exercises in chapter 8, pages 254ff.). In the first practice sessions, some people find it difficult to perceive the disturbance simply with the label "Distraction, distraction," and then to bring mindfulness back with the innerly expressed resolve "And now back to the breathing." After all, due to long years of conditioning it has become "normal" for us to relinquish the power over our experience to external objects. You yourself might conceivably get into a situation (don't let it discourage you!) that looks something like this: You make all the preparations, sit down comfortably, and begin the mindfulness exercise. You are able to follow at least seven breaths more clearly, undisturbedly, and intensively than ever before, and then you hear a car . . . "That reminds me—the last bill from the garage was so high that I serious considered . . . ," and so forth. Or: "That reminds me . . . this steady increase in the number of cars . . . It's high time some political action is undertaken to stop it. Better talk it over with X and Y at the next meeting. No, not with Y—he doesn't take such things as seriously as he used to. Now he only thinks about . . . It's amazing how you can fool yourself about people; and I've always been so dependable. . . ," and so on. The car (it could also be a fly lighting on your nose) triggered in your mind a whole chain of thoughts and ideas, and now the whole meditative mood is gone. You do remember that you actually had wanted to do a mindfulness exercise, and you try a few times to get started again. But it doesn't work. Fine. This sort of thing can certainly happen.

The wise way to deal with an extreme situation like this is for us to accept the reality of the situation as it is, but *without allowing our own action to be determined by the distraction.* No fly, and no car either, has the power to evict us from our meditation seat. If I have decided to sit for ten minutes, then I remain sitting for ten minutes—even if something makes it impossible for me to use the time as I had originally planned.[3] I let the disturbances take their course, but nevertheless I keep attempting to observe a breath now and then or to see what other kind of thing I might be able to perceive that belongs to the realm of mindfulness of body.

Probably you yourself sometimes get into situations that, though not as extreme as the one described above, ruin your mood in a similar way, to the point where you consider abandoning the exercise. There can be a number of causes for this. In interviews with meditators, one finds the most frequent cause is that the subjective expectation of progress is too high. In other words, the meditator is impatient and is too quick to overlook the fact that loving attention to each breath results in the deepening of a sublime anchoring in reality, just as every stroke of a saw deepens the cut in a piece of wood—and without any added pressure on the saw.[4] A totally different kind of reason is that for some people who are particularly apt at grasping details, or for others who do not want to repress anything, it is difficult to set the disturbances aside just as distractions. The problems arising from this can be helped through the use of two techniques.

The first technique is to label the "interesting" distraction with a catchphrase and make an "appointment" with it for later. After the end of the mindfulness exercise, one can come back to these interesting themes, formulate them in detail, and weigh their problematic or creative worth.

The second technique is at the same time a preliminary stage of analytic meditation, such as apprehension of elements and *satipatthāna-vipassanā*. In relation to the previous example in which extended chains of distractions were set off, let us be precise and note that it was not a car that we heard; what we heard was a noise that we presumed was associated with a car. But it might equally well have come from a tape recorder. Likewise, in relation to the fly, we perceive only a tickling, tingling, or an itch that might have had nothing to do with a fly; it could have been caused by a drifing dust mote. No matter what object our idea relates the perceptions to, we should remain (at least during the mindfulness exercise) realistic and note only what we actually perceive: sounds, noises, colors, lights, sensations of touch, odors, thoughts, wishes, intentions, and so forth. If we do yield to our tendency to distinguish the manifold qualities of the disturbances, then it is advisable to register only the actual processes, such as "Hearing, hearing," "Thinking, thinking," "Itching, itching," "Wishing, wishing," (and perhaps through mindful "Scratching, scratching" to get rid of them), and then return to that which we actually intend to do.

"Rising" and "Falling": Advanced Stage

Through our experimentation up to this point, you have very likely already found out what time of day (certainly not immediately after eating), what place, and what posture are best for your practice. (If you learned in the trial session that you feel the breath best in your nostrils, just skip this section and go on to the following section at the bottom of the page.

In the practice session, you experienced the rising and falling of your belly and its inner expansion and contraction more immediately than the flow of air caused by breathing. Perhaps you noticed other phenomena in your body connected with breathing, such as changes in general muscle tone, an impulse (without your body actually moving) to rock or make circular motions, associations connected with climbing and sliding, and perhaps still other perceptions and images. Any investigation of these secondary phenomena would hinder your progress in developing reality anchoring through mindfulness of body. Therefore, pay them no special attention; just let them be where they belong—on the fringe of your field of experience. Your vehicle for cultivating psychic power is the flow of rising and falling.

1. Sit up straight and comfortably in your accustomed posture for practice.
2. Feel the contact with the floor, the seat, and the back of the chair (if you are leaning back), as well as the contact between your lips with your mouth loosely closed, and the contact between your hands resting on one another in your lap.
3. In case you are not comfortable yet, adjust your posture so that no disturbance resulting from posture change is necessary during the exercise.
4. Make the resolution: "Now for five minutes[5] I will only pay attention to the rising and falling."
5. Breathe out deeply and with some emphasis, then let the breath follow its natural rhythm.
6. Feel your belly rising and note mentally "Rising, rising."
7. Feel your belly falling and note mentally "Falling, falling."

It would be helpful, after reading these instructions and impressing them on your memory and before making your resolution (step 4), to close your eyes and keep them closed for the entirety of the exercise.

"Breathing In" and "Breathing Out": Advanced Stage

In trying out the two methods of practice, you found that you could best feel the in- and outflowing air on the rims of your nostrils during inhalation and exhalation. (If this is not the case, it would be better for you to practice the other method of mindfulness of body as described in the preceding section.)

You have already discovered what time of day, what place, and what posture are best for your practice. In practicing, in addition to the sensation of the in- and outflowing air in your nostrils, perhaps you noticed that you were able to follow the flow of air into your lungs. Maybe still other phenomena connected with inhaling and exhaling cropped up, for example various currents in the body, or associations of space and form, or other distracting perceptions and images. Any investigation of these secondary phenomena would hinder your progress in developing reality anchoring through mindfulness of body. Therefore, pay no special attention to them; let them be where they belong, that is, on the fringe of your field of experience. Your vehicle for cultivating psychic power is the sensation in the nostrils.

1. Sit up straight and comfortably in your accustomed posture for practice.
2. Feel the contact with the floor, the seat, and the back of the chair (if you are leaning back), as well as the contact between your lips with your mouth loosely closed, and the contact between your hands resting in your lap.
3. In case you are not comfortable yet, adjust your posture so that no disturbance resulting from posture change is necessary during the exercise.
4. Make the resolution: "Now for five minutes I will pay attention only to inhalation and exhalation."
5. Breathe out deeply and with some emphasis, then let the breath follow its natural rhythm.
6. Feel in your nostrils the sensation of the inflowing air and note mentally "Breathing in, breathing in."
7. Feel in your nostrils the sensation of the outflowing air and note mentally "Breathing out, breathing out."

It would be helpful, after reading these instructions and impressing them on your memory and before making your resolution (step 4), to close your eyes and keep them closed for the entirety of the exercise.

Mindfulness of Breathing: Superior Stage

After you have practiced for a few weeks according to the instructions, you will probably be ready to fill out your practice with two additional elements:

- Clear comprehension concerning spheres of experiencing and transitions
- Examination of disturbances as secondary objects of mindfulness and analysis

For the superior stage of the practice the same instructions are applicable as for the advanced stage. However, at this point we attempt to apprehend the experiences in a more thorough fashion.

As soon as you sit down to do the mindfulness exercise, you are in a sphere of experiencing different from the one you were in before when you were involved with the things around you. Your experience is now concentrated within the most personal sphere of how you are in your body. You practice clear comprehension (*sampajañña*) by taking note of sitting there, mentally formulating it in the following words: "Sitting in order to practice anchoring in reality through mindfulness of the body." Then carry out steps 2 and 3.

After making the resolution to practice (step 4), note that you are now in transition to the sphere of your primary object of mindfulness, the breath.

As soon as you notice during the practice that you are being distracted by other perceptions or by thoughts, say to yourself mentally: "Distraction! distraction! . . . This is not what I sat down here for!" In doing this, you have already left the sphere of the primary object of mindfulness, and you should clearly recognize that.

At this moment you have the choice—and you should realize that it is exclusively your choice—to make the transition to the sphere of the primary object of mindfulness by once again placing your attention on your nostrils (or the movement of your belly) and labeling the sensation "Breathing out" or "Breathing in" (or "Rising" or "Falling").

The other alternative—before continuing the exercise in mindfulness of breathing—is to analytically distinguish whether the distraction belongs to the sphere of body (*rūpa*) or mind (*nāma*), some mental representation, wish, or thought. Thus you should note "Pressure," "Movement," "Pain," "Itch," "Warmth," and so on, if you are dealing with one of these physical things. If it is a mental distraction, note "Thinking," "Wanting," "Intention," "Imagination," and so forth, without getting involved with the particular content within the thinking, wanting, and so on. As soon as you have made such a mental note, go back to your primary object and observe your breathing.

There is no point in speculating about these instructions. Before you think about them, try them out in practice to see how they function. When you have progressed so far in the practice that you have mastered noting and distinguishing distractions and are able without difficulty to make the transition back from any distraction to the sphere of your primary object of mindfulness, then you will be ready for Mindfulness Exercise 2, *dhātu manasikāra*, which is the basis for shamanistic, magic, and healing techniques. However, before you begin with this further exercise, you must without fail master the transitional technique for return to everyday reality.

In making the transition to the sphere of mindfulness of breathing, as also in making the transition to the sphere of the elements, *dhātu*, or to any other sphere of the shamanic journey or meditation, be sure to make a resolution in which the length of time to be spent in the sphere is fixed. It is a very helpful security measure always to keep properly to the period of time decided upon. In this way, we train our own "inner clock," which then reliably gives the signal for return— also from spheres in which the ordinary thought and will are not available (return from meditation, from a shamanic journey, from normal sleep, etc.). The instruction for transition must be impressed on the memory before the exercise, so that it can be effective in waking us from sleep or ending a meditation (the exercise in mindfulness of breathing is a meditation). This instruction is as follows:

1. As soon as the decided period of time for remaining in the sphere has lapsed, become aware through inner impulses that it is now time for the transition. In case you are occupied with another object of consciousness, return immediately to mindfulness of the breath.
2. Start a countdown, following ten breaths mindfully and without distraction. Feeling the outbreath, note "Breathing out, breathing out . . . ten," "Breathing in, breathing in . . . nine," and so on down to "Breathing out, breathing out . . . two," "Breathing in, breathing in . . . one." (If you have chosen rising and falling as primary object of mindfulness, correspondingly note "Falling, falling . . . ten," etc.)
3. Immediately after breath-movement number one, note the contact between the hands, resting one on the other, between the closed lips, the contact with the seat and floor, each time in the same sequence.
4. Then become aware of the rest of your bodily sensations: odor, taste in the mouth, sounds of the environment.
5. Open the eyes and perceive the environment with the clear comprehension: "The transition to everyday reality is complete."
6. Decide to stretch an arm or a leg or to get up, and become clearly aware of this intention.
7. Carry out the decided movement. Mindfulness should be maintained in all subsequent everyday perceptions and actions—to the extent possible.

Now, dear reader, you possess the complete instructions for the practice of mindfulness of breathing. If you are interested in further details concerning this practice, and if you would like to understand it precisely in the context of *satipatthāna-vipassanā*, I would recommend to you Nyanaponika's book *The Heart of Buddhist Meditation* (York Beach, Me.: Samuel Weiser, 1988).

2. DHĀTU-MANASIKĀRA: APPREHENSION OF ELEMENTS

The apprehension of elements is an advanced exercise in mindfulness of body, which should be practiced only as a technique complementary to mindfulness of breathing (*ānāpāna-sati*) once the latter has already been mastered, or as a further stage of introspective examination of the thirty-two parts of the body. It is a means to bodily anchoring in reality through epistemological analysis of materiality (*dhātu-vavatthāna*) and a Buddhist therapy for mental illness (*bhūta-vejjakamma*). *Dhātu-manasikāra*, in this case, however, is concerned only with apprehension of the four basic elements, also called *mahā-bhūta*, and with distingishing them from elements of consciousness (*viññāna-dhātu*) as well as from possessing spirits and elements of delusion (*bhūta-gāha*). In the exercise we will learn what power exists in accurate labeling. In the chapter section entitled "Reality Anchoring through Labeling" (page 130ff.) we will return to this theme.

When *dhātu-manasikāra* is practiced as a complement to mindfulness of breathing, instruction for it is simple. Begin the exercise in accordance with the instructions for the superior stage of mindfulness of breathing (see p. 120) and supplement the resolution in the following manner:

4. "Now for thirty minutes I will observe only the breath and apprehend all distractions as *dhātu*."

Steps 5 to 7 as before.

8. Do not purposely provoke distractions, but wait "like a hunter" until a *dhātu* appears.
9. The distraction that has appeared is appraised: "Consciousness element or body element?"
10. If you determine that it is a consciousness element (thinking, intention, imagination, etc.), then return at once to the primary object of mindfulness, the breath.
11. If you note that it is "pressure," "touch," "heaviness," or "hardness," then give the appearance full attention. Realize: "This is the earth element," and stay with this perception as long as it lasts.

If you note that it is "flowing," "sticking," "soft," "viscous," "cohesion," then realize: "This is the water element."
If you note "movement," "flying," "vibration," "spreading," "expansion," then realize: "This is the air element."
If you note "warm," "cold," "shining," "glittering," "burning," "freezing," then realize: "This is the fire element."

12. Impress the direct inner experience of the respective elements on your memory at the moment that the perception seems clearest, and move back and forth between the remembered knowledge and the experiential knowledge for as long as the experience of the element lasts.

13. If the experience of the element becomes unbearably intense, return at once to the safety of the experiential sphere of the primary object of mindfulness, "Breathing in," "Breathing out."

14. After practicing apprehension of elements, rest in the refreshing, always peaceful mindfulness of breathing.

15. The exercise is ended with the "countdown" (see p. 122).

It would be misleading to speculate or theorize about the four *dhātu* or *mahā-bhūta*, because they are elements of experience and thus can be known only through direct experiencing. It is the same as with perception of colors; no theoretical knowledge about light particles and light waves can explain the subjective experience of a color, much less substitute for it. However, if you would like to know more about this exercise and the potential applications of its results, then read chapters 11 and 12 of Buddhaghosa's *Visuddhi Magga* (*The Path of Purification*: Berkeley: Shambhala, 1976).

3. IRIYĀ PATHA: NOTING BODILY POSTURES

This practice can be roughly divided into noting the four basic postures of sitting, lying, standing, and walking. It is traditionally taught, as in the Satipatthāna Sutta, right after mindfulness of breathing, before *sampajañña* and *dhātu-manasikāra*. Literally, *iriyā* means "movements" and *patha*, "way," "situation," or "range." In practice it refers to the experience of bodily postures and their alteration. It is natural for us to bend when we breathe out and stretch when we breathe in. One assumes more difficult postures (such as yoga postions) while holding the breath. Different bodily postures are characteristic of different states of feeling. Thus an insecure, frightened person has a cringing style of sitting; this gives an entirely different impression from the posture of the self-confident person who sits as though he were on a throne. And conversely, assuming various postures inwardly conveys different moods and feelings. Try now to sit for half a minute like an insecure, circumspect, anxious, and self-protective person. Then sit up straight for a while and self-confidently look down upon all that you see with the full weight of your personality.

It is possible to experiment in this way in all four postures. With eyes closed, slowly moving from sitting position to standing—possibly also stretching your arms above your head—then kneeling, then making the transition to lying on your belly, note how differently you experience yourself in the different postures. Also lying down, you feel different lying on your back than on your belly or on your side. If you have ever taken a course with a good yoga teacher, then you are already familiar with the fine shifts in mood that take place in varying the individual yoga positions (*āsana*) and gestures (*mudrā*). There is a dynamic breathing-feeling-position exercise that loosens up the whole space of mindfulness of body and has a very enlivening effect, especially during meditation sessions that last for many hours. For more than twenty years, I have enjoyed this exercise every morning before breakfast—that is, when I am not sick or otherwise prevented—even when I do not have time for any other meditation. The exercise is called *suriya-namaskar*. Literally, *suriya* means "sun" (inner and outer) or "the solar plexus" (of the body), *nama* means "name" (from *namati*, "bowing," "turning the mind to what has been named") and *kar* means "voluntary deed" (as in *karma*); *namaskar* also means "greeting." In English, the exercise can be called "greeting to the sun" or also "cloud dissolver," since, through a loosening up of all spheres of emotion or mood, it brings about a brightening of the mind; as soon as it has been well learned, it is capable of dissolving any kind of unpleasant mood.

The picture on the following page shows the steps of the greeting-to-the-sun exercise.

Begin by standing up straight with hands folded; be aware of the contact with the floor, the anchoring in Mother Earth. Realize: "I am steadfast and erect, upright, uniting the energies of my hands."

1. Breathing out heavily, think: "Out with old, stored-up dregs of air; I am empty, free, receptive."
2. Breathing in, stretch your arms upward into the cosmos, standing tense but firm, pushing the solar plexus forward into the world . . .
3. Breathing out, bend over, relaxed . . .

1
Strong outbreath
(following
standing concentration
practice)

2 = 11
Breathe in

3
Breathe out

10
Breathe out

4
Breathe in

9
Breathe in

12
Stand and relax
(after twelve
repetitions of
the exercise)

5
Breathe out

8
Breathe out

6
Hold without
inhaling

7
Breathe in

Discover for yourself what you feel with each of the positions and the transitions between them. It is a question of discovering the intelligence of your body, not some kind of rote learning or setting yourself right or imposing meanings. The greeting-to-the-sun exercise can be compared to a piano lesson in which we learn the mood coloration of different chords, how to feel them, to master them, so that later on, at a performance, we can fit them harmoniously into the whole. Thus we are attempting here to penetrate various mood spheres. It hardly needs to be said that in this situation also the joy in gentle penetration increases with repetition. And it should not be forgotten that a performance is enjoyed not only in the experience of individual chords and not only in the experience of melodic transitions, but also in fully savoring the pauses. Thus in the greeting-to-the-sun exercise, one can remain in any one of the positions for several breaths, or, for example, after six repetitions, can remain standing for a few minutes. In any case, after the twelfth (or with fewer, after the last) repetition, remain standing for a while in order to note what all has been aroused in the way of bodily sensation.

After the end of the greeting-to-the sun exercise it is helpful to remain motionless in standing position for a few minutes. First note:

- Am I standing straight?
- Is my head erect?
- Are my shoulders relaxed?
- Am I not rocking or swaying too much with the breath?

Then direct your attention exclusively to inner body feeling and savor the subsiding of all vibrations and currents that were activated by the greeting-to-the-sun exercise.

Collect yourself—in a literal sense—in a new equilibrium.

4. CANKAMANA: WALKING MEDITATION

You are standing there anchored in reality, and you decide to walk. What happens then? "Owing to what do we walk?" asks the *Papañca-Sūdanī*,[6] an Abhidhamma commentary, and gives an answer on the microanalytic level of experience. Without theories, Abhidhamma gives the answer in one word, even if it is a rather long compound word: *Citta-kiriya-vāyo-dhātu-vipphārena*. An English translation renders this as: "Owing to mental activity and the vibration of the wind or moving element brought about by it."

This indicates a directly experienced bodily fact, observed in the process of arising, which you yourself could also see after a certain amount of experience in the practice. In order not to make things too suspenseful, or indeed be accused of having left something unclear, I will cite from the commentary the matrix of wise apprehension for this "setting out to walk," which follows the one-word answer given above:

Thus the practitioner understands the process of walking in the following manner: The thought arises, "I wish to walk." This thought causes the wind element (*vāyo-dhātu*) to vibrate, and the wind element causes the bodily expression (*viññatti*) of walking to arise. The carrying forward of the whole body brought about by this mental activity (*citta-kiriya*) and vibration (*vipphārena*) of the wind element is called "walking."

Thus we have contented ourselves with an observation of beginning to walk made by others.[7] Observation of the actual process of walking makes accessible several spheres of experiencing that are of great importance for, among other things, shamanistic and magical techniques. Here, for reasons of space, we can only mention them as factors of far-reaching significance: the clearly comprehended experience of moving forward in general; then the clear comprehension of looking away and looking toward, connected with so-called tunnel vision; and the awareness of setting out and arriving. What particularly interests us in the *cankamana* exercise is once again bodily anchoring in reality, which is the basis for opening up other spheres of experiencing.

The purpose of *cankamana* is multilayered. Entertaining and instructive in this regard is the account of a conversation that took place between a participant in a course on mindfulness meditation and an Alpine herdsman behind the chalet where I was conducting the course. The herdsman had driven one of his cows out of the path of the course participant, who was mindfully striding along at a very reduced pace. But then the herdsman placed himself where the cow had been and asked: "What are you doing?"

"We're practicing walking mindfully," came the answer after a short pause.

"What is that good for?" The herdsman pursued the question slowly and deliberately in his rustic Alpine dialect.

"So that we won't have an accident hiking in the mountains," came the equally slow and deliberate answer of the practitioner. The herdsman, visibly satisfied, went on about his business.

In fact we do not exercise mindful walking on a mountain hike, nor while crossing a busy street for that matter. If you do not want to be distracted from your practice by explanatory conversations, you will be better off picking a corridor or two adjoining rooms for a practice site. The pathway should be even, straight and about ten yards long, so that in walking back and forth you can have a long enough stretch just to be mindful of the sensation in your feet. It is helpful to begin with a preliminary exercise in which you pay attention to component elements of walking only. By contrast, in everyday-life applications, as external demands increase one's perspective becomes more and more global. For example, if you were walking in the woods, you would not try to pay attention to the individual elements of your stride, but just to feel the alternating motion of your left and right legs. When hiking in the mountains or crossing a street, one pays attention mainly to the external dangers and moves mindfully without analyzing anything or trying to train in intensifying one's anchoring in reality.

Cankamana: Preliminary Exercise

1. Concentrate briefly, standing up quite straight and letting your gaze rest on the floor about two yards in front of you. Your arms are crossed on your chest or your hands joined behind your back.
2. Rather slowly but still naturally, begin walking.
3. While walking, notice the moment when each of your feet touches the floor and note this with the word "Placing."
4. After about four turns on your walking path, change the focus of your mindfulness to the moment when each of your feet leaves the floor. Now you pay attention only to each moment when contact with the floor ceases and note this with the world "Lifting."
5. After about four more turns, change back again to noting the moment of contact, of "placing." Alternating in this way, practice for five or ten minutes.
   To conclude, try for a couple of turns to note both lifting and placing without altering the slow but natural manner of walking.

Cankamana: Complete Exercise

1. Standing straight and collecting yourself in your body sensation, make the resolution: "Now I am going to walk."
2. Note the changes in bodily sensation connected with taking a step (shift in the center of gravity of your body, movement of your leg, etc.).
3. At the moment of cessation of contact between the sole of your foot and the floor, note: "Lifting."
4. As soon as contact between foot and floor reappears, note: "Placing."
5. Walk slowly but naturally, noting: "Lifting," "Placing," "Lifting," and so on.
6. If you become distracted, note this with the word "Distraction" and guide your mindfulness back to lifting and placing.
7. As soon as the bodily sensation of carrying the feet forward becomes apparent, note it with the word "Carrying." Now note all three: lifting, carrying, placing.

8. When you reach the end of your walking pathway, remain standing for a moment and note inwardly: "Arrived, arrived."
9. Turn around with the clear comprehension "Turning,
turning." Standing, collect yourself briefly, and then continue on to the next lap.

After the exercise bring to mind once again the insights and knowledge that during the exercise were noted merely as distractions. Perhaps heavy-feeling problems and moods have been resolved into processes and conditionalities that lift and are placed, that arise and pass
away. An occasion for joy? It can also happen that a catharsis takes
place, perhaps followed by an act of creativity, as was the case with
the Abhidhammika who, after this exercise, composed the following lines:

> Wind power moves the ship,
> The power of the bowstring speeds the shaft.
> So this body only moves
> When the wind *dhātu* pushes it.
> Like the puppet on a string,
> This body-puppet, bound to its mind string,
> Can only walk, stand, sit
> Through its force.

> Where is there a being here
> Who can walk about or stand
> Free from cause and condition,
> Moved and driven by its own force?
>   [PAPAÑCA-SŪDANĪ]

REALITY ANCHORING THROUGH LABELING

Labeling experiences is an important tool of mindfulness. It is ancient
knowledge—which, moreover, has been confirmed in the latest psychological experiments—that we only differentiate things in perception if we can label them as different. There are many examples that
illustrate this: Inhabitants of tropical countries, who know snow only
from television programs, would hardly be able to distinguish between rime, frost, powder snow, crusted snow, slush, and sleet. On
the other hand, the Eskimos see about fifteen different things that we
know only as different kinds of snow. But you do not have to be
an Eskimo to have trouble distinguishing the roughly ten kinds of
tropical fruit that all look like bananas, but all of which have completely different names. Anthropologists have established that there

are peoples who do not see certain colors. Because, for example, they have no word for blue, they classify this color either as a kind of green or a kind of black. Conversely, in the textile industry in Switzerland, five kinds of black are recognized that have different names in different sectors of the industry.

The act of labeling brings reality and experience together in a way that builds up a special power of word over thing. This is highlighted by a bit of folk wisdom from the fairy tale "Rumpelstiltskin." A demonic being, that is, a personification of unknown and thus uncanny experiences, has the protagonist of the fairy tale in its power. The princess—for us the noble observer, mindfulness—gains power over the demon as soon as she is able to name it. In a similar way, through your first practice experiences you yourself have already gained power over unusual objects of experiencing, those, for example, labeled as elements, *dhātu*. That is a power far greater than the power of labeling as "disturbance" whatever does not belong to the main meditation object, the breath. This power of naming or labeling becomes increasingly evident as we master further exercises. At that point the practical value of the matrices of knowledge and the psycho-algebra of *akkheyya* also becomes clear once again. Now you can perceive on the basis of your own experience those factors that were distinguished at the beginning of this chapter as truthfulness, accuracy, reality-relatedness, and bodily anchoring in reality. On the basis of your mindfulness of body, you can now also understand elements of the joke about the neurotic, the psychotic, and the psychiatrist that remain closed to those who have no experience in reality anchoring.

Practicing the exercises of mindfulness of body experientially clarifies the implications and significance of bodily anchoring in reality, and it does this in a way that no story, theory, or lesson can replace. Even the reader who was only able to retain a few fragments of the material conveyed in the previous chapter will now have seen these fragments filled out with a deeper meaning within the context of bodily experience. We can now understand how our linguistically fragmented world becomes a whole once again in bodily experiencing if we cultivate this consciousness. Within the sphere of bodily reality, there are no mistakes and no lies. Though we can physically pretend, that which is pretended is true as soon as it is physically carried out. It cannot be a deception, because it really is what it is. Only the explanations and interpretations—in other words, the thinking related to it— can be untrue or deceptive, if reality anchoring is lost or apprehension of the bodily reality is incomplete or unwise. And this brings us to the theme of clear comprehension. Clear comprehension goes beyond reality anchoring and truthfulness; without it no liberational increase of happiness would be possible.

MINDFULNESS AND CLEAR COMPREHENSION IN ACTION

Mindfulness (*sati*) notices what is really there; it opens the mind for complete reception of all that is present, without rejecting any particular kind of thing. It directs the mind to reality, which is labeled so that the process of knowing takes place with wisdom. Mindfulness notices what is, without interfering; it registers. In concrete life situations, we cannot just observe what is happening. We also cannot rely on our automatic reactions and just notice and label them. Daily life demands not only that our experience be anchored in reality and that our thinking be true. In order to live fully, we must also act—indeed, we must act with clear comprehension (*sampajañña*).

In order to fulfill the immeasurable potential of human existence, we must work it out in a completely concrete way through the course of a happy life. Happiness is something we ourselves must sincerely want. No one can order someone else to lead a happy life. When we really want something, then we invest more in it than when we are doing something just because we think it is advisable. Diagram 8 (page 94–95) showed that decisions related to action take place on a level that is closer to bodily experiencing than to thinking. During the exercise in walking meditation, it becomes experientially clear how a decision to act is transformed into action. Deciding, wishing, striving, and acting happen outside the sphere of thinking.

When we want something and decide to strive for it, then we collect ourselves in order to be able to bring all our mind's powers to bear: willpower, confidence, concentration, wisdom, and mindfulness. We are acting, hence we are not simply thinking. However, if we want our action to produce happiness, we have to act mindfully and with wisdom. This particular coming together of mindfulness (*sati*) and wisdom (*pañña*) in action is known in the Abhidhamma terminology as *sampajañña*, which means something like "clear comprehension." We have already spoken about various aspects of clear comprehension of the spheres of experiencing, clear comprehension of purpose, and so on. Now, through the practice of mindfulness of body, we have reached the point where it makes sense to examine clear comprehension more thoroughly and systematically. Since we have experientially established a concrete point of reference, we do not run the risk of degenerating into theorizing. However, for the moment let us limit ourselves to a discussion of clear comprehension related to quite simple actions. In this way, we will more easily be able to grasp clear comprehension as related to complex actions in the larger framework of our mental ecosystem. In the following chapter, we will see that the basic principles of *sīla* serve clear comprehension as criteria of value in promoting happiness even in the most complex undertakings.

For the moment we will steer clear of questions regarding clear comprehension of social and political action. General considerations with regard to New Age politics were presented in chapter 2, when we were working with the question of personal relationship to world affairs. Now let us work with this experientially based sense of personal connection on a (so to speak) microanalytic level. Only when we get to the strategies of sympathy will we dare to enter the realm of structuring social interactions. In the following exercises, we will begin by also excluding clear comprehension as applied to action in the inner world, which belongs to the strategies of ecstasy and power.

Before beginning with the exercises, however, let us familiarize ourselves with a few more distinctions, which will provide us with apprehension matrices (*yoni*) for clear comprehension. According to Abhidhamma, four kinds of clear comprehension are distinguished:

1. Clear comprehension of the domain of experiencing
2. Clear comprehension of purpose
3. Clear comprehension of suitability
4. Clear comprehension of nondelusion

A synoptic view of how these four kinds of clear comprehension fit together can be gained from a study of Diagram 9 (page 166). Here we will discuss them individually a bit more in detail.

1. Clear comprehension of the domain of experiencing (*gocara-sampajañña*) in its concrete form is an extension of the essence of what is outlined in the Abhidhamma literature as clear comprehension of a meditative domain, which is described as "not losing track of the object of meditation." In the framework of the strategies of reality anchoring, we use clear comprehension of the domain of experiencing to establish

   a. the current object of consciousness
   b. the sphere of reality in which the event experienced is taking place
   c. the orientation of mental movements and transitions between states of mind and spheres of experiencing

In all the exercises and strategies it is important to know the answers to the following questions:

a. What am I experiencing now? What is the current object of consciousness? Is it the main object of the meditation that I am practicing at this moment?

b. What sphere of reality am I presently experiencing? Is it an event of the bodily directly experienced external world? Am I experiencing an imagined event? Is the event a content of my thinking? Am I in the domain of meditative experiencing? Am I in the process of preparing for a meditation exercise? Am I oriented with regard to my spatial surroundings? Am I experiencing the current state of my body? Do I have physical sensations related to a past (future) event? Am I presently experiencing a mental movement (decision, effort, intention, perseverance, alteration of consciousness, exploration,[8] discrimination, calming, disappointment, etc.)?

c. If more than one answer to the question of my present domain of experiencing is possible, what is the transition I am in the midst of? Toward what is the present change in my experiencing oriented?

The psychological background of the various domains or spheres of experiencing were dealt with extensively in the chapter section "Levels of Experiencing" (page 87). Here we have progressed to the point of practical application. The questions we are addressing have matrices for the liberational apprehension of reality as their basis; thus they have nothing to do with any kind of psychological theorizing or, for that matter, with a scholastic classification of reality. There is a widespread misunderstanding in the West that Abhidhamma is an intellectual affair. Such erroneous views are particularly prevalent among biblical scholars who are psychologically naive and without experience in meditation. Abhidhamma also cannot be reduced to a psychology or a psychological ethics, as happened in the earliest English translations. As an example, the entire first book of the Abhidhamma canon, the *Dhammasangani*,[9] serves the advanced practitioner as a compendium of matrices of clear comprehension. Thus every experience can be related to as a field for practice. Nyanaponika, one of the greatest contemporary meditation masters, expresses this fact in the following words:

> But if one's meditative practice is all-round Mindfulness, as advocated here, there will be no need ever to lay aside the

subject of meditation, which, in fact, will include everything. Step by step the practice of Right Mindfulness should
absorb all activities of body, speech, and mind, so that ultimately the subject of meditation will never be abandoned.
How far one succeeds in that, will depend on the presence
of mind available at the single occasions, and on the habit-
forming and growing strength of diligent practice. The aim
to be aspired to by the disciple of this method is that *life*
becomes one with the spiritual *practice*, and that the *practice*
becomes full-blooded *life*.

The "domain" (*gocara*) of the practice of Right Mindfulness has no rigid boundaries. It is a kingdom that constantly grows by absorbing ever new territories of life. It
was in reference to this all-comprehensive domain of the
Satippatthāna method, that once the Master spoke as follows: "Which, O monks, is the monk's domain (*gocara*), his
very own paternal place? It is just these Four Foundations
of Mindfulness."

Therefore the disciple of this method should always ask
himself, in the words of Santideva:

*"How can the practice of Mindfulness be performed under these
very circumstances?"*

One who does not forget thus to question himself and
also to act accordingly, may be said to possess "Clear Comprehension of the Domain" of Right Mindfulness. [Nyana-
ponika Thera, *The Heart of Buddhist Meditation*, pp. 50–51]

2. Clear comprehension of purpose (*sa-atthaka-sampajañña*) helps us
to adopt suitable goals and purposes and keeps us from falling under
the spell of ill-considered actions. There is no such thing as goalless
action until we are completely enlightened. Each action is either effective in serving a purpose or not. If we deceive ourselves into thinking
that we are acting "just like that," without a goal, it simply means that
we are not yet ready to become aware of what we are aiming at. Perhaps we are not even capable of grasping what our aim is. Perhaps we
are not mindful enough to see that our action conflicts with our aim.
Perhaps rejected, unheeded, and repressed needs of ours are manifesting in our action, which in retrospect we would see as completely
senseless and irrational. It can also be the case that we are ashamed
of our goal and are unwilling to acknowledge it; thus we prefer a
vagueness that leaves us under the pseudoprotection of ignorance.
The type of education customary in our latitudes, poisoned by the
cyanide of moralism, often makes it impossible for us to affirm purposes and goals that are in complete conformity with natural requirements of life.

In order for us to make necessary progress in mindfulness, we must recognize that a severe, impatient, and intolerant attitude toward our own weaknesses and lack of purposiveness is in no way helpful; on the contrary, it increases our alienation from reality. Only when we see this does it become possible mindfully to note intentions and aims that embarrass us. Cultivation of a loving and patient attitude toward oneself as well as toward others, as developed in the context of the strategies of sympathy, is also helpful for clear comprehension of purpose. Though an Abhidhammika's sole purpose is progress toward truth, liberation, and happiness, he or she finds it entirely understandable that, under the manifold influence of *papañca*, other goals can temporarily come to the fore, even goals that, in a higher sense, are unsuitable. Clear comprehension of purpose is called in Abhidhamma *sa-atthaka-sampajañña*. *Attha* means "purpose," "gain," "benefit," "well-being," "sense," and "meaning." Clearly comprehended action is not only purposive but also gainful, beneficial, good, sensible, and meaningful. Above all, though, it is carefully considered.

Quite concretely speaking, how do we act with clear comprehension of purpose, and how can we practice this clear comprehension? As with all exercises of Dhamma strategies, let us begin with simple, unproblematical, and clearly laid-out processes. When the thought of doing something develops—let us say, for example, the thought of going somewhere—it does not immediately have to be translated into action. After all, we should not be at the mercy of every thought. We should mindfully note the intention to act (*chanda*) and before we make a decision (*adhimokkha*), we should ask ourselves these questions: What good will going there do? What effect will it have? Does this intended action really correspond to my goal?

In advanced practice of clear comprehension of purpose, we also take into account in relation to actions in society what impression they make on other people. We do not live alone in this world and are not independent of the experience and action of other people. Our activity not only triggers mental and karmic reactions. Even if you, dear reader, are not a politician or a leader in society, you nevertheless have a sense of what impression your actions make on other people and what you aim for in this respect. Of course we cannot please everyone, but we can still, up to a certain point, guard our autonomy, integrity, and dignity from the doubts of others by mindfully thinking through the suitability of purpose of our actions and foreseeing the possible consequences of them. We would be foolish if we acted strangely and then complained that we were treated accordingly by others. It would be ludicrous for us to carry on like an enfant terrible or behave arrogantly and then reproach others for not being nice to us. But it can also happen that we act a little differently than expected and merely thereby awaken suspicion and mistrust. In deed as in word, one can always be misunderstood. There is no absolute protection against blame, false conjecture, and accusation other than trust (*saddhā*) in truthfulness and the equanimity (*upekkhā*) that grows out of it. (About these, we will speak in detail in the next chapter.) Thus it remains indisputable that the purity of our own way of thinking and of setting our goals is crucial for clear comprehension of purpose.

Clear comprehension itself has the purpose of creating a clear vision of the possible effects of our actions, so that we can evaluate them and freely choose what to do. With clear comprehension we avoid the danger of simply spinning our wheels. It guards us from falling prey to the merely incidental, from distractedness and the resultant weakening of willpower. Where otherwise we might be at the mercy of blind drives and influences (*āsava*), clear comprehension makes it possible to maintain our initiative and sovereignty.

3. Clear comprehension of the suitability of an action (*sappāya-sampajañña*) takes into account the limited possibilities of given external situations. It enables us to make a critical self-evaluation by recognizing the extent of our competence in a situation. Not all the skills we have that are useful and applicable toward liberation and well-being are appropriate in every situation. We can protect ourselves from failure and disappointment by asking ourselves the following questions before carrying out even a well-practiced, happiness-furthering action: Is this action suitable at this time in this situation? Will I be able to accomplish what I intend in these circumstances? Is it the right approach for these conditions?

Clear comprehension of the suitability of an action chooses the right means (*upāya-kosalla;* see page 74f.) and makes sure that we do not apply it naively. Thus it is an art of the possible and at the same time a protection against hasty application of learnt routines. Clear comprehension of suitability has a special significance also in choosing meditation objects and techniques, which we will look into in connection with the strategies of ecstasy and power. At this point, let me mention only as an illustrative example that meditation on death, which has as its purpose the overcoming of inertia and indifference, is not suitable for a person who is insecure. In the same way, meditation techniques like the contemplation of colors and *devas*, which are meant to calm violent temper and restlessness, are hardly appropriate for a reckless, avidly indulgent person.[10] The same applies to suitability of actions, techniques, programs, and entire strategies as to suitability of herbal preparations and chemicals—the point in time when they are to be used, the dosage, and how they are combined requires precise understanding and trial testing.

4. Clear comprehension of nondelusion (*asammoha-sampajañña*) is the result of thorough wise apprehension (*yoniso manasikāra*), which without any confusion or delusion, perceives things as they really are: composite, changing, and mutually conditioned. There are no solid entities that are discrete from one another and exhibit any kind of immutable identity. This is the supreme clear comprehension. It goes beyond concepts, using them only as labels and paradigms—like a psycho-algebra (cf. page 69f.)—without imputing any reality to them. Conceptual classifications of things into "mine," "alien to me," "I," and "not-I," as well as other distorted views and preconceptions, are dissolved, because clear comprehension of nondelusion brings about complete reality anchoring in the structure and process of the interrelatedness of events.

Clear comprehension of nondelusion is more than an antidote to delusion (*moha* or *avijjā*), which we recognized in the course of our analysis of the social roots of suffering as one of three. We also encountered these three, greed, agression, and delusion, as the roots of suffering in our analysis of conditioned arising (*paticca-samuppāda*) in chapter 3. In chapter 4, we became acquainted with the three roots of suffering in their role of distorting and blocking the healthy normal flow of feelings. Also our discussion of cathartic processes in the purification of the mind (*citta-visuddhi*) showed up the distorting mechanisms of delusion, aggression, and greed. It repeatedly became clear that in a technical sense the path of liberation is based on cultivation of wisdom (nondelusion), generosity (absence of greed), and kindness (absence of aggression). Liberation is the purification of the mind, becoming free from everything that obscures our mind and distorts our perception. The less our inner world is tainted and the more liberated the way we experience ourselves is, the more competent our action in the external world becomes. This competent way of acting also includes the generation of ethical rules that promote a purification of our subjective basis (*sīla-visuddhi*).

Clear comprehension of nondelusion not only includes all the other three kinds of clear comprehension (domain, purpose, and suitability), but also embraces the ethical wisdom of *sīla-visuddhi* and the skill-fulness of *citta-visuddhi*, which was discussed at the end of the previous chapter. Thus clear comprehension represents the culture of nondelusion, in which the exercises of mindfulness of body play a major role. It is for this reason that mindfulness of body, along with clear comprehension, receives so much attention in the strategies of reality anchoring. However, clear comprehension of nondelusion is just as important for the strategies of sympathy, which are the primary basis for cultivating generosity without greed and kindness without aggression. Before we focus on these stategies in the next chapter, let us turn our attention to a few practical exercises. They will give our discoveries concerning clear comprehension a living relationship to the body. This in turn will provide us in all subsequent strategies with a clearly comprehended foundation for any action.

EXERCISES IN CLEAR COMPREHENSION

The Abhidhamma teachers of old developed numerous exercises for clear comprehension during everyday activity as well as during meditative retreats. A representative selection of these is found in the previously mentioned work *Papañca-Sūdanī*. Here the teachers have worked out minutely detailed practice instructions for each of the following elementary life-spheres:

1. Bodily postures
2. Going to sleep and waking up
3. Eating and excreting
4. Bending and stretching
5. Looking toward and looking away
6. Dealing with objects
7. Speaking and remaining silent

The exercises take into account all four kinds of clear comprehension in each sphere. In the framework of methodical *satipatthāna-vipassanā* meditation, the spheres of clear comprehension constitute the secondary objects of meditation—the primary objects being the breath (*ānāpāna*) and walking back and forth (*cankamana*). During a meditation retreat, speaking and dealing with objects are reduced to a minimum; thus they are much easier to apprehend according to the criteria of clear comprehension. Looking toward and looking away, which will be discussed further in connection with training in concentration in chapter 7, as well as the remaining spheres, are not less present at times of strict meditation than otherwise. Some of these spheres are less problematic and are therefore accessible to mindfulness (*sati*) and clear comprehension (*sampajañña*) without great difficulty.

Since in our civilization everything having to do with the experience of excretion has a special importance in the mental economy, let us devote a few thoughts to this theme at this point. Most people are unable to adopt an objective attitude toward matters having to do with excretion. An internationally prevalent view holds German toilet-training—or indeed, compulsive toilet-training wherever it is found—to be prototypical for all causes of miserliness, ego-identification, compulsive orderliness, and intolerance. Psychiatrists surely have their reasons for asserting that an adult's relationship to money recapitulates that individual's relationship to excrement, and that this is also responsible for the structure of all of one's interpersonal relationships. Thus they attribute all extremes such as sadistic beating in upbringing and education, masochistic submissiveness in sexuality (cf. my observations on pages 103ff.), as well as all extremes of compulsive effort "not to lose control" in any sphere of life, to one's relationship to the primordial causal entities excrement and money. Various degenerations connected with this type of phenomenon make this inability to let go highly evident. A characteristic feature of our civilization is (physical and mental) constipation and distension, which are spasmodically eliminated through the use of purgatives, and the eliminated material is frequently then held up as a showpiece of technology, science, or art.

Whatever may be the case with the alienated realities and the philosophies of psychiatry, psychology, modern art, and so forth, the exercises of clear comprehension aim for genuine anchoring in reality. To put it figuratively, clear comprehension of nondelusion stops us from building castles in the air out of materials resulting from the mental process of elimination; it opens up the ivory prisons, the houses of "I" and "mine," and permits the awareness that has hitherto been imprisoned there to take increasingly long sojourns in the open air of homelessness. All this does not mean that clearly comprehending persons no longer make use of conceptual casings; it is just that for those who clearly comprehend, there is no longer any self-imposed house arrest. Once we have the certainty of clear comprehension of the domain, we can move freely in the domain represented by the castle in the air and the ivory tower.

We could come up with further metaphorical thoughts about the "immutable substance" of excrement and money and ego. . . . However, let us not forget that what we are concerned with here is the purification of the mind and, in particular, elimination. The suffering that comes from experiential constipation resulting from some kind of indigestible, immutable substance of the mind is the worst kind altogether: in that situation one is also unable to let loose a completely outmoded conception of self. Letting go as a psychological skill can be profitably practiced through meditating during defecation. These remarks seem necessary to me just because in our civilization the process of excretion is laden with so many taboos.

J. H. Schultz, a prominent German psychiatrist who developed a system known as autogenic training, particularly studied the Abhidhamma notions of clear comprehension and of "bare attention," which latter also has the quality of letting go. He expressed his appreciation of Nyanaponika's book on the *satipatthāna* method and also foresaw the difficulty discussed above. As Schultz wrote:

> It is a matter of developing on the one hand the approach of bare attention toward one's own experience and on the other that of "clear comprehension," that is, clearly aware and clearly cognizing thought and action.
>
> On this path, first of all one strives for a high degree of detached inner and outer objectivity; . . . "clear comprehension of nondelusion" consists in the clear and present knowledge that in the functions carried out by the other three kinds of clear comprehension, there is no ego, no soul, no kind of immutable substance. Here the practitioner will have to confront the strongest resistance.[11]

If we apprehend resistance as a challenge and have confidence in our ability to deal with it, then overcoming resistance becomes enjoyable and has an enlivening effect. Dealing with resistance can also be a source of joy. Lack of any challenge, on the other hand, is boring and has a fatiguing effect. It has often been stressed, and has been frequently pointed out in these pages, that joy (*pīti*) is the most important motivating force. Thus there is nothing wrong if in the following exercises we run into resistance. But we should not force ourselves to do any exercise that would mar our joy. This will probably apply primarily to clear comprehension exercises connected with going to sleep and waking up or eating and eliminating, because it is these spheres of experience that are most often encumbered by fears, prejudices, and delusive conceptions of self.

All the exercises in clear comprehension can be carried out in the midst of everyday life. They require no special practice times—unless, for example, during a week of vacation you decide to drop all demanding activities so that for the whole time you can systematically practice clear comprehension in all seven elementary spheres. In contrast to the exercises in mindfulness of body described at the beginning of this chapter, with these exercises it is not necessary to resolve to continue to dwell on certain phenomena. One simply practices clear comprehension in relation to whatever happens to present itself to one's mindful attention.

CLEAR COMPREHENSION OF BODILY POSTURES

When from time to time the knowledge arises, "Now I am sitting," or "Now I am sitting here in order to read quietly," this is basically already enough for clear comprehension, and we need not consider any further. Thus far there are also no changes of posture either planned or thought about. Only if we lie down to rest or get up with the intention of stretching is it appropriate to note mentally: "Sphere of bodily posture." It is also helpful to use this phrase in observing bodily expression of moods (*iriyā-patha*, p. 124) in order to remain in the elementary sphere of bodily postures instead of losing oneself in secondary thought-reactions to the given experience. Indeed, we could deal a bit more frugally with thinking, especially when it is without purpose, and in this way stay with our bodily experiencing more. For the intelligence of the body makes possible knowledge that cannot be obtained through reading or thinking.

CLEAR COMPREHENSION OF GOING TO SLEEP AND WAKING UP

Clear comprehension of going to sleep is an important requirement for all techniques for experimenting with dreams, for training the "inner clock," and for preparing our manner of waking up. Some people use the time right before falling asleep for reflecting about the day just past. This is to be recommended only if we are well practiced in a clear method of reflection (see p. 181f.) or when, after a tiring day, we really want to think things over a bit. Clear comprehension of going to sleep combines well with a certain ritualization of the process of falling asleep, which is also useful for getting rid of any sleep problems one might have.[12] Deciding about the time and manner of waking up is an important part of such a going-to-sleep ritual. Perhaps the following description may be useful, as an example and inspiration for you in experimenting with and developing your own ritual of going to sleep.

You should do this exercise only when you really feel tired and sleepy enough to go to sleep. When you have noted the intention and made the resolve to go to sleep, check to make sure that everything is finished for the day. Then you are disburdened and open for clear comprehension of the following:

1. Where am I now? In what posture?
2. What do I have to do to reach my sleeping place (stand up, walk to the bedroom, get undressed, brush my teeth, etc., . . . until I am standing next to the bed that has been prepared for going to sleep)?
3. Mindfully I sit down on the bed, lie down, cover myself— all with clear comprehension of the purpose "Going to sleep."
4. Lying down, I become aware of contact with the bed-clothes and perhaps also of my breath.
5. Now comes the resolve: "Now I am going to sleep peace-fully until, exactly at a quarter to seven, I wake up re-freshed and strengthened. The first thing I will do when I wake up is become aware of my breath and feel the con-tact with the bedclothes."
6. Feeling the contact with the bedclothes, one falls asleep, once there has been a fair amount of practice, after just a few breaths.
7. In accordance with the resolve, wake up, become aware of the breath, and feel the contact with the bedclothes.

This exercise of ritualizing the processes of going to sleep and wak-ing up is usually practiced primarily by participants in meditation courses during "siesta" periods. In this case, experience has shown that the sleeping period should be no shorter than fifteen minutes and no longer than forty minutes. Waking up from sleep, like the end of a meditation period, is a transition between spheres of experienc-ing, a new entry into everyday life. The first activities you undertake after waking up have a lasting effect on the succeeding mode of expe-riencing, just as in a musical jam session, the first notes and rhythms shape the improvisations that follow. A person who wakes up and unmindfully begins to participate in frivolous or even unwholesome activities instigated by others will find it difficult, as the situation de-velops, to win the way back to meaningful activity.

An ideal waking confers on the daily-life situation a happy underly-ing tone as well as providing a sense of self-confidence, indepen-dence, and ability for accomplishment as a foundation for clearly comprehended action. Such a waking-up process might take place as follows:

1. You wake up by yourself at the decided time (without being shocked from sleep by an alarm of any kind).
2. Although various possibilities present themselves to our awareness, turn your attention to your breath (as decided before going to sleep).
3. Resting in yourself in this way, open yourself to take in the current environmental situation. Listen to the sounds of the birds, smell the fragrance of the basil plant on the windowsill, look at the play of light and shadow on the curtains. Tune yourself into the world here and now.
4. If you dreamed, now is the moment to recall the dream and summarize it in three to five main points. (More main points could hardly be remembered later in re-counting or writing down the dream. Moreover, more detailed recall of the dream would give it too much weight in shaping the day. This is not the time for a dream analysis.)
5. Return again to the actuality of current bodily experiencing and relate to your other physical sensations as well as your breathing.
6. Make the resolve: "I will set up my day self-confidently, openly, happily, and efficiently with regard to my goals."
7. With mindfulness and clear comprehension, carry out your first actions—sitting up, stretching, and so forth. Pausing, mindfulness, and clear comprehension—these three key words, which refer quite clearly to particular skills, convey the guidelines for a successful and happy day.

This detailed account of how clear comprehension of going to sleep and waking up can be practiced may possibly serve as an incentive to work up other similar strategies of reality anchoring for other spheres of daily life. It would far exceed the framework of this chapter, and would also inhibit your own creativity, were I to provide here similar schema for clearly comprehended eating and so on, even if they were descriptions of personal experiences. The general principles of clear comprehension in dealing with objects have been explained in the chapter sections on "Wise Apprehension," particularly on p. 71f. We should not forget that all the instructions and descriptions of principles are meant only as encouragements and never as commandments or directives. What we are doing is practicing mindfulness and clear comprehension, not training ourselves in the "right way" of sitting, waking up, eating, speaking, and so on. Nevertheless, by way of conclusion a few indications about how to relate to food might be interesting, especially considering the fact that there are many taboos concerning this subject.

CLEAR COMPREHENSION OF EATING AND ELIMINATION

Alienation from reality in our civilization is perhaps most clearly evident in relation to food. Prevalent superficial and foolish attitudes toward food frequently degenerate into extremes of destruction and adoration, which we find expressed in our civilization in various ridiculous customs. On the one hand, through unnecessary cooking and conservation, food is stripped of vital ingredients and poisoned with chemicals; on the other, we indulge in gluttony as a ceremonial occasion at the family table or eating out. So it goes with the "establishment." In the "alternative" culture, food philosophies such as "raw food only," or "the saltier, the more religious," or "no *yang* vegetables" sometimes represent the whole purpose of life. Members of the alternative culture as well as those of the establishment rarely get beyond their ideologies. The content of their experience in relation to food would remain the same even if they were actually to consume dietetic cookbooks and French menus. Mindfulness and clear comprehension of eating? Sounds weird.

When a child is trained to eat, touching food with the fingers—or even kneading it, as is done in non-Western cultures—is condemned. Savoring the taste and odor of food has been rendered impossible by anti-authoritarian distractions such as television and lack of discipline at the table. Yet tasting and relishing, chewing and swallowing can be interesting experiences. They are amazing discoveries that are usually made for the first time during a course in mindfulness meditation.

How often have you granted yourself the time calmly and thoroughly to contemplate the same food as it is served, chewed, digested, and eliminated?

How clear is your comprehension of the different way food feels on the lips, the tongue, the gums? For the moment, let us set aside clear comprehension of the sensations connected with elimination of feces and urine. In psychiatric institutions, one sometimes encounters people whose toilet training was so thoroughly carried out that in their world such processes as elimination of feces and urine never occur at all; awareness of such processes and disposal of their results must therefore be delegated to the nursing staff.

Neither institutional changes nor a revolution in education is the aim of our book. We do not need to exercise self-criticism or submit to psychoanalytic treatment because of our eating behavior or our excretory habits. *It is enough to see and admit the truth.* The technique of labeling opens the door to this possibility—especially in the case of spheres of reality that are so important for our well-being and are so neglected in relation to their importance, such as the spheres of eating and eliminating. Thus the exercises for mindfulness and clear comprehension in their regard may well turn out to be quite rewarding and also instructive in relation to other similar processes in other life-spheres.

Dear reader, you are already competent in applying the skills of *yoniso manasikāra* and labeling. Now it is necessary in addition to take enough time during eating and eliminating to permit the natural processes to take their course unhindered. Although in eating active movements predominate, such as carrying food to the mouth, taking it in, and chewing it, there are also processes involved that can be passively allowed. Discover them. In the case of elimination, clear comprehension of experiences that are allowed to happen predominates. The active part there is mainly deciding to relax the sphincter muscles, to let the urine flow, to release the feces, to let the elimination take place. Even here you can make the exercise easier at the beginning by proceeding in a certain order as we did, for example, with going to sleep and waking up. Develop your own ritual, one which provides a protective framework for your natural needs, your health, and your well-being.

THE VALUE OF RITUAL

Behavioral sequences designed with clear comprehension (*sīlabbata*) provide protection for the undisturbed progression of vital functions that cannot be actively "done." In this sense, we could see appropriate rituals as strategies of letting be. They provide us time that we would otherwise use for the fulfillment of obligations. To be sure, these assertions require further elucidation. In our civilization, practically all daily activities and almost all of conscious life is directed toward the fulfillment of external tasks and obligations. Passive recreation, integrative harmonization, and intimate reality anchoring are little valued, because they do not profit outer tasks in the short term. When something has little value, we also give it little time. After all, we have to save time so that we can produce and consume more. This is the way "productive" people think, who consider rituals meaningless. Values shaped by science and technology consist in hoarding time and in supplanting living processes with dead mechanisms, which if possible run automatically after one has pushed a button. Our society values this as "efficient" and applies the same criteria to people. Feelings, everything having to do with emotional life, are only perceived when disturbances appear. By contrast, in cultures in which production and consumption are given less value than the enjoyment of play, celebration, and meditation, feelings are appreciated. In such less "diligent" cultures, rituals also thrive. Because for a ritual one needs time. Time is different in every reality. Machine time (the clock is a machine, too) is determined by the lifeless functioning of a mechanism. The time of the immutable concepts of a purely formal logic stands dead still. By contrast, the inwardly experienced time of bodily reality, of feelings and actions, is borne along by the rhythm of life. In this sense, a meditation session can be seen as a ritual, as a strategy, that lets reality anchoring in the processes of life take place. *Sīla* as the inwardly instigated self-regulation of a living person is the reliable subjective basis for designing wholesome rituals (*sīlabbata*), which provide the needed time for experiencing anchored in the body. In bodily anchored rituals, there is no "right or wrong," only different degrees of good, beautiful, and useful, depending on the extent to which they are conducive to happiness.

Through overemphasis on external acts, a ritual loses its usefulness for anchoring experience in reality. Such loss and alienation of worth and effectiveness takes place when the meanings of the ritual actions and precise conformity to rules and regulations for their performance win the upper hand. In this way a ritual can become an artistic performance or a ceremony. With such rituals, which are performed without the four kinds of clear comprehension, we find ourselves once again in the value sphere of production and consumption. It is true that we can take active part in a ceremony and even perhaps express our experience—to the extent that the rules of the ceremony permit—but nevertheless, following the outer rules is the important part. Ceremonies can also (perhaps on account of their artistic qualities) put the onlooker in a good mood. However, they have no liberational worth in the sense of a purification of experiencing (*visuddhi*). Participation in ceremonies requires adaptation to external rules, regulations, and directives that repress everything that is subjectively alive and are therefore damaging to the reliable subjective support base of *sīla*. Someone who is attached to rules of behavior no longer related to a purpose (*sīlabbata-parāmāsa*; *parāmāsa* means contamination and infectious contact) must lose his anchoring in reality and become mad like the Pavlovian dog that we discussed at the beginning of chapter 4.

For that dog, however, there was no chance to alter his environment. But what is the case with us?

Our discussions in this chapter show the high priority of mindfulness and clear comprehension in the strategies of reality anchoring and give some perspective on their significance for action in everyday life. Effective action is only possible on the basis of reality-true perception extended to true thinking, reflecting, and planning. True statements about real events are results of thorough, wise apprehension, *yoniso manasikāra*, which, as the most elementary of the techniques of liberational wisdom, we already practiced at the end of chapter 3. In chapter 2, we came to know the roots of suffering and happiness through consideration of broader social questions and thus learned the value of *sīla*. The following chapter builds on the foundation of our previous findings by showing us the pathways of the possible in the sphere of interpersonal relations.

6

Strategies of Sympathy

The better things are going for the people around me, the better external conditions are for things going well for me too. However, my happiness is not conditioned by external circumstances alone. A much greater determining factor for the quality of my life is my capacity for happiness.

The strategies of sympathy, through systematic practice and application in concrete everyday life situations, unify and develop both approaches: sharing happiness with our fellow human beings and cultivating our own capacity for happiness. Purification of the reliable subjective basis, *sīla-visuddhi*, and purification of the mind, *citta-visuddhi*, are the basic methods for developing the strategies of sympathy. Wisdom, *paññā*, provides the needed holistic vision as well as understanding of conditioned arising (*paticca-samuppāda*) and the teaching of cause and effect (*kamma*)—all of which themes will be familiar to you from the previous chapters. On the other hand, new for you at this point are the methods of meditative training in interpersonal relationships and methods for building up *sīla*, which comprise the core of this chapter. These methods lead to the culture of the heart, which culminates in the meditation of universal kindness, *mettā*.

The importance of *sīla* was elucidated in chapter 2 from a sociological point of view. There we saw the necessity for a reliable subjective basis to serve as protection against societal dangers. Peripherally, I also mentioned how *sīla* provides security from magical attacks and from drifting into spheres alienated from reality. In what follows, we will approach *sīla* more from a psychological point of view in order to clarify how regulation and control of speech and action affect our clarity of mind. We will concern ourselves little with theory, but will try to assimilate this more on the level of poetry. When I speak of the regulation and control of speech and action, I am referring not to some kind of self-punishment, but rather to a mastery that makes us feel like a sovereign power in our own ecosystem.

Joy in our own abilities sets energies free that permit action and speech to play an ever more creative role in the realization of happiness. Control goes hand in hand with overview or vision, and vision is necessary to create free space for trying out new things. The complicated life of our unhealthy industrial civilization provides many examples (some of which were mentioned in chapter 2) of unskillful action and empty chatter that are the result of inadequate vision, incompetence, and excessive and overtaxing demand. Not only do politicians and leaders speak and act in a muddled and aggressive fashion; their constituents, too, including our youth, have little choice but to compensate for inadequate vision and lack of creativity through consumerism and intolerance. Frustrated, disoriented, and overburdened people are incapable of living creatively, and so tend to be tied to authority and to simply vegetate, either in submissive obedience or in reactionary revolution. This situation has brought about the contemporary psychoboom, an overabundance of psychological techniques and group activities, of which even professionals cannot maintain a complete view.

Contemporary group activities, which go beyond the framework established by professional psychologists and (especially in self-help groups) have sympathy or solidarity as one of their goals, are much indebted to the work of Carl R. Rogers.[1] Rogers was the first to investigate not only the conduct of therapists or group leaders, but beyond that those therapeutic approaches that are conducive to liberation, sympathy, and mental health. In his investigations, he found three "therapist variables" that are crucial for successful therapy and—this is particularly important—in which therapists can be trained through interpersonal relationship. Rogers training groups for therapists as well as self-help groups for nonprofessionals are meant to provide a protected environment in which participants can investigate the effects of their actions, discover what approaches are conducive to their well-being, and further practice what they have found good. Thus there is an effort to "discover autochthonous patterns of behavior regulation." This corresponds in part to the definition of *sīla* formulated in chapter 2. The reference to actually experienced events and feelings that are currently physically present is also one of Rogers's principles. The three "therapist variables" psychologically investigated by Rogers and his colleagues do not, however, yet constitute the "culture of heart." They can be compared to only three facets of a crystal that are polished individually so that mindfulness and clear comprehension can shine through. Mindfulness of Rogers's "therapy variables" is directed toward the interpersonal, as we see from the following definitions:

1. *Empathy* or sympathetic understanding, in which one places oneself precisely in the concrete experience of one's partner in dialogue.
2. *Emotional warmth*, kindness, an attitude of loving acceptance of people that is not tied to any condition.
3. *Genuineness*—expressing only feelings and intentions that are actually present. This does not, however, mean ruthlessly externalizing every mental impulse, nor does it mean lack of consideration in speaking.

Empathy is a function of mindfulness (*sati*). All mindfulness exercises lead first to a more precise feeling and understanding of physical as well as mental impulses and states. Later they bring us to understand the contexts and relations that they are part of. In mindfulness meditation, we notice that different states of mind express themselves in different bodily postures, that breathing rhythm, muscle tone, and mobility are dependent on our inner state. With progress in the meditation, it becomes increasingly easier to recognize states and mental processes more precisely, in others as well as oneself. In order to recognize something, to apprehend it thoroughly, we must first accept it as given. Nothing that is immediately rejected can be understood. For this reason, controlling and restraining are not conducive to understanding. Thus emotional warmth, which is meditatively unfolded as kindness (*mettā*), is closely related to empathy.

However, it sometimes happens in desperately striving for empathy and warmth that a person may work him- or herself up into a state of ungenuineness and even believe, affirm, and carry out things that currently have little to do with that person's bodily reality. Genuineness also requires mindfulness, which leaves us open to all levels of experiencing. Only when empathy and warmth of feeling are not in conflict with our bodily state and its manifestation are they genuine and do they come through as authentic. A genuine person is one who does and says what is felt bodily and actually experienced.

When we do not feel threatened in interpersonal situations, it is easier to manifest empathy, kindness, and genuineness. And we do not feel threatened when we have a reliable subjective basis that makes it possible for us to do without risk even things that other people usually take advantage of. Thus we look toward gentle, increasingly genuine personal relationships that are free from struggle, obsequiousness, and blind faith but based instead on mutual respect, trust, and noble friendship. "Noble friendship" is the exact translation of *kalyāna mittatā*, the term for the relationship between the Abhidhamma teacher and his student. In contrast to Indian religion, where there is a guru, and in contrast to Western psychotherapies and other Western psychological procedures where there is a therapist or leader who determines the situation for his clients, the *kalayāna mitta* or noble friend provides support to his companion on the path by mindfully respecting the companion's needs and inclinations, by placing his capabilities at the companion's disposal, and by offering personal feedback. Noble friendship is close to those types of interpersonal situations in which the three "therapist variables" described above are present to a high degree.

Noble friendship has as its goal first and foremost to assure the practitioner a supportive and unthreatening interpersonal space in which self-exploration and shaping of autochthonous patterns of behavior regulation in the manner of *sīla* are possible. Let us look at this subject more thoroughly. Several other aspects of noble friendship will be elucidated in connection with the strategies of ecstasy and power. The point does not need to be pursued here that noble friendship can be lived more intensively in the retreatlike situation of a meditation center, in a New Age strategy workshop, or in a self-help group than is possible in everyday life. Nonetheless it is possible and helpful increasingly to try out genuine, nobly friendly relationships outside such protected environments. Even if conversations that provide feedback are often not possible here, we do not regard this attempt purely as a part of our own practice, but also as a way to affect the general mental ecosystem.

CULTIVATING SĪLA

The patterns of behavior regulation of *sīla* are autochthonous, that is, they spring from our inmost personal spheres; they are developed through insight and they are tested by experience. The basic principles of *sīla* simply provide *orientation* and are to be regarded as training principles. *They are neither norms nor commandments,* because for New Age strategies based on the Abhidhamma no criterion is higher than that of bodily actuality, as has repeatedly been made clear. This, however, does not exclude the possibility of influencing our action, speech, thought, and mode of experiencing for the purpose of increasing our capacity for happiness. The first chapter already made evident that it is not so easy to influence our thinking and our mode of experiencing. It is much easier to regulate our action and speech wisely and thus to exercise influence on our inner speech and action—that is, on thinking and experiencing—and thus increasingly to gain mastery over it until we achieve sovereign rulership over our entire inner household.

The basic principles of *sīla* can be most simply formulated in terms of five criteria, which aim at stopping aggression and greed in word and deed and preventing people from sinking into delusion and obscured awareness. The intentionality (*cetanā*) or goal-orientation (*kamma*) of states of consciousness that are free from suffering-causing tendencies constitute the reliable subjective basis.

According to the *Vibhanga*,[2] the second book of the Abhidhamma canon, the reliable subjective basis of *sīla* is made up of all states of consciousness that meet these five criteria, regardless of whether they are associated with knowledge and resolve, regardless of what object of consciousness they are directed toward, and also regardless of whether they are sensual (*kāma*) states of consciousness or meditative (*jhāna*) states that are devoid of sense perceptions and devoid of all activity of verbalization or thinking. It is crucial that no intention that goes against the five criteria be present; the momentary experience must be unshakably rooted in *sīla*. So it is not the verbal formulation of your resolve to practice that is important, but rather noting if and when the five criteria of *sīla* are met. It goes without saying that it is also helpful to note when we are fulfilling the criteria of *sīla* outside of special practice periods as well, because this is a valuable occasion for joy. The traditional formulation of the resolve to practice is as follows:

1. From the destruction of breathing beings, I will abstain!
2. From taking that which has not been given, I will abstain!
3. From sensual excesses, I will abstain!
4. From suffering-causing, untrue, and harsh talk, I will abstain!
5. From the diminution of mindfulness through ingestion of intoxicating substances, I will abstain!

It is a matter of giving up suffering by distancing ourselves from actions motivated by greed, aggression, and delusion. We are giving up that which causes suffering (*dukkha*) to ourselves and others. To repeat once more: we are talking not about prohibitions or commandments, but rather about the conscious resolve to cultivate a reliable subjective basis during practice periods in unthreatening situations. Then it becomes increasingly possible to venture actively into new territory with more self-confidence and trust (*saddhā*) in our own competence and without fear of failing or of external dangers.

The resolves to practice *sīla* are connected with action in the external world, in contrast to the resolves in the practice of mindfulness of body that we dealt with in the previous chapter. There we were concerned with mastering our inner household by means of reality anchoring in inwardly felt physicality. In the strategies of sympathy, we direct our mindfulness also to the externally perceived bodies of others, whom we are now better able to understand, because we have a more complete understanding of ourselves. Thus in other breathing beings injury results in pain and the intention to annihilate the aggressor, just as it does in us. Or: If someone took something from us that we had not given, we would probably take measures to get it back and to penalize them—how would another person behave in such a situation?

But all five principles of *sīla* shield us even much more directly from suffering. We need only recall the considerations at the beginning of chapter 4 concerning what goes on within a scientist who torments experimental animals. How does such a person treat the animal in himself? Or a person who, for whatever reason, makes up something untrue and circulates it—how much space and energy in the inner household must that person's lies require (insofar as he can still distinguish the true from the untrue himself)! It can be readily seen that stealing is bound up with fear and that, through increasing our greed, it diminishes our capacity for happiness. How sensuality is "managed" in much of the West has already been discussed in detail in the chapter section "Sex without Sensuality?" Thus it will already be clear to you what is meant by "sensual excesses"—any degradation of myself and others. Sensuality that is coupled with greedy craving can lead to actions that violate basic morality or are even criminal. We need only think of the widespread sexual abuse of children, of the sexual exploitation of employees and other dependent persons, of the practice of "date rape," of all the family dramas triggered by the breakdown of a marriage, and so on. However, sensual excesses are not confined to sexuality. Gluttony, drug addiction, enjoyment of the suffering of people and animals—in bullfighting, for example, or crude kinds of sports like boxing, and not least, watching brutalistic videos—are also greed-bound sensual excesses.

Interestingly, according to the Abhidhamma commentary to the *Anguttara Nikāya*,[3] greed-bound sensuality is a "lesser evil" than hate-motivated acts of destruction, because indulging the former offends less against public opinion and general morality than do the "heinous crimes" committed out of hate, such as murder of one's parents and so forth, which always have grave karmic consequences. Still, however, the risk always remains that sensual greed may turn into hatred as soon as hindrances to its satisfaction arise. A person who is at the mercy of his passion generally becomes so blinded and his mindfulness so reduced that he is capable of fully disregarding all harm he does to himself and others.

By cultivating *sīla*, we protect our capacity for happiness. If, however, we let our greed and aggression run rampant, it will be diminished. In addition, we prevent any suffering that might otherwise arise in our outer surroundings and our mental ecosystem and have further painful results. As a result of training in the five principles of *sīla*, our reliable subjective basis gains more backbone and at the same time we develop our ability for action. Our own formulation of the *sīla* rules and their application is also the first effective step toward mastery of our inner household and harmonization of our mental ecosystem. For it is far easier if we learn to master our outer actions before we go ahead to liberational reshaping of our mode of experiencing.

Wise apprehension of, and reflection on, the personal knowledge that you yourself draw from the treasury of life experience gained in working with the five *sīla* principles can already bring about an unexpected catharsis. Your personal treasury of knowledge is worth more than the psychological theories about *sīla* that I could easily trot out here. But it is better to experience the joy of your own insight and creativity! Formulate your own *sīla* principles and your own formula for the resolve to practice. The formulation of the five resolves for practice on page 153 as well as the following basic principles from the *Dhammapada*[4] may provide some inspiration. They have been recited and contemplated by countless practitioners over the last twenty-five hundred years.

25. By endeavor, diligence, discipline, and self-mastery, let the wise man make (of himself) an island that no flood can overwhelm.
67. That deed is not well done, which one regrets when it is done and the result of which one experiences weeping with a tearful face.
120. It is ill, perhaps, with the doer of good until his good deed ripens. But when it bears fruit, then he sees the happy results.
131. He who, seeking his own happiness, torments with the rod creatures that are desirous of happiness, shall not obtain happiness hereafter.
133. Attack no one with harsh speech; the answer could be harsher. Hateful words breed pain; beware the answering blow.

197. Happy indeed we live without hate among the hateful.
     We live free from hatred amid hateful men.
201. The conqueror begets enmity; the defeated lie down in
     distress. The peaceful rest in happiness.
223. Conquer anger by love, evil by good; conquer the miser
     with liberality, and the liar with truth.
 96. Calm is the thought, calm the word and deed of him
     who, rightly knowing, is wholly freed, perfectly peace-
     ful and equipoised.

UPLIFTED STATES AND SYMPATHETIC ACTION

Upliftedness, self-confidence, and competence are the conditions
for sympathetic action. We are uplifted if we know that no attack and
no accusation can really harm us, because our way of life meets the
criteria of *sīla*. If we are not attached to anything, if we do not crave
anything, no obstacle and no intrigue and no hostility can shake our
certainty. When our *sīla* has been purified, there are no uncertainties
in our inner household to rise against us in the form of self-reproach,
guilt feelings, or bad conscience. In the strategies of sympathy that
you will generate on the basis of this reading, your competence and
ability, which no one can take away from you, is the key. Even when
you are confronted by superciliousness and cynicism, you maintain
uplifted equanimity (*upekkhā*), because your self-confidence (*saddhā*)
is grounded in your direct knowledge of your *sīla* and your anchoring
in reality.

I need not reiterate here that the conventional measures for your
protection, which were discussed in detail in chapter 2, are not rendered superfluous by your upliftedness. Rather the point is that now
you are able also to break new ground and learn new things; without
great risk you can generate your own New Age strategies, try them
out, and later apply them spontaneously. Specifically, it is the four
strategies of kindness, compassion, sympathetic joy, and equanimity
that are practiced here, as well as in formal, systematic meditation.
These four strategies have as their source certain states attained in
meditation, which in Abhidhamma terminology are called *brahma-
vihāra*, sublime, divine, or uplifted states or abodes.

Kindness, sympathy, sympathetic joy, and equanimity are "worthy
of Brahma," "sacred" or "divine," because they are properties of the
character of Brahma, the creator god of Indian mythology. Brahma is
called the "aggressionless one," because he—in contrast to many
other gods of East and West—is incapable of any form of irascibility,

envy, or wrath. He is also uplifted above any so-called "justified indignation," because after all he himself is the lord of all creation. Brahma and those like him dwell in the spiritual spheres (*vihāra*), to which one obtains access through *brahma-vihāra* meditation. The *brahma-vihāra* are open spaces that are without limitation and are therefore known as the "immeasurable states" (*appamānna*). Once one has practiced them well, they can be applied in every situation, as it is said in the *Mettā Sutta* ("Unlimited Friendliness"):[5]

> Standing or walking, sitting or lying down,
> during all his waking hours,
> let him establish this mindfulness of goodwill,
> which men call the divine state.
>
> [*Sutta-Nipāta*, 151]

From these uplifted states actions can be instigated that can be concretized into strategies of sympathy—and also into magical strategies of power, as we shall see in the next chapter. I have myself several times witnessed radiation of kindness, *mettā-bhāvanā*, being used in forestry projects in such countries as Burma and Sri Lanka. When a work elephant for any reason goes berserk, the incident ends (sometimes after the mahout, or elephant driver, has been trampled) only after a mahout specially trained in *mettā-bhāvanā* succeeds in bringing the disturbed elephant under control. Radiation of kindness is also used extensively with snakes in these countries. In addition I myself have used these methods with rockers, customs officials, policemen, and others who in my estimation were behaving dangerously— successfully, I think, though scientific verification was not possible in those situations. (For a first exercise in *mettā*, however, one should not choose a large animal.)

The application of *brahma-vihāra* strategies definitely requires two techniques that you have already practiced: *yoniso manasikāra*, wise apprehension, and *sampajañña*, clear comprehension of purpose, suitability, and sphere of experiencing. These two techniques, as specifically applied to the four *brahma-vihāra*, are described in the next chapter section (page 162ff.). In addition, before we can make use of the *brahma-vihāra* strategies, we need discriminating investigation (*vīmamsā*, treated in detail in chapter 8), which is used in the process of interpreting concrete situations. All of these prerequisites—to which the chapter sections "Matrices of Knowledge" (page 50ff.), "Wise Apprehension" (page 66ff.), and "Levels of Experiencing" (page 87ff.) are devoted—together make up "proficiency in right means" (*upāya-kosalla*). They are an application of the algebra of wise apprehension (page 69ff.), which we practiced so intensively in connection with the matrix of conditioned arising.

Vīmamsā, wise investigation, is, in the case of the uplifted states, a consideration or reflection that permits us to distinguish the genuine *brahma-vihāra* from distorted forms of them and to define them by contrast to their opposites. Abhidhamma refers to the distortions of the following four uplifted states as the "near enemy" and to their opposites as the "distant enemy":

> *Mettā* is nonpossessive love characterized by benevolence; it is the opposite of all forms of hate, anger, and ill-will.
>
> *Karunā* is compassion based on sympathy and understanding; it is the opposite of cruelty, vengefulness, and gloating.
>
> *Muditā* is sympathetic joy in the welfare and success of others. It is the opposite of envy, jealousy, and competitiveness and does not permit self-defilement through bitterness, boredom, or resentment.
>
> *Upekkhā*, or equanimity, is an uplifted independence of flattery and threats. *Upekkhā* is characterized on the level of Abhidhammic microanalysis as evenness of mind resulting from the liberationally oriented harmony (*tatra-majjhattatā*) of all mental factors and powers, which balances every excess or deficiency, eliminates all bias, and holds to the middle.

Meditatively, one trains in the *brahma-vihāra* in three phases up to immeasurable ecstasy, as will be explained in the next chapter. The first phase is based on an analysis of tendencies related to intentions to act (*kattu-kamyatā-chanda*). In the second phase, through purification of these, one is able to develop control over pathological tendencies. On the level of strategies of sympathy, we are concerned only with tendencies related to intentions to act and with the concrete interpersonal relationships to which they lead. Practical instructions for practice will be given later in this chapter via the example of radiation of kindness (*mettā-bhāvanā*).

Even when execution of New Age strategies is based on learned programs—I spoke at the beginning of the book about our biocomputers—it is worth repeating here that reality anchoring in the given situation and a wise selection of programs suitable for furthering happiness always remain crucial. Abhidhamma strategies are more than beautiful new worldviews concocted by New Age writers and more than a mechanical unrolling of behavior patterns and ways of talking that are learned at New Age programs. One-sided, reality-alien application of even the noblest programs would favor the near-enemy and distant-enemy distortions of the uplifted states. True New Age strategies, once we have thoroughly apprehended them, must be developed by each one of us for ourselves in our own special, personal everyday-life situation. The matrices for thorough apprehension (*yoniso manasikāra*) must clearly distinguish between the happiness-furthering approaches and the distorted forms of them.

1. Kindness, *mettā*, can degenerate into either subservience or possessive adoration, which, though they may be motivated by love and good will, are not compatible with *mettā-brahma-vihāra*. Subservience and possessive adoration are "near enemies" of *mettā*. In this connection, three types of love are distinguished: *kāma-rāga*, sensually intense, possessive, passionate love; *sineha* or *pema*, which also chooses on the basis of liking and prefers though it does not limit by possessiveness (*sineha* also means "oil"); and *mettā*, love that is purer, more uplifted, and more wish-fulfilling than the two other types. In the most sublime love, as soon as it selects and prefers, there are tendencies toward exclusiveness that could cause suffering. A love that expresses favor or preference also usually slights someone—which can also be the lover him- or herself. In this way subservience, another "near enemy" of *mettā*, arises.

A love relationship denatured by subservience harms both partners. This can also be observed in situations in which the one who is traditionally supposed in society to be the stronger becomes the subservient one. This we encounter frequently in members of the helping professions, like social workers, doctors, and educators, who permit themselves to be taken advantage of. Another thing that frequently happens is that men who are aware that our civilization has long disadvantaged and abused women, with supposed kindness turn the tables and let themselves be abused. In many cases in psychological relationship counseling, we learn that the woman favored in this way becomes increasingly arrogant and destructive toward the kind partner, but then unconditionally submits to a primitive macho type. Also in other areas, distorted kindness can be seen to have a similar effect: The favored protegés of anti-authoritarian members of the helping professions and educators, whose demands know no limits, later become subservient to fascistic authority figures.

The highest love, *mettā*, is free from all seeds of exclusivity, subservience, and possessiveness—and in training in the strategies of sympathy, the practitioner must perceive these distinctions precisely.

2. The "near enemies" of compassion, *karunā*, are sentimentality,

despondency, foolish helpfulness, and arrogance. A person who fails to note that he projects his own problems onto people who are suffering is incapable of providing effective help and can, moreover, easily drift into sentimental grief. For this reason it is necessary to make a clear distinction between our own situation and our own mental ecosystem on the one hand and the situation of a person we want to help on the other. Only then is sympathy and empathic understanding, *karuṇā*, possible. When, reality-anchored and from the reliable subjective basis of *sīla*, we thoroughly apprehend the situation of the other, no despondency resulting from identifying with that other is possible. If, however, we were to drift into the other extreme of considering ourselves superior, forgetting that anyone, including ourselves, could wind up in the same situation as this other person, then our compassion and our help become arrogant. Examples of this are the majority of charitable activities, condescending assistance measures for the poor, and aid to developing countries that is bound up with exploitative calculations. Such "compassionate" self-aggrandizement has little in common with the understanding and compassion of *karuṇā*. Sometimes people in misery are used as a means to an end in political or other kinds of contests. We need only think of the use that is sometimes made of the suffering children in separations and divorce disputes. Find examples for yourself in the world around you of suffering that has been exposed and problems that have been brought to the surface—not for the purpose of empathizing, understanding, and helping, but rather in order to wreak vengeance on the supposed culprits. Very little concern is wasted on the people who are suffering. Another distortion of compassion is foolish helping. Through this we make it easier for a person to get entangled in activities that will cause still further suffering. This is the case, for example, when we give alcohol or drugs to an addict or cover for a criminal instead of confronting him with his situation. Such foolish help simply makes it harder for the suffering person to break out of the vicious circle of his suffering. Many helpful measures taken by our society are foolish; the only function they serve is that of an alibi, by covering up guilt feelings and providing a distraction from the actual problems. The genuine compassion and understanding of *karuṇā* thoroughly and undistortedly apprehends reality as it is.

3. *Muditā*, sympathetic joy, in its purified form of calm cheerfulness, is rather rare in our latitudes. Finding joy in the happiness of others happens mostly in the framework of celebrations set up by society to provide an occasion for having an uninhibited good time. Still, celebrating the happiness and success of another comes quite

close to *muditā*. Good celebrations are enjoyable and edifying, and we are strengthened and cheered up by the mere fact of being there, of being one of the fortunate and happy ones. The energies, which otherwise might have fed envy and jealousy, go into participating in the celebration or possibly even are utilized creatively in preparing for it. By the fact that we ourselves are actively moving in the direction of success and happiness, resentment is resolved, and the conflict-oriented content of hostility can then be seen from an uplifted viewpoint as one of the "curious contrasts that cause one to smile." (Remember the analysis of humor and the smile on page 82?)

So celebrating provides diversion and makes it possible to go beyond our usual limits. And it is just at this point that the "near enemies" of *muditā* can gain ground. If dissipation of the resentment continues on to become general dissipation, our energies fizzle and fail to achieve the purpose of sympathetic joy. If we lose our mindfulness, our capacity for enjoyment also abates; we lose ourselves beyond our usual limits, become confused, and wind up entangled in things that otherwise we would have nothing to do with. In this way sympathetic joy can easily become uncontrolled frivolity, and the party can end with a "crash." Another distortion of *muditā* consists in reckless disregard for dignity. It results from the false view that joy precludes seriousness. Gaiety and gravity, dignity and fun are only opposites on the level of words. On the level of reality, they are different aspects of the same thing, *muditā*.

4. *Upekkhā* has been described as evenness of mind or equanimity. *Upekkhā* evens out all swinging between opposites and leads to continuous refinement of happiness. *Upekkhā* is an open equanimity, thus disinterested indifference is its distorted form. *Upekkhā* accords to each thing an equal value and eliminates all bias. If egoistic indifference is accompanied by conceit, another "near enemy," arrogance, arises. Arrogance is bloatedness rather than evenness, even if from the outside it might seem like independence vis-à-vis threats and flattery. Genuine equanimity is a result of competence and openness. By contrast, bloated arrogance is a combination of singling oneself out as special and pretending competence. Arrogance is a very dangerous enemy of equanimity that causes much suffering and is very difficult to overcome. The best thing we can do to counter arrogance is actually to develop competence. Only when the pretence of competence, which only appears when we are inwardly unsure, becomes superfluous—only then can we take direct measures against our arrogance and do away with its unwholesome consequences, which isolate us and limit our sense of perspective. *Upekkhā* is thus the characteristic

of a way of life that is competent and open to reality and that goes hand in hand with a harmoniously integrated personality.

Upekkhā can be neither systematically practiced nor meditatively developed. There are also no direct strategies for learning equanimity. In the *Visudhhi Magga*, the instructions for equanimity meditation, *upekkhā-bhāvanā*, begin with a long sentence in which all the benefits of *upekkhā* in comparison with the other three *brahma-vihāra* are enumerated. *Upekkhā-bhāvanā* comes in only at the point where we can go no further with the strategies of ecstasy. Although for the present *upekkhā-bhāvanā* must remain only a theory, investigative knowledge (*vīmamsā*) concerning the opposites and distortions of equanimity is helpful for our evaluation of ourselves and our perception of our state of balance in concrete situations.

THE STRUCTURE OF ACTION STRATEGIES

Strategies of sympathy are action strategies that are used to direct concrete behavior in the interpersonal sphere. These action strategies are distinct both from strategic management of the mental powers in our inner household, which will be presented in the following chapters, and from dealing with objects of the external world, which was discussed on page 30ff. Strategies of sympathy can also be used in connection with personifications of psychic and cosmic energies that we encounter in our dreams, visions, and meditations, and also with animals when we perceive them as persons. Thus we speak of application to the "interpersonal" sphere, which is more comprehensive than the sphere of human relationships. Strategies of sympathy aim at a harmonization of relationships in the interpersonal sphere that increases our capacity for happiness.

The structure of strategies of sympathy joins together personally learned elements for the purpose of actualizing liberational principles. We began seeking out the elements of Dhamma strategies in chapter 1 and formulated their seven principles (page 12ff.). Then we looked at various elements of experience and by means of Abhidhamma paradigms apprehended and named them: *vīmamsā, sampajañña, sīla, paññā, upāya-kosalla, yoniso manasikāra,* and others. Each of these experiential elements has an inherent method and purpose. These can be summarized as follows:

- *Yoniso manasikāra* is wise apprehension that leads to anchoring in reality and makes possible processing by means of psycho-algebra.
- *Upāya-kosalla* was rendered as "proficiency in right

means"; it is the skill of proceeding in a sensitive and nonviolent manner.

- *Sampajañña* is clear comprehension of the domain of experiencing, of purpose (*attha*), as well as of the suitability of individual strategies, programs and actions. Without clear comprehension we would often fail to achieve our goal and end up in confusion.
- *Vīmamsā* is a master or metaprogram for cognizing, investigating, and reflecting based on knowledge of our abilities (*paññā, upāya-kosalla*) and their potential applications (purpose, suitability), which we infer from reality and from awareness of our goal. *Vīmamsā* uses the principles of *sīla* as ethical criteria; in accordance with them it coordinates and directs the utilization of strategies.

Diagram 9 (pages 166–67), "Connection with Reality and Coordination of Strategies," illustrates the most important relationships in the structures of the strategies of sympathy.

With the help of this technical overview, it becomes clear what was meant at the beginning of the discussion of the matrices of the four *brahma-vihāra:* Abhidhamma strategies are more than beautiful new images of the world proposed by New Age prophets and more than a mechanical unreeling of behaviors and ways of talking learned at New Age programs. To repeat it quite clearly: Without concrete connection with everyday reality through thorough apprehension and without coordination by investigative reflection, the strategies would miss both outer and inner reality and would thus not have a happiness-furthering effect.

EXERCISES IN THE BRAHMA-VIHĀRA

The following instructions are once again an invitation to experiment. The effect and usefulness of the methods should be verified by each one of you for yourself. Our own experience has a greater power of persuasion than any theoretical proposition.

In terms of method, the strategies of sympathy are practiced in conjunction with the sitting meditation of mindfulness of breathing or during an evening's reflection concerning the day just past—or, when well enough learned, they can be applied directly in concrete daily-life situations. First, dear reader, we are going to practice the first stages of the "development of kindness," and we are going to do so with the intention of discovering what basic tendencies toward kindness are already present in us, bringing them to the fore, and nourishing them in their growth. In doing this, we will be operating within the experiential sphere of *kattu-kamyatā-chanda*, intentions to act arising on the preverbal level. These are not words, not thoughts, but wordless movements of the mind. Only reflection and decision-making happens on the verbal level, except when (as we are about to do) we use words to note, apprehend, and label states of mind and mental events. Once we have reinforced the connection between word and reality with awareness of purpose in this way, we will try to make use of the words to trigger the desired mental events.

1. PRELIMINARY EXERCISE IN METTĀ: DEVELOPMENT OF KINDNESS

For all *mettā* exercises, we should first of all choose attractive, pleasant, undisturbed surroundings. In order to deactivate habitual daily concerns, to begin with enjoy a few minutes of mindfulness of breathing according to the instructions on page 114. Two or three minutes should be enough.

Apprehension of Well-Being

1. Check to see that you are actually sitting comfortably and free from disturbances.
2. Recall a concrete situation in which you were content, free from hostility and stress—calm and happy.[6]
3. Imagine this situation visually. You can also bring to mind any other sense perceptions that were connected with this situation.
   Stay with this memory for about a minute.
4. Note the feeling that you feel in your body in connection with this recalled situation.
5. Tag this pleasant feeling with a word like "happy," "relieved," or "content"—perhaps you will find a better word to label the mood you felt.
6. Now let the details of the imagined situation fade out and just stay with this mood.
7. Permit yourself the wish "May I be happy!" (as in the recalled situation), which after all expresses a healthy desire for well-being.
   Mentally repeat a few times the words "May I be happy!"

Apprehension of Goodwill

1. Sit comfortably and collect yourself for a short time by means of mindfulness of the breath.

2. Think of a situation in which you wished things to be pleasant, carefree, and without strain for another person or even caused this to be the case. (For example, when you gave a child a piece of candy or made it happy in some other way. Or you could recall a situation in which an old person was trying laboriously to climb on the bus, and you thought: "I hope he (she) makes it!" You were just about to leap to the assistance of the old person. Just this "just about to, just about to leap to the assistance" is *kattu-kamyatā-chanda* and very important for the strategies of sympathy, ecstasy, and power. Or recall a situation in which you felt your goodwill when you tried not to disturb somebody who was sleeping.)

3. Let the important sequences of the situation repeatedly pass before your inner eye.

4. In doing this, focus your mindfulness ever more on your inmost sense of goodwill.

5. During the repetitions, note your benevolent inclination with the word "*mettā*."

2. METTĀ-BHĀVANĀ: RADIATING KINDNESS

In the preliminary exercises you progressed to wise apprehension (*yoniso manasikāra*) of well-being and goodwill. Now you are experientially acquainted with the reality known as *mettā*. You are also able to distinguish *mettā* from its distorted forms, which have already been analyzed. Thus you are ready to begin with the exercise in radiating kindness, which can also be used in concrete daily-life situations. Basically, there are two methods for radiating kindness, which are combined with each other in the advanced stage of *mettā-bhāvanā*: development of kindness directed toward persons and immeasurable radiation of kindness. In both methods the starting point is just bringing to mind goodwill, benevolence.

Directed Kindness-Radiation

Choose from your circle of acquaintances a person who is kind and who has never caused you any harm. You can presume that in the case of this person *mettā* is present to a high degree. For this reason it is probable that the extrasensory radiation of this person can be helpful to you in this exercise. You should choose only living persons for the exercise in directed kindness-radiation. By not choosing anyone who has died, we rule out the possibility of pathological entanglements. In order to prevent proliferation of distorted forms of *mettā*,

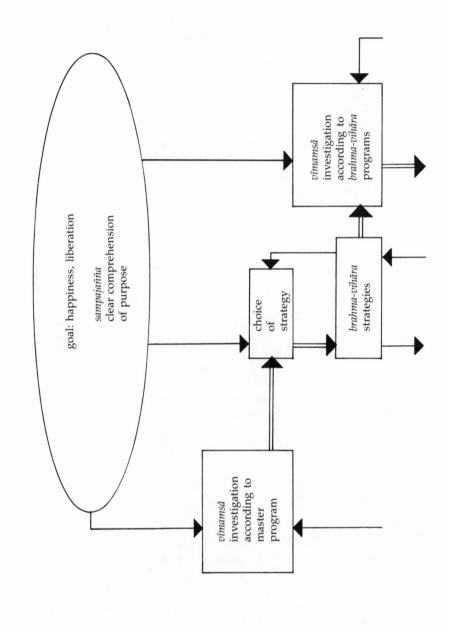

goal: happiness, liberation

sampajañña
clear comprehension
of purpose

vīmaṃsā
investigation
according to
brahma-vihāra
programs

choice
of
strategy

brahma-vihāra
strategies

vīmaṃsā
investigation
according to
master
program

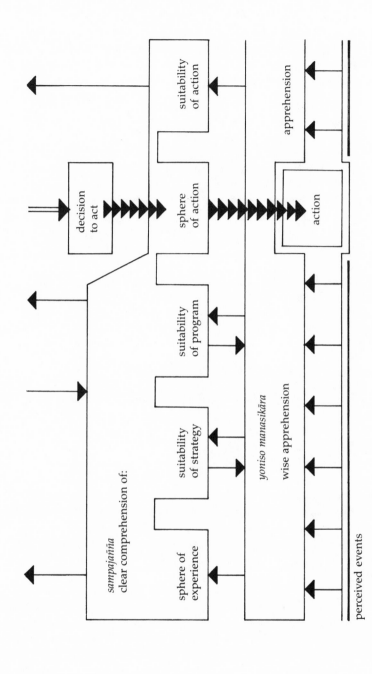

Diagram 9. Connection with Reality and Coordination of Strategies

let us also not choose anyone to whom we are tied by erotic desires or any kind of possessive demand. We should also not be involved in any kind of unfinished business with the person whom we choose for the exercise in directed *mettā-bhāvanā*.

1. After a few moments of mindfulness of breathing, sitting comfortably, bring to mind the sense of well-being of a happy, calm, satisfying situation.
2. Recall the face of a kind, lovable person with whom you have no entanglement. Try to hold the image of this person still before your inner eye.
3. Recall once again the good and benevolent feeling triggered by the imagined situation in the previous exercise.
4. Return to the image of the face of the lovable person. Reflect: "Just as I would like to be happy, let him (her) be happy!"
5. Apply the trigger words "well-being," "well-wishing," "*mettā*," and observe what happens in your mind.
6. Say mentally: "May————be happy!" keeping the face of the person before your mental eye.
7. Rest for a few minutes in the experiential reality of *mettā*.

Experimentation with variations and repeating your attempts is the key to success in arousing and strengthening *mettā*. It can also happen that during the exercise, negative feelings are aroused, and nasty impulses (for example, wanting to insult or slap somebody, etc.) might appear. Simply apprehend such negative tendencies and impulses with the label "disturbance, disturbance" and return to the focus of your exercise. If it should happen that the disturbances begin to pile up, then break off the exercise for that day. In thinking about this, take heed not to get involved in a process of self-accusation on account of it; such disturbances often accompany progress in the exercise and are a sign that you have penetrated into a deeper experiential domain. Later you will be able to make use of techniques in dealing with such disturbances that are part of the strategies of ecstasy and insight.

Immeasurable Radiation of Kindness

In this exercise, your sense of well-being is diffused as a source of kindness from the middle of your chest in the region of the heart. Often, while doing this, spontaneous experiences of light occur. You can help these light-experiences along a little by imagining yourself as a radiating ball of light, which takes in energy from all directions and transforms it into light. You should not, however, try to color the light in any way. Even if you notice that honey-colored, reddish, yellowish, greenish, or bluish hues sometimes appear, pay no particular attention to them. In any case, we know that uncolored light is the best suited for radiating *mettā*.

In learning radiation of kindness, it can be helpful at the beginning to record the following instructions—which are a little longer this time—on a tape recorder and play them back during the exercise. It may suffice, however, to leave the book open to these pages during the exercise so that you do not lose track of the order of the steps.

1. After a few moments of mindfulness of breathing, recall the sense of well-being of the happy, peaceful, satisfying situation.

2. Use the following formula as a trigger and reinforcement: "May I be happy, free from hostility and stress—happy!"

3. Imagine the person in relation to whom you practiced kindness radiation before, and direct your *mettā* to this person as you say the formula: "May————be happy!"

4. I.   a. Now imagine all the beings existing in the direction in front of you—stretching to infinity.

   b. Open up your inner space to the direction in front of you.

   c. Mentally bend forward (without changing your physical position), as though you would like to move toward the beings in front of you in order to give them something beneficial.

   d. Reinforce this mental gesture with the formula: "May all beings in front of me be happy, free from hostility and stress—happy!"

   II. a. Now imagine all beings existing behind you.

   b. Open up your inner space to the direction behind you.

   c. Mentally lean toward the rear, as though you would like to move toward all the beings behind you and give them something beneficial.

   d. Reinforce your mental gesture with the formula: "May all beings behind me be happy, free from hostility and stress—happy!"

  III. a. Now imagine all beings existing to your right.

   b. Open up your inner space toward your right.

c. Mentally bend to the right as though you would like to move toward all the beings on your right in order to give them something beneficial.

d. Reinforce your mental gesture with the formula: "May all beings to my right be happy, free from hostility and stress—happy!"

IV. a. Now imagine all beings existing to your left.

b. Open up your inner space toward your left.

c. Mentally bend to the left as though you would like to move toward all the beings on your left in order to give them something beneficial.

d. Reinforce your mental gesture with the formula: "May all beings to my left be happy, free from hostility and stress—happy!"

V. a. Now imagine all beings under you: the living beings in the earth, Mother Earth herself as she breaths and pulsates in the ebb and flow of her oceans; all beings of the lower worlds, demons of the underworld and hell-beings—to the extent that you have images for them.

b. Extend the radiation of kindness in the direction below you.

c. Perceive benevolently any images that might arise from the lower worlds, without, however, moving in their direction.

d. Use the formula: "May all beings below me be happy! May their suffering abate! Happy!"

VI. a. Now imagine all beings in the direction of the zenith: birds and insects; galaxies expanding and contracting as they breathe, as in the manner of systems they exchange energies and radiate intelligence; the beings of the higher worlds, gods, *devas*, angels—whatever images you have relating to cosmic forces and concentrations of intelligence.

b. Open yourself toward the cosmic beings.

c. As though you would like to ascend to them, radiate kindness upward.

d. You can also, in awareness of their superiority, ask the cosmic beings for their goodwill and accept their help.

e. Reinforce your opening upward with the formula:

"May all beings above me be happy! Benevolent! Happy!"

5. Now open yourself in all the surrounding directions, above and below, radiating *mettā* along with the formula: "May all beings be happy!"

6. Return into yourself, to the source of the radiation, which can be visualized as a ball of light, with the formula: "May I be happy!"

7. Expand the ball of light, until it has spread out to the entire cosmos, with the formula: "May all beings be happy!"

To emphasize the point once more: The seven steps of *mettā-bhāvanā* do not constitute a thought process; we are not working with thoughts here. Rather what we are working with are preverbal movements of feeling and mood, openings and expansions of experiential spaces. The words of the instructions and reflections and the wishes in the form of verbal formulas are only there as triggers and reinforcements that refer and lead to experiential realities.

3. BRAHMA-VIHĀRA STRATEGIES

To utilize the *brahma-vihāra* strategically in daily situations and in reflections on the day's events, we first have to understand their rational basis and impress it on ourselves, as when you want to use multiplying and adding while shopping. For this learning process we should make use of unproblematical, clearly defined situations. We should also clearly comprehend which of the four *brahma-vihāra* is suitable when. Diagram 9 (pages 166–67) illustrates the global context of clear comprehension, reflection, and thorough apprehension. We now turn our attention to the inner rationality and suitability of the individual *brahma-vihāra*.

Upekkhā is connected with a matrix of reflection that is particularly suitable for apprehension and processing of unclear interpersonal situations. Someone who wishes to create confusion makes use of threats, negative signals, and empty warnings (like a paper tiger), and other intimidating means meant to bring about submission and pleas for mercy. Just as dangerous are appeals to our vanity, which can distort our perception and apprehension even in quite clear situations. To instigate intrigues and create complications, it is necessary to work with lies and to pass over facts in silence.

Not acting, pausing, apprehending possible flatteries and threats, establishing distance and upliftedness vis-à-vis the situation; attempting to proceed with the greatest possible independence from partisan influences—these are the principles of *upekkhā*, equanimity. Only evoking our equanimity can create a state that is a suitable basis for choosing among the other strategies.

Mettā is suitable for any situation, as long as we are strong enough to radiate kindness and as long as we are not being menaced or harmed by some external agent.

The effective power of *mettā* can only be developed through meditation—we know how this is done from the preceding exercises. However, even *mettā* has a rational principle that we should impress on our memories so that we can use it as a matrix for *yoniso manasikāra:*

Never in this world can aggression
be pacified by aggression.
But kindness puts it to rest.
This is Dhamma, timeless in virtue.
[*Dhammapada*, verse 5]

For the purposes of wise apprehension, we can formulate other principles that are connected with *mettā* and are understandable for us. We can then recall these in suitable situations. Here are a few examples:

Just as I want to be free from hostility and distress, so do
all beings want to be happy.

Hostility, after all, only originates when somebody feels threatened, pushed, and unhappy. Even our love can be threatening if it becomes possessive. When such a distortion of *mettā* appears imminent, we can summarize it in a formula:

Through possessiveness I am limiting this person's freedom
and am causing him (her) pain.
If this person, who is dear to me, suffers,
then I too will not be happy.

The following formula for *yoniso manasikāra* pertains to thorough apprehension of situations that to begin with do not seem suitable for the application of *mettā:*

Just like everything that comes into existence,
this person also is impermanent.
We suffer from the passing away and loss of what we desire.
Love that is greedy causes suffering.

In situations of parting with a loved one that are unsuitable for the development of *mettā*, we can switch to the openness of *muditā*, which, through joy, lets things go. If the one we love is suffering, we can switch to *karunā*.

Karunā, compassion, provides a solution even for situations in which we do not possess the inner strength to radiate kindness. Even when every attempt to take control of our experience fails, we can at least remain "reasonable." When, for example, we are directly confronted by aggression and feel pushed, we can still call to mind the rational principles of *karunā*:

a. An angry, hate-filled, violent person does not feel good.
b. A person who lets himself be drawn into this kind of state of mind (through resentment or vengefulness), loses perspective and clear comprehension and defiles himself inwardly.
c. By creating karmic debts, hate-driven action diminishes our capacity for happiness.
d. If the suffering of an aggressor is empathically worked through, it is possible that appeasement or calming will take place.

It is easy even for someone not well-versed in psychology to see the connection between timidity, despair, and fear in a person and that person's inability to find peaceful solutions—that is, to see the connection between the person's suffering and his or her aggressiveness, vengefulness, anger, or resentment. A person for whom everything is going well and who feels good has no reason to attack other people, fight with them, or try to convert them. Such a person is secure in himself; he sticks with his views but does not impose them on others. A terrorist or militarist advocates violence and makes use of it out of insecurity, fear, and inability to proceed nonviolently; out of cowardice he shifts the responsibility for his action onto the external authority of a leader or an ideology, or ascribes it to "natural" impulses. A strict and unyielding teacher or supervisor, a nagging and quarrelsome spouse, a juvenile delinquent, or an angry police officer—all these act out of insecurity and fear. Are not such deluded people worthy of our compassion?

An inner attitude of compassion is even more helpful when we are actually exposed to the violent action of such people and are inclined to become afraid of them. If, however, we feel inwardly superior to the adversary, it is unlikely that our perception will be distorted through fear. Thoughts of compassion, even if coupled with disdain, make us independent of the definition of the situation as a fight that the adversary wants to impose on us. Thus we let ourselves be drawn into neither headlong flight nor an angry act of vengeance. When we have achieved a safe level of detachment and feel superior to the adversary, perhaps we gain the strength needed to soothe him with *mettā*, to resolve his aggressive impulses by radiating kindness. If, however, we still find ourselves exposed to injury from his words and actions, then resting in compassion makes it possible for us not to submit inwardly to the aggressor. In this way his power, perversion, and simplemindedness do not become the principles by which we organize our cognition (see principles of *yoniso manasikāra*, page 71).

We know that the time of being in the aggressor's power will pass (*anicca*) and that he himself will have to suffer the consequences of his actions (*kamma*). We have not defiled our mental ecosystem, and so have also not diminished our capacity for happiness. We remain inwardly independent, even though we were unable to alter the external circumstances. We have not permitted ourselves to be drawn into joining in the aggression and so have not worsened our present situation. We have maintained perspective and clear comprehension of purpose. Therefore, we have remained capable of seeing possible ways out of the situation. Even if we are disdainful toward hate and aggression and thus enter the sphere of the "near enemy" of *karunā*, arrogance, this is a lesser evil than the karmically unwholesome reaction of hate. And, indeed, the short road to genuine *karunā* remains open!

The following episode, which was recounted to me by a German patient after he had put *karunā* into action in everyday life, shows how even an externally stronger aggressor can be pacified by his victim. As a secondary school student, Bruno wrote good compositions. He also admired his teacher, who, however, seemed to find nothing better to do than to ridicule him continually. After having worked through the broader implications of this problem with Bruno in psychotherapy, I taught him the rational principles of *karunā*. Guileless as Bruno was, after his teacher's next outburst he went up to her when the lesson was over and said: "Doctor S., I also mentioned the child's affection in my composition on relationships, because usually people only write about the mother's love. It seems to me that in doing this, I somehow hurt you. I'm sorry. I admire you as my teacher and it hurts me to have to conclude that you made fun of me today because something in my essay touched a painful point in you." Since that time, Bruno's teacher has left him in peace.

Yoniso manasikāra takes place in situations suitable for *karunā* when we recall the insights and principles mentioned above and apprehend wisely:

> This person is full of hate and angry
> because things are not going right for him (her).
> If I respond with hate and violence,
> I will only increase suffering and aggression
> in this suffering person
> and, beyond that, defile my inner world.
> May this poor person become happy!

Muditā is an intensification of our sense of well-being into a selfless happiness that is connected with giving, nonattachment, goodwill, and joy in others' happiness. Joy (*pīti*) is, after all, under various names, the main theme of this book, and the rational principles of *muditā* were set out in our discussion of the distorted forms of sympathetic joy (page 160). So here let us only summarize the main points of what meditative insight and psychological understanding tell us about *muditā:*

a. Envy, miserliness, jealousy, scorn, mockery, and competitiveness are accompanied by bitterness, outrage, and malaise—they do not give a person a good feeling; they do not make a person happy.

b. Generosity and selflessness make it possible for us also to perceive others' success and happiness as an occasion for joy.

c. The more I am able selflessly to identify myself with those who are happy and successful, the sooner will I myself be able to accomplish the same.

d. The greater the capacity I have to perceive occasions for joy, the more often will happy experiences arise and the greater will be my capacity for happiness.

Thus our capacity for happiness can be developed by deciding through wise reflection to do what is happiness-furthering (*kusala-kamma*) and abandon what is unwholesome (*akusala-kamma*). In this way we multiply the occasions of enjoyment and joy in the karmically conditioned stream of our feeling. Through cultivation of selflessness (*anattā*) we extend the sphere of joyful occasions also to the happy experiences of others. We realize that our own chances of being happy are greater the happier the beings around us are. Goodwill and generosity are beautiful (*sobhana*), karmically wholesome (*kusala*), and bear enjoyable fruits as karmic results (*vipāka*). By contrast, all thought, speech, and action motivated by greed, aggression, and delusion diminish our capacity for happiness. Perhaps you will find it helpful to go back at this point in your reading to page 160 and scan the approaches to sympathetic joy once more. Take them as an inspiration for your own reflection about the principles of *muditā*.

Yoniso manasikāra happens in situations suitable for *muditā* in the following manner: Whenever you perceive anybody's happiness, relief of suffering, welfare, and success, extend the scope of your own happiness by registering: "Occasion for joy!" If a fellow human being achieves success in an area in which you have been vainly striving for success, envy and jealousy might threaten to arise. As soon as you notice such a tendency arising, clear away this disturbance by calling to mind the following:

> I would be stupid to defile my inner world
> with bitterness and resentment.
> My capacity for happiness would be reduced
> and my own prospects for success diminished.

Then as a trigger for *muditā*, you can use a formula such as this one:

> Well done! This person is happy.
> Suffering in my surroundings has been reduced
> and through this my own prospects for happiness have
> improved!

If it would give you pleasure to devise your own formula for wise apprehension, please do so. However, you can also enjoy sympathetic joy in regard to the formulas provided here. The main point is to take the instructions given in this book and make them the basis of your own practice in such a way as to further your happiness.

Brahma-Vihāra as Meditative Reflection

Meditative reflection on the events of the day combines elements and programs of several exercises already familiar to us into strategies, which, when we master them, can also be used in concrete daily-life situations. Meditative reflection is retrospection (*paccavekkhanā*) that can be carried out in accordance with the paradigms of conditioned arising, of wise apprehension of useful objects, and others. For us, however, retrospection will serve mainly as an instrument for developing personal *brahma-vihāra* strategies in connection with recalled events of the day.

In the evening, when we have ended the day's routine and have calmed ourselves through systematic meditation, such as mindfulness of breathing, radiating kindness, or walking meditation, then we are ready to carry out retrospection. Recollections of important, emotionally charged situations of the day or those involving unfinished business generally arise by themselves. First let these situations simply play back once more before your inner eye without trying to change anything. The important point in doing this is not to reproach yourself or anyone else. Then repeat the sequence several times and in doing so, go through the seven steps of the general exercise for wise apprehension that we have already practiced according to the instructions beginning on page 74. In this way you can make use of unsuccessful or embarrassing situations as a practice ground for increasing your capacity for happiness, because this imaginary exercise trains our ability to interrupt the development of similar situations that might occur in the future or to prevent them from arising altogether.

We should not work through more than one unsuccessful situation per day in this manner. It is very important each time to recall also one successfully mastered situation and to assimilate it thoroughly by means of intensive meditative reflection. We should dwell more on our potential and abilities than on our mistakes. False humility at this point would lead to a shrinking of our competence, disappearance of our sense of certainty in action, and reduction of our capacity for happiness.

We should recall each time that we have successfully extended the base of our reliable subjective basis of *sīla*. We do this by recalling events in which we acted according to the five principles of *sīla* (nonviolence, greedlessness, self-control, truthfulness, and clear overview). We think of situations in which we also, at least initially, put our own liberational strategies into practice. Joy in success and the knowledge that the generosity, nonviolence, and truthfulness in our actions will bear their fruits, are an important incentive in developing our culture of the heart.

In meditative reflection on the events of the day, we apply the same strategic measures from the *brahma-vihāra* principles as we do in a daily-life situation.

Brahma-Vihāra Strategy in Daily-Life Situations

In every situation of everyday life it should be possible for us to interrupt what is happening and become aware of its meaning or purpose (*attha*). This is making a great demand, a demand for a life that is meaningful moment by moment. Though meaninglessness is considered completely normal in our civilization, a way still remains open for us to a culture of loving encounter, to a culture of the heart. The freedom to make things meaningful to ourselves and to choose how we will go forward are basic principles in the liberational culture of the heart. These basic principles can be actualized by means of the following steps:

1. Pause after breaking off a meaningless routine or after getting out of a situation that has gone wrong.
2. Relax if you are tense; rouse yourself if you are listless. Both are done by anchoring your experiencing in reality.
3. Clear comprehension of your capabilities, range of choices, and nondelusion.
4. Wise apprehension of the situation in your own inner household.
5. Clear comprehension of the purpose of the specific actions to be undertaken and awareness of the entirety of what makes it meaningful.
6. Clear comprehension of the suitability of the strategies possible in a given situation.
7. Make your decision and begin meaningful action.

In relation to each of these steps you have available to you the treasury of your personal wisdom, *paññā*. You can recognize behind each of the seven steps one of the spheres of experience you systematically investigated in the course of the first five chapters of this book. Now, before we go on to the questions concerning systematic accomplishment of these steps, take time for your own associations with regard to each step to arise. Also note the expertise that you already have at your disposal pertinent to each step.

Strategic accomplishment of these seven liberational steps requires a combination of three kinds of skills: programs for apprehension of outer and inner reality, coordinative investigation and reflection through metaprograms, and application of techniques for altering our approach to our experience. How truth-perceiving apprehension and coordinative reflection work together is shown in Diagram 9 (pages 166–67); from this inner cooperation arises outer action. *What* we do depends on *how* we experience and *which* purposes we are attempting to fulfill. We would definitely like to change an approach to experience that might cause us suffering to one that will bring us happiness. Hence we are now learning a strategy that in seven technical steps brings about such a change in our approach to experience. Let us look at each individual step in greater detail and then summarize the flow of this whole approach to experience.

1. Pausing means pulling back from the entanglements of external circumstances. The best way to pull back from a heated discussion, from a dispute, or even a fight is to move out of the range of the adversary, go into another room, increase the physical distance, or occupy ourselves for a time with something else. We execute the retreat with composure and dignity, by which we demonstrate that it is not running away, not an expression of defeat, and that we might well be coming back. Such a retreat can also be carried out purely on an inner level simply by directing our mindfulness to our inner state and our bodily posture. With a little practice, one of these techniques will become possible in any situation, even in a very complicated one filled with "factual constraints."

In using *brahma-vihāra* strategies in meditative reflection, simply stop the internal playback of events by making a quick physical movement and bringing yourself back to the present by observing it. You can also interrupt the playback of recollections by opening your eyes for a moment.

2. Reviving yourself by means of relaxation or refreshment has the effect of freeing you from your inner adjustment to the problematic external circumstances. The problematic course of events that we interrupted—whether we are talking about a meaningless, boring and wearisome routine, an intolerably pointless activity, an alarming increase in the danger of harm, or being at the mercy of somebody's unpredictable whim—whatever it was externally, it drew us in to the point where our inner state became the correspondingly problematic counterpart of the outer circumstances. We have worked ourselves up into a deluded state; we have become the victim of illusions, manipulations, and determination from the outside. Therefore we must now find our own reality again.

This alienation from ourselves can be best overcome by restoring our anchoring in bodily reality. The most effective method is mindfulness of breathing (*ānāpāna-sati*), because breathing is our most central and important life process. By relating to our breathing with mindfulness, respect, and loving care, we are paying heed to what is most vital in us, and as experience has shown (and as it also says in the *Visuddhi Magga*), "from the first, the practice of mindfulness of breathing is peaceful and uplifted in character."

3. Clear comprehension of our range of choices consists in awareness of the liberation and freedom that we have already achieved. The more we have become free from situational compulsions and inner drives, the greater our range of choices has become. Thus freedom of choice is a result of our upliftedness and our independence; we experience it as clear comprehension of nondelusion (*asammoha-sampajañña*).

This means that in this concrete situation that we are using as a ground for practice, we do not let ourselves be deluded by either threats or flattery. We rely on our equanimity (*upekkhā*), integrity, and evenness of mind, to the extent we possess them already. In this way *saddhā* arises, trust or confidence in our ability. We experience equanimity and upliftedness in relation to the possible outward loss that we might risk by forging ahead to greater freedom. Very concretely, in daily-life situations this means being clear in our minds that there is not just one right way, which alone is possible, right, and reasonable. Beyond that, there exists for an Abhidhammika in every situation the choice of acting or not acting.

4. Wise apprehension of the situation in our own inner household means that, all our upliftedness notwithstanding, we do not ignore our inner inclinations. We treat all inner urges as of equal worth. Without training, we would only heed a strong inclination, or only one that is "permissible," and act on the basis of that. Wise apprehension of the situation does not mean some kind of analysis of motivation; it is simply a question of perceiving and making ready (taking into account) the available potentialities for action (*kattu-kamyatā-chanda*). In the exercise this step takes only a few seconds. After sufficient training, in daily-life situations it will require no more than a fraction of a second. The role of wise apprehension of the inner-household situation here is very quickly to take stock and register (notice) what inclinations, conceptions, and intentions are present. In this way we head off a process of suppression that might well backfire against us in the course of carrying out our strategy. If we do not seek to banish anything from our experiencing, then we also need not fear any kind of outburst from our unconscious. Practically speaking, this step is accomplished by quickly labeling all impulses toward action that present themselves. Noticing, labeling, and remembering, these three acts of mindfulness (*sati*) are sufficient here.

5. Clear comprehension of purpose (*attha*) calls to mind both the goal and the possible effective ways of proceeding toward that goal. Now all the strengths on which we based our self-confidence in step 3 become practically applicable. Here the rational principles of the strategies that we assimilated as meditative formulas for the application of *yoniso manasikāra* are called up. The formulas represent the algebra[7] that we use in devising and evaluating strategies; they are our tool kit, our repertoire of happiness-furthering programs. In the exer-

cise of meditative reflection on the day just past, we should also leave ourselves enough time to think through these formulas a number of times. The verselike formulations of the rational principles of happiness through sympathy, *sīla*, and so on should be looked at again and again in the light of our own treasury of experience. Then in applying the *brahma-vihāra* strategies in everyday life, clear comprehension of the purpose of the specific actions to be undertaken will arise spontaneously. We will be able to choose the right programs and skills, so to speak, intuitively. After all, the goals always present themselves when we ask the question about the meaning of life. Acting effectively with awareness of our goal will require increasingly less conscious effort. Spontaneously leading our lives in a meaningful fashion will become more and more natural, more and more a matter of course.

6. Clear comprehension of the suitability (*sappāya*) of actions to be undertaken and their application to a chosen strategy is the result of checking over the planned course of action one last time before actually carrying it out. Once more we thoroughly apprehend the situation—this time from the point of view of the strategy under consideration. The repetition of wise apprehension (*yoniso manasikāra*) and selective investigation (*vīmaṃsā*) are here combined into a unified interactional overview. As a result of it, the most suitable of the four paradigms of *brahma-vihāra* comes to the fore and takes over the function of a master program. We know then that the planned course of action is suitable.

7. Making the decision to carry out the chosen strategy means making the transition to action. We know that the action makes sense. It is realistic because wisely planned and therefore has the best possible prospects of success. With this knowledge, not distracted by doubt, we can use all our mental powers for the accomplishment of our intention. We can act with the full weight of our person.

When these seven strategic steps are successfully carried out, they make this moment into the best possible opportunity (*samaya*) for a liberational leap (*abhisamaya*). With the first step, we free ourselves from a difficult situation, which in the succeeding steps we transform magically, as it were, into a favorable one, and in the seventh turn into a situation that produces happiness. You probably noticed that the seven steps swing back and forth between inner and outer—until that swinging brings us to an interactionally integrated wholeness, out of which we become creators of a new world. Beginning on page 45, we saw this liberational process as taking place in two steps that resulted in our becoming sovereign masters of our own ecosystems. Diagram 9 (pages 166–67), too, is concerned with the logistics of this process. The principles involved are not logical; these processes are not thought out; rather they consist of movements of the mind, of arousing of potentialities, of alteration of consciousness, of direction of mindfulness (*sati*). These seven steps represent changes in the way we experience. All five mental powers (*bala*), confidence, willpower, concentration, mindfulness, and knowledge participate in them.

How can we now apply this strategy in a completely concrete fashion?

The most difficult part for us is going to be breaking off the entanglement and pausing. Let us take as an example a conversation that has degenerated into an argument or a fight. I could introduce an interruption by saying: "Please wait a minute. At the moment, I can't continue." I could ask for a glass of water or go get one myself. I could break off by signaling with my hand and then demonstratively occupying myself with another activity—for example, changing my seat, taking off my jacket, starting to make some notes, or something of this nature. I could also leave the room—with or without indicating that I will be right back. The main thing is to create some distance, a pause, some space in which to pause. So I have now broken off the proceedings that I apprehended as having gone astray and become senseless. I gauge how much time I have for the seven strategic steps, turn away from the external situation, and carry out the steps on the basis of the following self-instructions.

1. "Pause. I am going to become aware of my bodily state."
2. I say to myself mentally: "Relax, be refreshed—watch ten breaths," and grant myself this brief (or possibly fairly long) moment of recovery.
3. I recall: "In any situation I have the right to make a free choice."
4. I ask myself: "What do I want to do now?" and leave myself a little time to see what comes up in me.
5. I say to myself: "My goal is to lead a meaningful and happy life. What can I contribute toward this now?" and permit an answer to arise in my mind.
6. I ask myself: "What course of action is most suitable in this situation?" and choose.
7. I designate the decided strategy with one word: "This is what I *want* to do now!" and carry out what I have decided.

BRAHMA-VIHĀRA IN COMMUNITY LIFE

Joy in the uplifted states becomes even greater if we can share them with others. Also, it is much easier to develop genuine interpersonal relationships with people who consciously value mutual respect, trust, and noble friendship. The practice instructions given thus far have presumed that the practitioner is a pioneer in the culture of the heart. If that is the case, we rely to begin with only on ourselves and harbor no expectations about cooperation with others. With this outlook, we persuade our peers through the effects of our behavior, without having too much to say. In a community of people who have recognized the value of the strategies of sympathy, however, we can cultivate an exchange of views for the sake of clarification and coordinating our working together.

In the chapter section "Cultivating Sīla" we talked about the principles to be observed in such a situation. Here we will consider just two experiential facts that are important for the uplifted states in communal situations. Out of sheer enthusiasm we easily forget that, for one thing, everything in life cannot be dealt with by means of the strategies of sympathy and that, for another, even the most interesting insights and discoveries become tiresome for others when they are the subject of too much discussion.

Experiments with applying the *brahma-vihāra* principles in group work, in directing and supervising group-therapy teams, in communes, and in marital situations have proved very encouraging. One thing they have shown is that it is helpful if every member of the group or community is working on himself or herself and is practicing mindfulness meditation (*satipatthāna-vipassanā*) so as to be able to gain introspective access to his or her own inner household. It is considered incontrovertible in this connection that each person can only offer to the others a report of personal introspection and self-exploration. It is impossible to explore someone else, as many psychotherapists try in vain to do. We can at most express our own conjectures about the experience of others and ask to what extent they are correct; for each person is the highest authority where knowledge of his or her own experience is concerned. The only thing we can do for a partner is to listen mindfully.

When we try through talking together to find out what events arose as a result of what conditions, we quickly learn that the same events can be perceived entirely differently by the various participants in them. Thus we learn to respect the truth of *anattā* (no identity) experientially. This should be left as it is. In this way we become more tolerant and come to the understanding that there is no monadic essential being in things or people. Each thing and each "I" can become something different when it enters another interaction or when its inner structure changes. Nonetheless, it is extremely important in these types of discussions to remain objective and concrete and not get lost in theorizing or generalizations. We should respect the uniqueness of each event and experience and realize that there are no identities there, only similarities in arising, application, relationship. Our cognition works with paradigms, which, though they do bring some system to the multiplicity of things (*papañca*), can never really take hold of them.

Any apprehension or any paradigm is goal-oriented. The goal-orientation of Abhidhamma is happiness, decrease of suffering, liberation, freedom. As we saw in detail in chapter 2, the paradigms of politics, law, technology, and science are concerned by contrast with conquering, controlling, exploiting, limiting, and manipulating. Both liberational and control-oriented courses of action have their justifications in life, also in the life of the community—at least so long as all its members have not become either Brahma-like or fully enlightened. What is critical is the degree to which conventional paradigms are utilized or opportunities for the application of liberational Abhidhamma paradigms are made use of (whenever one is feeling confident enough).

In community life there will always be leaders and followers, those who are set above the rest and those subject to them, those who are responsible and those who go along, experts and their assistants. However, in predominantly liberational communities, we can from time to time try to exchange roles. If, however, you are not content with the state of relationships in a community of which you are a part, then reflect on your range of choices:

- to try to change the community through your own example in working with the strategies of sympathy
- to reconcile yourself to the outer circumstances and in this way cultivate in yourself the culture of the heart
- to give up the cozy home of this community and enter into a more all-embracing homelessness

It may be that you will find other alternatives beyond these three. An example: You live in a community with your children or your spouse and, although you are not content with the situation, none of the three paths described above can be traveled. You would like to develop your own personal power and bring it to bear in such a way that, without oppressing or abusing anyone, you bring about a better way of life for all members of the community. You also do not want to slight yourself in the process. To this end the strategies of ecstasy or the strategies of power, which are described in the next two chapters, will surely be useful to you.

Strategies of Ecstasy

Concentration is the key to ecstasy. Every person has a capacity for concentration, which can be meditatively cultivated until it becomes a power of mind. Since in the realm of the mind, monoculture cannot really succeed, concentration grows best in the company of other psychic powers. These powers were discussed in chapter 3. What confidence (*saddhā*), mindfulness (*sati*), and wisdom (*paññā*) consist of and how they can be developed as powers has already been explained. In this chapter, concentration will be treated in detail. We shall save the development of willpower for the next chapter. At this point, let us only note the following: Concentration of the mind is something different from effort of the will. Willpower (*viriya*) and concentration (*samādhi*) are actually two mental powers that counteract each other and that must be kept in balance through mindfulness. In concentration training, we nevertheless combine all the mental powers in a "proficiency in right means" (*upāya-kosalla;* see page 74), on the basis of which a systematic choice of a course of action can be made.

In this chapter we will repeatedly try different approaches to ecstasy. We do so in the hope that you, the reader, in accordance with your particular makeup and inclinations, will spontaneously like one or another of these approaches. Because what you like is what your mind can concentrate on.

What does ecstasy consist of? Total absorption. According to Abhidhamma, only that concentration is apprehended as absorption (*jhāna*) that, through detachment (*viveka*) from multiplicity, leads to one-pointedness of mind (*citta-ekaggatā*) and so brings about a feeling of well-being and happiness (*sukha*). In other words, when our process of experiencing is protected from disturbances and needs less and less to discriminate intellectually, then all difficulties subside, everything separate becomes unified, and the resulting concentration (*samādhi*) intensifies joy (*pīti*) to the point where happiness transforms into the limitless fullness of ecstasy. Have you already experienced something of this nature, or is this too theoretical for you?

Ecstasy contains something of transcending boundaries, of heightening of the feeling of life, rapture, and expansion of consciousness. In the popular view, however, ecstasy is connected with intoxication, wildness, excitement, or madness. In colloquial terms, it tends to be connected with "flipping out." On the whole, ecstasy appears as something beyond the rational-control level of everyday life. In the common narrow-minded point of view, the various derogatory characterizations all coincide with the threat that ecstasy poses to those who are not familiar with it. On the other hand, we find that many people have just the opposite outlook, equally based on erroneous prejudices. These people regard anything "flipped out" as good, because it flies in the face of today's "normal" dullness and boredom. For them, ecstasy means turning off your head, throwing all rational principles overboard, losing yourself, throwing caution and consideration to the winds, sentimentally abandoning yourself, as well as others, to some idea or other—simply flipping out. All this, however, has nothing to do with the enjoyable and enlivening beauty of the peaceful ecstasy to which the Dhamma strategies lead.

CONCENTRATION WITH COMPOSURE

Concentration is based on the enjoyment that is connected with the subsiding of wanting. Two principles are important for the accomplishment of concentration: first, granting ourselves the possibility of dwelling on what is dear to us; second, skillfully dealing with distractions and disturbances. To do both, we must be left in peace. Then we can give our attention more and more to happiness-furthering objects of concentration, such as mindfulness of breathing and radiating kindness, and let them become dear to us.

Before we consider suitable objects of concentration in greater detail, let us ask ourselves what composure really is. In organizing this book, I have adopted the strategy of leaving you, the reader, in peace and always respecting your right for self-determination. If there is anything I question, it is the idea that you ought to become different from how you are. Perhaps you recall that you were able to develop best when your parents and teachers left you the choice of being the way you wanted to be. In those times, you flourished and as a result were able to open yourself. Free from interference, you opened yourself to receive what was offered to you. Because of this, it is my conviction that what is offered in this book will also be best received if it remains up to you to take what is helpful to you, what grows dear to you because your unforced attention turns toward it. That constitutes your composure with regard to this book and lets you happily concentrate as you read it.

When, more than ten years ago, I asked my teacher Nyanaponika Thera how, in the advanced stages of concentration, to get rid of unwanted perceptions that distract one from the meditative object, he replied: "You don't get rid of anything. The mind concentrates itself on what interests it when it is left in peace." Then he had me think about the example of a child who is so absorbed in playing with a toy train that he does not even hear his mother's voice when she calls him to come and eat. At that time, I had been involved for months with the introspective analysis of mental processes that take place during the onset of meditative absorption and had made a fairly great effort to understand them conceptually. This led to my temporarily losing the ability to attain the higher stages of concentration in my meditation. Only when I once more left my experiential process in peace, left off making it an object of investigation, did I once again find the composure to enjoy concentration. I then only continued my analytical investigation when observing children at play.

I will come back later to some discoveries I made in this connection. Let us provisorily sum up the moral of this story with the following formulation: The composure necessary for concentration consists in part in leaving oneself in peace.

In order to attune ourselves to an object of concentration that is dear to us, all distractions must leave us in peace. You have probably noticed by now in reading along that "letting be" is always emphasized in connection with concentration. This is intentional, because I am trying here to make available the insight that we cannot create concentration. We can let concentration happen by letting our awareness enjoyably dwell on the object of concentration. How do we create this possibility? Certainly not by fighting off the distractions, because the rejected and suppressed distractions, in reaction, exercise a kind of counterpressure as soon as suppression leaves off—and we cannot concentrate as long as we have to keep suppressing distractions. The only help here is dealing with the distractions skillfully. This leads to detachment of the mind from disturbances.

OVERCOMING DISTURBANCES TO CONCENTRATION

There are two kinds of disturbances that hinder us in attaining concentration: first, the kinds of disturbances that make it completely impossible even to begin concentrating at all, because they counteract it directly; and second, distraction by things that are closely connected to the object of concentration and are immediate neighbors of the concentrated awareness itself. This corresponds to the distant and near enemies of *brahma-vihāra*, which we dealt with in the last chapter.

The distant enemies of concentration consist in greedy hunting and pursuit of the manifoldness (*papañca*) of things. We indulge in this multiplicity, become scattered, and jump from one thing to another, so that awareness becomes fragmented. If we actively try to establish relationships in the multiplicity by spinning threads between things, to integrate them into a whole and thus "create" concentration, we just get entangled. If we reach any result at all this way, it is something contrived and just patched together externally. Concentration cannot be "created."

It is best to avoid confrontations with the distant enemies. Any tendency or temptation in the direction of possible involvement with the distant enemies we should resolutely oppose by stopping these fast-proliferating, unwholesome programs as soon as they are noticed.[1] Here we should have recourse to clear comprehension of purpose and suitability and consider the painful consequences of such unwise reflection and action. If we are not yet advanced in mindfulness training and we notice something unwise when we are already in the middle of carrying it out, there is still the possibility of interrupting the action. For this, wise apprehension (*yoniso manasikāra*) and investigative reflection (*vīmamsā*) in the following sense can be helpful:

> Doing this reduces my power of concentration.
> It creates unwholesome distractedness and gets me
>   entangled.
> My goal is ———.
> I would be stupid to do anything counter to my goal.
> This action is unsuitable.
> So: Stop!

Entanglements that ruin our power of concentration and capacity for happiness can take different forms: knowledge that seems interesting, but is actually disappointing, constricting, or creates confusion; activities that at first promise relaxing diversion, but then begin to captivate our minds and become addictive pastimes; short-term enjoyments, which, however, drag us down below our standards—in general all kinds of things that make a disproportionate demand on our time, energy, and attention and for which in the long term we have to pay more and more. You might make a list of things in your everyday life that perhaps work against your power of concentration.

Perhaps you now see that there are a few things that, although they are not conducive to concentration, are nevertheless a bit too dear to you for you to give them up: a Thursday evening card game, where though you drink a bit too much and there is a lot of meaningless conversation, the people "are such good buddies"; the concerts that you enjoy so much that you do not care how far you have to drive to get to them; a hobby that you so gladly lose yourself in; afternoons in the game arcade or playing the pinball machines, which provide you with an unrisky adventure. After all, we have no intention of becoming hermits or ascetics! But wouldn't you like to strengthen your power of concentration, perhaps even have an ecstatic experience?

We do sometimes enjoy a diversion—and we think we need it. Is this really the case? When we are tense, when a situation has gone wrong, when we have just had enough, then we look for diversion. Diversion in the form of a cigarette, in the form of reading an idiotic fashion magazine or pornographic magazine, or even getting involved in senseless intrigues. Anything is fine, as long as it takes us away from the unbearable situation that we have had enough of. This, however, is only the case for people who are not strong enough to apprehend their situation thoroughly and truly, as it is. In your case, on account of your reality anchoring in your body and the support of *sīla*, you are strong enough. You have the capability of wise apprehension, *yoniso manasikāra*, and you will have learned, by the end of this chapter, effective methods of relaxation through which you will be able to get rid of what you have had enough of so that you can concentrate on what is dear to you—instead of, unwisely, becoming too scattered. Harmless little diversions that you nevertheless do not want to give up do not preclude getting together time, space, and composure for the practice of concentration. There are solutions with whose help you can achieve perspective and organize your time better:

1. Check through your relationship with objects using the instructions for *yoniso manasikāra* (page 71f.). What things do you relate with in a way alien to their purpose? What things do you neglect? Interestingly enough, the meditation manual *Visuddhi Magga* also regards an orderly relationship to everyday objects and bodily cleanliness as a prerequisite for training in concentration.
2. Devise a few personal rituals (*sīlabbata*), which provide you with a protective framework for satisfying private needs and which make possible a concentrated inner experience. Sometimes through a five-minute pause we can gain hours of more effective coping with tasks.
3. Reorganize your daily schedule. A half hour before breakfast is the best time for concentration exercises, because at that hour the distant enemies of concentration can exercise hardly any influence. Consider in relation to your schedule whether there are any tasks that draw you into entanglements that you can shorten timewise or avoid altogether.

4. Take one weekend a month for time in seclusion. Go some-place where you can practice concentration intensively.

By controlling your outer everyday circumstances in this manner, you are creating free space in which you can be left in peace. This way you are granting yourself more of a chance lovingly to investigate happiness-furthering objects of concentration, giving them more of a chance to become dear to you. By organizing your time and mastering your material circumstances, extend your periods of free time, periods when there is nothing you have to do. The purpose here is not to plan your leisure time, but rather to bring about greater gaps. We are planning in order to obviate disturbances, in order to have to do nothing during concentration. Only from doing nothing can the concentrated action of composure arise.

When we have progressed to a certain point, the following reflection becomes possible: External circumstances are now mastered and organized, and I have the time and space for composed concentration at my disposal. Now how do I deal with disturbances that crop up during the concentration practice itself? How do I cope with them when they arise? How can I prevent distractions from arising?

Answering these questions and finding solutions to them is the task of actively investigating reflection (vīmamsā), which does its work outside the actual concentration exercise. There are right means (upāya-kosalla) for this, which consist of little tricks. One of these tricks we can practice while reading a newspaper, before using it for the purpose of meditative concentration.

The "impatient" reader will quickly leaf through the pages ahead to see where an enumeration of these tricks can be found. At this point, in this particular case, such an "unconcentrated" approach is helpful: On page 216, you will find Diagram 11, which illustrates a technique in which effective newspaper-reading is combined with the meditation of joy. However, there are major differences between the two practices, as we shall see later.

We read a newspaper differently from a book, and for that reason the layout of a newspaper page is different from that of a book. The headlines try to catch your eye and are therefore composed in sensational language. The articles themselves usually have little to offer, and no one expects that they will be read with concentrated attention. For the most part, after a few sentences the reader's attention is distracted by the sensational headline of another article. In this way the mind jumps from article to article, becomes scattered, and never really penetrates at any one point. The reader gets the impression of having obtained an overview, albeit a superficial one, and puts the newspaper down. And this is also the intention; a newspaper has no purpose beyond this.

If, however, I select one of the many items on the newspaper page because I find it very interesting and worthy of a thorough examination and want to read the whole article with full mental concentration, then there are some meditative techniques I can use for this. I make use of the right means of concentration, which consists in the following steps:

1. I make sure of seclusion from distant disturbances by closing the door to my room, taking the telephone receiver off the hook so that I do not get any calls, and so forth.
2. I seat myself comfortably in order to prevent disturbances in the form of physical discomfort.
3. I clearly recall the purpose (*attha*) of my activity: "This article is about one of my favorite subjects." Or: "I wish to examine intensively the attitude of the author of this piece, as well as the intentions and effects of this report and the influence it might have on what I am doing." Or: "I wish to apprehend thoroughly the significance of the facts reported here and their consequences for my own plans."

    In this way I attain clear comprehension of my motivation.
4. Now I make use of the technique of transforming distractions into supports of concentration, which is explained in the next chapter section.
5. I make my resolve and carry out my intention (intensive apprehension in reading the selected newspaper article) with complete composure and total concentration.

TRANSFORMING DISTRACTIONS INTO SUPPORTS OF CONCENTRATION

In reading an important newspaper article as well as during the meditation exercise, concentration can get lost by being distracted by nearby things. We have already talked about dealing with distractions in connection with the exercise in mindfulness of body (at the end of chapter 5) and kindness meditation (in chapter 6). The procedure there was, first, simply to label the disturbance and return immediately to the main object of mindfulness and, second, to use the disturbance as a secondary object of meditation, as for example, in apprehending the elements. We did not treat the distortions of kindness, compassion, and sympathetic joy explicitly as distractions, but rather termed them "near enemies." Probably it occurred to you even then that the "near enemies" (for example, frivolous good humor) actually might function as preliminary stages of the pure form not yet attained (for example, calm sympathetic joy). Thus an enemy can be made into a helper or harbinger. At this point let us discuss this principle more technically and in greater depth.

Let us carry on with the example of the newspaper article. The page of a newspaper bearing many sensational headlines lies in front of me. I pick out the headline of an article that interests me. I have shielded myself from gross disturbances and prepared myself—through the use of a technique I know—for some concentrated reading. I am composed and I have time. I allow myself the time and do not let myself be bothered about it. Once more I leaf through the whole newspaper and conclude that there is really nothing interesting in it. Then I return to the chosen article.

The newspaper page with the article I have chosen is in front of me, and I know: "This is the most interesting one." Nevertheless I glance at the neighboring article and say to myself, "This is interesting." Nevertheless, I shift my gaze back immediately in the direction of my chosen article and comment mentally: "But this is more interesting!" and stay with this for a few seconds. Then I glance again at the other neighboring article and acknowledge: "This is also interesting," but go back again immediately to the chosen article and say to myself softly but with emphasis: "Yes! This is more interesting!" I continue in this way deliberately to distract my attention from the object of concentration, but each time immediately going back to the chosen one, because it is more interesting. Of course it could happen that during this process my gaze shifts unexpectedly away from the newspaper altogether, onto an open box of candy (a bowl of fruit, a package of cigarettes) on the table, and immediately the intention almost arises to reach out my hand for a piece of candy (an apple, a cigarette). . . . However, I know: "There are so many interesting articles here in front of me" and let my gaze come back to the newspaper page. And now the technique that I learned before spontaneously comes into play: Clearly knowing the purpose, I let my glance come back to the newspaper page. Once there again, I yield to my reinforced tendency to give my attention to what interests me the most.

You have certainly understood, dear reader, that this is an application of the clear comprehension of looking away from and toward that we practiced in chapter 5. It makes use of the following three principles:

1. Continual returning of attention to the object of concentration that takes a possible distraction as its starting point and turns the distraction into a preliminary stage of concentration
2. Attending to something interesting and from there to the still more interesting object of concentration creates the orientation toward one-pointedness (*ekaggatā*) of mind
3. The shortest, most direct movements of attention onto the object of concentration create the focal point and thus intensify concentration

These three principles determine the techniques through which distractions can be made into supports of concentration. The same goes also for the experiential sphere of meditation: Things immediately connected with the object of meditation can be used as a support field for one-pointedness of mind. Here it always important that the movement of apprehending attention (*manasikāra*) goes direct in a centripetal fashion from the preliminary stage to the focal point and seeks it out with as few detours as possible. At the onset of distraction, it is the task of mindfulness (*sati*) to notice as soon as possible that the focus of apprehension is shifting off the point of concentration. When such a looking-away takes place, we immediately try to bend the centrifugal movement of attention back, to weaken it, and to catch it at the level of the preliminary stage, as is illustrated in Diagram 10.

Let us also look back at the right means (*upāya-kosalla*) involved here, with which we are already familiar. The more intensive mindfulness (*sati*) is, and the more lucid the clear comprehension (*sampajañña*), the more effective are the techniques of concentration. Here thorough apprehension (*yoniso manasikāra*) of the object of concentration and clearly comprehended enjoyment of the joy (*pīti*) of concentration also contribute. Thorough apprehension is also a means of increasing joyful interest in the object of concentration, in that it deepens our knowledge of everything pertaining to the object. For this reason, not all objects are usable for liberational meditation. However, before we go on to discuss the objects of concentration that are particularly suitable for meditation and for the strategies of ecstasy, I invite you to make a test.

Please read this chapter on "Strategies of Ecstasy" over again from the beginning. (In other words, go back to page 186.)

Key to Symbols:

◯ neighboring feeling

- - - → distraction (looking away)

▭ related thoughts

← increase in concentration (looking toward)

Diagram 10. Transforming Distractions into Supports of Concentration

Now you have reread the chapter, and in so doing you have made unexpected discoveries—for the text was especially designed with this in mind.

Beyond that, you have also surely noticed certain shifts in mood, alterations of consciousness, and mental events, for example your emotional reaction to the invitation to read the chapter over again from the beginning. Please note your subjective responses to the second reading before you read further.

What kinds of things did you notice in your mind? Did you perhaps use the paradigm of the four foundations of mindfulness (*satipatthāna*) to distinguish between bodily experience, feeling, state of mind, and mental contents?

Did you take so much pleasure in your deepened understanding that you stayed fully concentrated on this mental content without interruption? Or did you perhaps feel from the beginning an aversion or even anger at "having to" read the whole chapter again? If that is the case, there is some lack of composure. Or did you completely reject the invitation to reread? Did you notice alterations in your state of mind: inquisitive openness, blunt rejection, swinging back and forth between different spheres of experience?

What does your mind tend toward, at what point does it flow all together as one?

OBJECTS OF MEDITATION: THE GATES TO ECSTASY

The beginning of the way to ecstatically concentrated awareness was shown through the example of concentrated reading of a newspaper article. We are acquainted with the right means for bringing about ecstasy from concentration. Diagram 10 synoptically illustrates how distractions can be reworked into preliminary stages of concentration, to wit, by the same trick we used with reading the newspaper. This technique encloses the inevitable fluctuations of attention in a circle in such a way that gross deviations are forestalled. In this way, awareness is separated from the more distant manifoldness of things. According to the definition of ecstatic concentration introduced at the beginning of the chapter, it requires detachment (*viveka*) from manifoldness so that concentration can be intensified into one-pointedness (*citta-ekaggatā*); also, dwelling on the object of concentration should be accompanied by a feeling of happiness (*sukha*).

Concentration achieved by means of repression of distractions and without an accompanying feeling of happiness would not be a concentration leading to ecstasy. Such a tense and loveless concentration would not even allow effective comprehension of a newspaper article. Unfortunately, such a way of looking at concentration is all too widespread. Taking this approach, for example, school psychologists, psychiatrists, teachers, and childcare personnel try to suppress obstacles to concentration and get children painfully to give up their spontaneous interest in things by the most diverse means. They know nothing about affection toward the object of concentration, nothing about detachment and composure. They do not know that the so-called obstacles to concentration are in fact healthy reactions of a mind defending itself against violation by boring, wrongly conveyed, and meaningless material. Not only newspaper-reading and meditation, but also learning, traveling, discussing, playing, and working can be ecstatically experienced and enjoyed.

The ecstatic experience is characterized by the even flow of a feeling of well-being (*sukha*). There are two possible ways for such an unobstructed current of feeling in a perfectly harmonious form to arise. The first way is in the experience of an enlightened or "noble" person (*ariya-puggala*) treading on the path of seeing (*dassana magga*) or on the path of power (*bala magga*)—this is the theme of the next chapter. The other possibility is absorption in *jhāna*.[2] Here we are designating as "ecstasy" an experience that approaches this ideal, and as "strategy of ecstasy" a course of action that is conducive to the actualization of this ideal. Thus an ecstatic everyday life would be one in which we lived meaningfully and happily and, by means of a composed and competent way of dealing with the manifoldness of things, attained to a simple integrity. If we are successful in simplifying the manifoldness of experience, then we are able, in a concentrated or collected fashion, to enter the higher worlds of ecstasy.

Concentrated dwelling on a suitable object of meditation makes it possible to overcome the fragmented and conflict-laden multifarious world of *papañca*. If we can succeed in taking leave of the manifold, it becomes possible, in cultivating an increasingly peaceful ecstasy, to experience a higher unity (*ekaggatā*).

Concentration can be applied to any object. Any thing or process in the outer world, as well as any process or content of the inner world, can be an object of concentration. Concentration while reading the paper opens up spheres to us that obviously are filled with other matter than the spheres of ecstasy reached by meditating on sympathetic joy (*muditā-bhāvanā*). Thus the comparison between eye movement over a newspaper page and the movements of the mind on the edges of *muditā*, as illustrated in Diagram 10, is valid only to a very limited extent. Not only a nonviolent skillful procedure (*upāya-kosalla*) for reaching concentration, but also choosing a suitable meditative object, are critical for experiencing the joy, well-being, and peace of ecstasy.

Choice of the meditative object is in part determined by the goal (*attha*) that is to be reached and in part by its suitability to the personal situation and character of the practitioner. For the exercises in this book, only those objects have been chosen that can be used without harm by anybody. We shall emphasize the various characteristics of meditative objects that are of key importance for their application with particular Dhamma strategies. Meditative objects are classified in terms of these characteristics into categories such as actual states, mental representations, etc. Abhidhamma teachers are familiar with forty different meditative objects, which they utilize in accordance with their suitability for the six basic psychological character types.[3] This is a very far-reaching subject, which in practice is reserved to the area of expertise of highly qualified meditation teachers. Leaders of meditation courses in Europe and America usually limit themselves to *mettā* (radiation of kindness), *cankamana* (walking meditation), and *ānāpāna-sati* (mindfulness of breathing) in conjunction with secondary objects from the sphere of mindfulness of body, certain devotional meditations on deities, mantra and other prayerlike activities, which, however, do not lead to total ecstasy.

At this point a detailed discussion of the individual meditative objects would serve no practical purpose. The following brief enumeration will merely provide an overview of the general field out of which the meditative objects used in our book are selected. In the exercises introduced so far, you have already become familiar with meditative objects possessing various characteristics. Now in this chapter we will have in addition exercises with objects consisting of an extremely simple mental picture that are particularly suitable for bringing about complete absorption (*jhāna*). All meditative objects can be classified according to the following characteristics:

1. Contemplation of actual states (*sabhāva-dhammā*) of mental qualities and abilities, like *sīla*, the reliable subjective basis, or the basic nature of one's character type; and *dāna*, the ability to let go or generosity, and so on. The preliminary stage for these meditative objects consists in calling to mind one's own acts of joyful giving (*dānavatta*) and noble morality (*sīlabbata*). These themes were dealt with in detail in the previous chapter. We can also imagine the actual states of the very subtle world of the senses as personified, as for example, in the contemplation of

the *catudisso devā* (gods of the four directions), *yāma devā* (god of the underworld), *tusita devā* (blissful gods) and *nimmānarati devā* (the joyfully creating gods),[4] before going ahead to experiential evocation of our own qualities. The contemplation of the gods just mentioned is embedded in a psychocosmology that, interestingly enough, was further developed in Tibetan Buddhism (Lamaism) and Euroasiatic shamanism.

2. Development of the suprasensual uplifted states (*brahma-vihāra*) and the interpersonal ideals that occupied the entirety of chapter 6.

3. Absorption in a unitary mental image (*nimitta*) of a primary color or a disk (*mandala*) that represents one of the four elements (*dhātu*). These meditative objects are based on visual perception of external supports known as *kasina*.

4. Concentration on objects related to mindfulness of body (*kāya-gatā-sati*), such as the breath, walking, eating, etc., which we discussed in chapter 5.

5. Analytic penetration of actual states and processes apprehended as *akkheyyā-vatthu-dhammā* (contents of Abhidhammic psycho-algebra). These are objects of *vipassanā* meditation, which is becoming increasingly popular in Europe and America. The next chapter will concern itself in detail with this subject.

In everyday life all these meditation objects are accessible to us as things in the world of multiplicity (*papañca*). However, they are different from other things in that penetrating them meditatively shows the way to altered states of consciousness of ecstasy. They are gates to spheres of higher unity of consciousness, in which completely new experiential perspectives open up that are not comparable to the manifoldness of everyday life. Metaphorically expressed, the meditative object is the keyhole; the personal capability developed through our training in Dhamma strategies up till now is the key. The technique of concentration given in this chapter is putting in and turning the key. Thorough apprehension of the meditative object is opening the door. This is followed by absorption's entering into the unitary image of a new space of consciousness. Joy brightens this open space and broadens our perspectives in the direction of a kind of ascent. If we have left behind all limitations and divisions of the world of multiplicity and eliminated every defilement of the mind from the space of our experience, then immeasurable freedom arises.

STAGES OF CONCENTRATION

The complete absorption of *jhāna* is characterized by an undisturbed unity of experience. Technically this means that there is only one object present in consciousness and all mental formations like noticing, concentration, will, joy, and so forth are in equipoise and flowing evenly. Such a harmonization is the result of a painstaking labor of mindfulness in which, through frequent repetition, skills for accomplishing the transitions between states of consciousness are trained. By progress in practice the meditator is able to discover technical tricks within the process and to apply them appropriately.

For the sake of illustration, let us once more compare meditative concentration to a child playing with a toy train. With the help of an adult (here parallel to the meditation teacher), the child first learns simply to lay a circle of track and to put the locomotive on it—that is, to establish the meditative object and direct mindfulness toward it. This corresponds to the stage of preparatory concentration (*parikamma-samādhi*). This is the level on which a beginner's meditation takes place. Though the beginner remains concentrated on the meditative object alone throughout the session, his meditation is characterized by many distractions and discoveries that are not part of the unitary image of the primary object. With time the child learns to round out his game to a greater level of completeness and at the same time to neutralize the events of the outside world so they will not cause interruptions. Continuous time spent in playing with the train is extended by perceiving any external events—such as the mother bringing something to drink or a piece of furniture having to be moved in order to extend the track—as a useful part of the game. During periods of meditation when, in a similar way, the primary object is held at the peak of the hierarchy of attention (*aggatā*), we may speak of a "neighboring concentration" (*upacāra-samādhi*).

Only when no more changes are taking place on the peripheries of the meditative object and no things neighboring on the meditative object are drawing attention to themselves—only at that point, a new experiential space opens up that is completely filled with a single object of consciousness. This is full concentration (*appanā-samādhi*). In the experiential sphere of meditation, full concentration goes together with the harmonization of all mental formations (*sankhāra-upekkhā*). Without any longer having to control outer or inner disturbances, we enjoy the even flow of awareness. Only the most elementary forms of thinking are still necessary in order to apprehend the reality-anchoring impressions of the meditation object (*vitakka*) and to administer the inner household (*vicāra*). Joy (*pīti*) keeps interest in continuing alive, and the feeling of calming, pleasant freedom from care (*sukha*) strengthens the one-pointedness of mind (*citta-ekaggatā*), which shuts out (*viveka*) perceptions from other spheres of experiencing. This is the full concentration of meditative absorption (*jhāna*), which goes beyond ecstasy of the sensuous world (*kāma-bhava*).

We must be clear here that it is no more possible to convey such an experience by means of a description than it is, for example, to convey color perception to someone who has been born blind; and indeed, we are usually born without experience of *jhāna*. Thus perhaps we will get a better idea if, with the help of clear comprehension of the sphere of experiencing (*gocara*), we try to understand ecstatic concentration through the example of the child playing. The child is functioning in the experiential sphere of family life, and playing with trains is part of the manifoldness of this sphere—just as meditation exercises are part of the manifoldness of the sphere of training in Dhamma strategies. Within this manifoldness, the child shows preference toward those things that help him to prepare for intensive play. While playing, he concentrates his perception in such a way as to exclude everything that does not touch on his game. However, the paths of transition between the experiential sphere of family life and that of the train game remain open; it is just that whatever is connected with playing with the train is favored. However, from the moment when the world of trains is established and the child's interest is fully given over to the functions of train traffic, all other spheres of experiencing disappear. As long as there are no disturbances, the ecstatic train journey continues alone or, who knows, perhaps in interaction with new companions whose natural habitat is the sphere of ecstasy. This metaphor could be pursued further into the investigative sphere concerned with the psychocosmology of gods and demons who dwell in the worlds accessible by means of meditative objects. For the development of Dhamma strategies, however, such a geography is less important than the development of skills that assure our competence in all spheres of experiencing and especially in making transitions between them.

HINDRANCES AND ELEMENTS OF ECSTASY

Although the techniques of concentration are best developed during meditation, they represent program elements from which we can build strategies of ecstasy in all spheres. The special quality of these programs, however, consists in the fact that they can serve as links to higher—or, wrongly used, also to deeper—spheres of existence. They are means for transcending the boundaries of everyday consciousness. If the mind is relaxed and concentrated in the meditative object, then it is removed from the treadmill of everyday tasks and open to receive other kinds of influences. During meditation we experience this as an opening toward other worlds and as encounters with their inhabitants. These worlds differ in degree of ecstasy if they are in the direction of *jhāna*, or in degree of agony if they lie below the level of human existence.

The purpose of Dhamma stategies is a purification of consciousness (*citta-visuddhi*) that manifests in an elimination of suffering (*dukkha*), an intensification of awareness, and a heightening of the quality of life. Thus all programs that work against ecstatic refinement of experiencing hinder liberational progress. Such hindrances—we could also call them "strategies of agony"—are programmatic elaborations of the three roots of suffering—greed, aggression, and delusion—which we discovered in chapter 1 in analyzing social and psychological misdirectedness. We must recognize, bring under control, and stop these suffering-producing programs by apprehending the images and thought chains associated with them with the help of the paradigms of *nīvarana*. Thus here once again the Abhidhammic psycho-algebra of *akkheyya* comes into play. *Nīvarana* is a matrix for understanding and controlling mental defilements (*kilesa*) as they arise as by-products of concentration. *Nīvarana*, or hindrances, can be assigned to five categories in accordance with their characteristics, as follows:

1. Sensuous desire (*kāmacchanda*), which scatters the mind among the multitude of things and keeps it fettered in this world of multiplicity (*papañca*). It distorts perception and renders impossible any comprehensive overview or uplifted perspective. Awareness defiled and fragmented by sensuous desire is incapable of intensifying or unifying consciousness.

2. Ill will (*vyāpāda*), which creates divisions and darkens and cramps the mind. Awareness impeded by malevolent inspirations cannot flow in a continuous manner, because it is always entangled in animosities. At best, enemies yield temporarily in order to gather themselves for another attack.

3. Sloth and torpor (*thīna-middha*) are connected with the impenetrable debris of unprocessed contents of consciousness that we have not let go of. They befog our

awareness and also manifest as physical fatigue. If they gain the upper hand, the mind becomes intractable.

4. Agitation and worry (*uddhacca-kukkucca*) consume the mind by causing it to jump about restlessly. Mental energies have no interest to give them a sense of direction. Although a decision may have been made, there is no frame of reference to integrate past results.

5. Doubt (*vicikicchā*) is irresolute vacillation, an unwillingness or inability to understand, resulting from unwise, inadequate apprehension. Once doubt is present, any further thinking only reinforces skepticism and increases uncertainty. A mind troubled in this way is unable to enter the way to the ecstatic unitary object (*ekatta-ārammana*).

The only effective way of dealing with these hindrances to ecstasy is, as soon as they arise, to notice, label, and stop them. We must recognize them for what they are: sensuous desire, ill will, sloth and torpor, agitation and worry, or doubt. We must in no way become involved with their content; thus we avoid becoming exposed to the suffering-ridden worlds that lie at the base of them. By mindfully noting the presence of one of the five hindrances and labeling it as *nīvarana*, we have thoroughly grasped it by means of a matrix (*yoni*) of wise apprehension (*yoniso manasikāra*); we have managed to remain in the experiential sphere of meditation—to be precise, in the sphere of *akkheyya* as meditative object (cf. page 198).

Later it will be possible also to deal with the inner mechanisms of these hindrances on the level of microanalysis, that is, to break them down and rechannel their energies. For that, however, well-built roads of power (*iddhi-pāda*) are necessary. They alone ensure the success of such an undertaking. We will discuss this in the next chapter.

In the framework of the strategies of ecstasy, we notice when the hindrances arise, label them, and turn away from them. We regard them not as enemies worthy of attack, but rather as unwelcome guests in our experiential space. We remain restrained when the *nīvarana* come to us personified as demons. We do not become involved with these beings, who though they may appear full of pomp, promise, and highly adorned, nevertheless make it known that they are motivated by one of the five *nīvarana*. In the tradition of Zen Buddhism, all such tempters and shady specters are called *makyo*, "devil's work," which distracts us from the true purpose of meditation. With regard to all such beings, we should adopt an attitude of equanimity (*upekkhā*) or compassion (*karunā*), without, however, undertaking anything further. We turn our energy and attention instead to more happiness-furthering occupations—the strengthening and further building up of the constituents of ecstasy.

We have already encountered in various ways the mental factors that are to be developed into constituents of ecstasy. They appear, more or less prominently, together with many other mental factors in everyday experience. In the higher stages of concentration and in peaceful ecstasy, however, they become especially intensified and refined, and—this is crucial—are harmonized with each other in an even flow. We will now try to understand the constituents of ecstasy better by examining them individually in their process-related character. There are actually five of them, but they are described here as part of a series of eight steps toward intensification of concentration, so that the entire transition from the world of the manifoldness of things (*papañca*) to the world of ecstatic unity of *jhāna* can be shown.

1. In a preparatory phase, the object of concentration is selected out from the manifoldness of experienced things and, in connection with its utilization for meditation, thoroughly apprehended. Awareness is thus selectively anchored in the reality of the meditative object. Resolve and anticipation, among other things, participate in this preparation as motivators. This step is summarized in the following drawing, which can serve as an aid to memory.

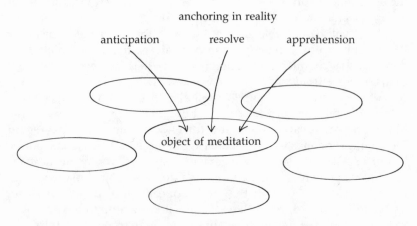

2. After having taken measures to prevent gross disturbances of the meditation, establish detachment (*viveka*). This is done by means of, among other things, transforming distractions into preliminary stages of concentration (cf. Diagram 11).

detachment

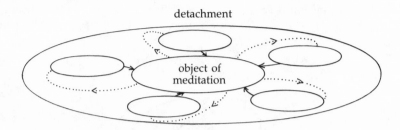

3. Now the first element of ecstasy, *vitakka*, is repeated in relation to impressions of the meditative object. *Vitakka* is the connection between apprehensive labeling and sense perception that penetrates the object and is absorbed in it. *Vitakka* is the most elementary form of apprehension by means of thought, which by tracking down the object again and again, leaves tracks on it, that is, it "makes markers that make recognition possible: 'Here it is!' just as the blind do in recognizing an elephant, and so on." (*Visuddhi Magga*)

vitakka

4. When the mind is completely absorbed in the meditative object, it lets discursive thinking, *vicāra*, rest in it. The thinking function no longer goes beyond the boundaries of it, but controls and manages (*vicārana* means "management") only in relation to the interior of the meditative object. In the commentary to the *Anguttara Nikāya*, the following comparison is used: "When a potter by pushing the handle

sets the wheel in motion and makes a pot, the hand pressing firmly
from the outside is like apprehension by means of thought (*vitakka*),
while the other hand that moves about here and there is like discursive thinking (*vicāra*)." *Vitakka* attunes the mind to the object, and
vicāra keeps it in movement.

vicāra

5. The successful attainment of nondistraction is accompanied by a
kind of rapture (*pīti*), which brings joyful energy and cheerfulness.
Pīti is joyful participation in the precious object that releases energy
and expresses itself as upliftedness. We discussed the continual refinement of joy (*pīti*) that intensifies the feeling of happiness in detail
on pages 102 and 103. According to the *Visuddhi Magga*, the mature
sense of rapture brings about a twofold tranquillity—satisfaction of
consciousness and calmness of mood—through the harmonization of
all mental factors.

pīti

6. "Wherever there is rapture (*pīti*), there is a feeling of happiness
(*sukha*). Where there is a feeling of happiness, however, rapture is not
necessarily present," the *Visuddhi Magga* tells us, and explains further: "Though the two are often not separate, nonetheless, rapture is
considered to be the contentment resulting from the attainment of the

wished-for object, and the feeling of happiness is considered to be enjoyment of the attained object of enjoyment." *Sukha* is a feeling of well-being that experiences no inadequacy and no discord. It is a kind of beatitude resulting from every physical and mental strain having subsided. It causes the sense of well-being to expand and supports it. It leads, through the subsiding of subsiding itself, to a fertile emptiness of ever subtler well-being.

sukha

7. One-pointedness (*ekaggatā*) overcomes all impulsive stirrings. It finds its momentary perfection in equanimity "that everywhere keeps to the middle" (*tatra-majjhattatā-upekkhā*), which is based in part on an even balance of the mental powers (*bala*), confidence, willpower, mindfulness, concentration, and knowledge. One-pointedness homogenizes awareness into a higher unity of ecstasy, which opens up a totality.

ekaggatā

•

8. When the transition from multiplicity to unity has been completed, ecstatic awareness attains an indescribable wholeness, might, and grandeur. We speak at this point of "mind that has become great" (*mahaggata-citta*), which through perpetual experience of nowness transcends time and binds it to unity. The experience of the mind that has become great is, however, only temporarily attainable until one has fulfilled the path of power (*bala-magga;* see chapter 8).

Often the very small steps of practical exercises bring better results than very grand notions that anticipate these results. How many minutes must you let your eyes rest on the point below before the circle disappears from your awareness?

CONCENTRATION EXERCISES

In what follows, instructions for three exercises will be given, in which you will learn to use for purposes of concentration the abilities and skills in mindfulness of body that you have gained thus far. Then, in addition, there is a fourth exercise that can only be fully practiced in a retreat, but is also very instructive even for attainment of the first stages of concentration. It is the *nīla-kasina* exercise for developing calmness of mind, which works with the unitary image of blue (*nīla*). As fifth, the exercise of the contemplation of death, *marana-sati*, is introduced, a concentration exercise used to arouse the mind and as a protective meditation.

All five exercises make use of meditative objects that are suitable for mentally healthy people of all character types. As long as the instructions given here are observed, there is no danger of unpleasant side effects. The application of the exercises described here for therapeutic purposes should be discussed with a psychotherapist who has personally had meditation experience. What positive effects the individual exercises bring about, you will find out yourself after a few days of systematic practice. The most beneficial approach is to try each of the exercises for a few weeks before going on to the next. At the end of this chapter, I will show how to combine the individual exercises into one comprehensive meditation practice.

1. SAYĀNA: RELAXATION

This method is well known in yoga circles in Europe and America mainly under the name *savāsana* (a short form of *sevā-* or *sayāna-āsana*). Strictly speaking, *sayāna* is a preliminary exericse for concentration, one which is especially important in our stress-plagued civilization.[5] This method of relaxation is fundamentally different from therapeutic methods of relaxation, which for the most part produce relaxation by means of verbal suggestion. In contrast to this, the process of *sayāna* is not verbally directed either by a leader or by the practitioner himself. In other words, we are not talking ourselves into something; rather we are wisely apprehending what we experience and making skillful use of the tricks we have acquired (*upāya-kosalla*).

To begin with, we recall the clear comprehension that relaxation cannot be produced, that we cannot will to relax, that all we can do to bring about relaxation is let it happen. What we can will and produce is the resolve (*adhimokkha*) to allow relaxation, to set aside time for it to take place in; and let us remember the value of ritual (discussed toward the end of chapter 5). As a practical means of bringing relaxation about, we can use the following trick.

What we can do is deliberately tense ourselves up and then abandon the tension, let the tension subside, but not just to the original state, but to a deeper stage. Let us look at this concretely through the example of the arm: Ball your hand into a fist, tensing the forearm. As long as you do this, the tension is there. Then *give up* maintaining the tension. Thus you make a resolve to abandon it. Let it go . . . just beyond the original level of muscle tone. Try it now! Without hampering the passive development of relaxation through intentional movement of the hand, release the energy caught up in the tension, give it up! Is this generosity? Yes, on a very basic level.

Relaxation of the whole body, the mood, the experiencing, should spread out from a central place. Total tensing and relaxation should be diffused from a muscle group whose tensing entails little movement. Best suited is the muscle group of the buttocks. The tensing (which happens only once at the beginning of the whole procedure) and the following relaxation is accompanied by slightly deeper than usual inhaling and exhaling. Moreover, pay no further heed to the in-breath. Let the relaxation go on out . . .

This process of allowing the bodily relaxation to go on out and that of the mind's going along with it are the two most important tricks derived from wise apprehension (*yoniso manasikāra*) of the process of relaxation. Any process, like a river, has the tendency to continue it-self, to go on. Whatever flows, lets other things go along with it. Try this out immediately, and if possible, lie down to do so.

In the outer organization of the relaxation ritual, you should heed the following:

1. Your posture (lying on your back on a hard mat) should be as comfortable as possible, so that it is unnecessary to move in the course of relaxing.
2. Clothing, jewelry, and so forth should not be in the way.
3. Now resolve that during the next ten minutes, all incidents or concerns will be a matter of complete indifference; during relaxation, everything external will be ignored. In addition to fixing the time, the resolve should also contain something about the manner of returning to the everyday level of tension, without, however, in this particular exercise, getting too technical. Something like this:
   "Now for ten minutes, I will not be concerned about anything. After that, I will feel fresh and good!"
4. With the next inbreath, begin tensing the buttocks.
5. With the outbreath, let relaxation occur. Let relaxation of the mind and mood go along with the bodily relaxation.

As far as the instructions for the manner of return are concerned, we need not be all too strict about them, since the point here is simply relaxation. Nonetheless, even this exercise can be further developed as a means toward clear comprehension of awakening (see page 142).

At this point, it might be appropriate to recount something of what practitioners usually have to report concerning the depth of relaxation they reach. They distinguish roughly the following stages:

1. Relaxation; just the normal relaxation of someone without training.

2. Relatively deep relaxation; a feeling of warmth, heaviness, sensation of the blood pulsing. Contact with the environment remains normal; inner sensation is slightly heightened.

3. Deep relaxation; both outer and inner sensation are very reduced, as though far away. From time to time there is a twitch in one or another muscle group—especially in connection with the arising and passing away of images and thoughts.

4. Very deep relaxation; no sensation at all. "As though the body had been put aside." Awareness, however, remains wakeful.

Since in deep relaxation contact with the external world is reduced to a minimum, the return should happen gradually. First, step by step, become aware of your own newly chosen state of mind, of your body, and your immediate environment. Then resolve, mindfully and with clear comprehension, gently to move your extremities—first the fingers and toes. Then comes a cheerful and mild tensing of the whole body, maybe a stretch as after waking up; then relax again to the normal level. Many people first notice at the time of return how deep their relaxation really was. Relaxation consists to a great extent in simply allowing the natural bodily processes to take place and wisely apprehending them, as well as in letting all thinking and wishing programs run down and stop.

The number of repetitions necessary to perfect the method differs from person to person. The crucial point is the extent to which the technique of outbreath-relaxation becomes a trigger for continually deeper relaxation. Progress in learning is helped by always practicing relaxation at the same time of day and place (the second half of the day is particularly beneficial). According to the accounts of a number of practitioners, if one practices three times weekly, after roughly four weeks a relatively deep relaxation occurs with the first outbreath. Soon after this point, one can also practice while sitting or standing. This is important for quick relaxation, which is used, for example, in the framework of the *brahma-vihāra* strategies and in other everyday-life situations.

On reaching the third stage of relaxation, one can switch to mindfulness-of-breathing practice—as introduced in chapter 5 and further elaborated later in this chapter—or to another exercise with the objects of concentration that will be described here. Even from stage 2 (which requires no particular level of previous training), it is possible to switch to the following exercise of *yoga-niddā*, which also produces a deeper level of relaxation as a by-product.

2. YOGA-NIDDĀ: YOGIC SLEEP

A technique of concentration is acceptance of distractions with a view to making them into preliminary stages or supports on the path to unity (*ekaggatā*). But these supports must also, once their job is done, come to a state of peace, so that concentration can develop undisturbed to its higher stages. Metaphorically speaking, as soon as the helpers receive their wage from the master and have been favored with attention, they may go to sleep. The master, however, watches over them. These are the techniques of *yoga-niddā*, which we will now learn to practice. My yoga teacher, Swami Satyananda Sarasvati, taught me this exercise (which he referred to by its Sanskrit name, *yoga-nidra*) in four stages:

1. Acceptance and overseeing of bodily sensations and their spontaneous falling-asleep during the relaxation of *sayāna*.
2. Rhythmic heeding of individual parts of the body (so as to satisfy and pacify them with attention) until the entire body has been worked through and thus become accessible to mindfulness (*kāya-gatā-sati*).
3. Acceptance and overseeing of spontaneous fine-material impulses, which can be used as vehicles for extracorporeal travel.
4. Pacification of all physical and mental impulses so as to contemplate the inner stillness (*antar mouna*), including even the unconscious mind (*ālaya-viññāna*), from out of which the directive formations (*abhisankhāra*) develop.[6]

The exercise described below is connected only with the second and third stages of *yoga-niddā;* in connection with them it also makes use of the technique for establishing directive formations (*abhisankhāra*) by means of a resolve. *Yoga-niddā* is practiced lying down. Only when concentration is good or gains the upper hand over willpower and mindfulness should we practice while sitting, just in order to prevent falling asleep in a completely ordinary way. The preparation for the exercise itself is the same as in *sayāna*, except that the resolve is formulated in a somewhat more specific fashion. The core of the exercise is the rhythmic heeding of parts of the body, through which one binds them into a unity in the sphere of bodily experience. The words are used only as *vitakka;* that is, only for the purpose of guiding the mind to sensation of the body part in question. We are not talking here about some spectacular experience, and it is sufficient merely to have some vague feeling of the body parts.

It would be helpful here to use the experimentation with body parts described on page 97 as a preparation. During the actual *yoga-nidda* exercise, we dwell on each sensation of a body part only very briefly, for about half a second. In doing this, it is important to move the attention from one body part to another with an even rhythm, working in this way through the entire body. This rhythmic round of the body is repeated from four to ten times. It is important to maintain the same order of the body parts. Finally, you will become aware of the whole body. Then turn the attention away from the body in order to concentrate on the purpose of the exercise as formulated in the resolve. In the resolve (*adhimokkha*), the following elements must be present.

A. Duration of the exercise.
B. The procedure for the exercise, which consists of (1) rhythmic attention to individual body parts, (2) pacifying them, (3) binding them into a unified experience of the whole body, (4) setting the whole procedure aside. This procedure could be summed up in the term "body check."
C. The purpose (*attha*) of the exercise, that is, "relaxation" or "extracorporeal travel," or "establishing a directive formation," and so forth.
D. Choice of a state of mind after ending the exercise.

Preparation of the resolve requires thorough investigative reflection (*vimamsā*), as you learned it in connection with the strategies of sympathy. Diagram 9 on pages 166–67 gives guidelines for it. Until you have become experienced in working with Dhamma strategies, you should use *yoga-nidda* only for the purpose of relaxation or cheering up. Therefore, I recommend practicing *yoga-nidda* for the first months in conjunction with the following resolve:

> "Four rounds of body-checking,
> then five minutes of relaxation,
> afterward, cheerful, composed, and confident."

The exercise is carried out in accordance with the following steps:

1. Comfortable posture, lying down, as in *sayāna*.
2. Compose your resolve.

3. Breathe in deeply and with the outbreath, relax, as in *sayāna*.
4. First round of body-checking (left-handers start with the left hand); do the following mental commentary along with the movements in attention:
"Right thumb, index finger, middle finger, ring finger, little finger, palm, wrist, forearm, elbow, upper arm, shoulder, armpit;
"Left thumb . . . armpit;
"Right big toe, second toe, third toe, fourth toe, fifth toe, sole; ankle, shin, knee, thigh, hip;
"Left big toe . . . hip;
"Buttocks, small of the back, shoulder blades, neck, back of the head;
"Skull, forehead, right eyebrow, left eyebrow, right eye, left eye, right ear, left ear, right cheek, left cheek, nose, upper lip, lower lip, chin, throat;
"Right breast, left breast, solar plexus, abdomen—first round."
(Without losing the rhythm, go on with the second round):
"Right thumb, . . . etc."
5. After completing the number of rounds you decided on, turn your attention to more inclusive areas of the body, and repeat three times:
"Right arm, left arm, right leg, left leg, bottom, head."
6. Then perceive the whole body as a unity of sensation:
"Whole body, whole body, whole body, sleep well!"
7. Remind yourself of the purpose of the exercise:
"Five minutes of deep relaxation; afterward, pleasant return."

A purpose of repeating the practice is to develop increasing trust in our inner clock. In fact we have already practiced the gentle, mindful transition to the experiental sphere of everyday consciousness in connection with the high level of mindfulness of breathing (see pages 120ff.), with *sayāna*, and with clear comprehension of awakening. It is obvious that transitions to other experiential spheres can also be accomplished from yogic sleep. Thus *yoga-niddā* is excellent as a preparatory stage for concentration with the breath as meditative object. Before, however, we go on to this application and to the next exercise, let us briefly discuss the basics of the already mentioned technique of extracorporeal travel.

Departure from the sleeping body should be wisely considered before starting the *yoga-niddā* exercise. The intention (*chanda*) to accomplish this and afterward to return in a clearly comprehended fashion should be established in the resolve at the beginning of the exercise. There are various techniques for departure and return that must be practiced to the point of perfection before daring to undertake lengthy journeys outside the body. Course participants tell me most frequently of spontaneously discovered techniques consisting of sitting up while the sleeping body is lying down, in standing up while the sleeping body is sitting, and in rolling out while lying or sitting. Rolling out is carried out while lying by making an effort (*kattukamyatā-chanda*) to lift half of the body. As soon as one has left the body, by way of experimentation one can do the *suriya namaskar* exercise and return back into the body. If anxiety should arise about being able to return into the body, the most helpful thing is to call to mind confidence (*saddhā*) in one's own competence in reality anchoring. And in turn the best method for rooting oneself in reality is mindfulness of breathing.

3. ĀNĀPĀNA-SATI AS A CONCENTRATION EXERCISE

While practicing mindfulness of breathing, we also notice the differences between inhaling, exhaling, and the pause between them. After mastering the exercise fairly well, as time goes on joy and contentment concerning this success appear. This releases energy and intensifies motivation to practice more. We should now thoroughly apprehend these three constituents of ecstasy with clear comprehension and label them:

1. "Apprehension by means of thought (*vitakka*) related to the meditative object is present."
2. "Reflection (*vicāra*), which remains within the experiential sphere of the meditative object, is present."
3. "Joy (*pīti*) is present."

At the same time we know, however, that the peace of happiness is not yet complete, because the unity of experience is not yet flowing solidly. Movements of attention are still creating too much unrest, and consciousness of multiplicity is present. So we begin to search for a unity[7] that will focus the awareness of breathing. I would like to stress that this does not mean searching for some kind of general concept to bring the labels of the individual aspects of breathing under one roof; rather what we are looking for is a unitary image (*ekatta-āramanna*) that will give prominence to what the sensations associated with the breathing have in common. This could be a sensation of softness, of

Apprehension by means of thought, *vitakka,*
of sensations connected with breathing

Reflective thoughts (*vicāra*) related to the breath

Diagram 11. Apprehension and Reflection as Supports of One-
Pointedness of Mind

gliding, of lightness or brilliance, which coalesces into the unity of a light source, a peg, a water surface, or a small cloud. My Burmese meditation teacher Mahasi Sayadaw, as we were walking together, had me look at and touch a little ball of fluff floating from a tree; this helped me a great deal to let a unitary image related to the breathing unfold in my meditation. You know what a dandelion looks like after it has finished blooming—does Diagram 11 perhaps have a similar form?

Nevertheless, such complicated phenomena are not unitary images, even if they are diagrams or symbols depicting a unity or the most beautiful paintings of flowers or mandalas. They simply distract us from the breath. During absorption, the unitary image is quite simple. What do we do, however, when our concentration is quite good but a composite image arises anyway and remains? We know the technique of transforming distractions into preliminary stages of concentration. This same technique can be utilized in this case. In the same way, coarser forms of joy, reflection, and apprehension by means of thought can be made into supports of one-pointedness of mind (*ekaggatā*). And when they have completed their task, we can let them go by means of the technique of *viveka* (detachment) or, so to speak, let them fall asleep—by applying the technique of *yoga-niddā* we have learned, of course. And if this also succeeds, then the overseeing focal point of mind experiences the peaceful contentment of happiness (*sukha*) in a unitary flow of consciousness.

Breathing is a concretely experienceable process, although "breath" is a word that is associated with many abstract thoughts. Meditating on the breathing is a concrete experience. This concrete experience consists in noting the inhalations, exhalations, the pauses between, the tactile sensations connected with the rising and falling of the belly, the tactile sensations on the rims of the nostrils connected with blowing out air. We should investigate all these experientially and learn to distinguish them. Knowledge arising from such investigation (*vīmamsā*) is an important prerequisite for concentration. In advanced concentration, however, the focal point of the mind is on a single object. Let us illustrate this with the example of sawing wood. The movements of the saw correspond to the breathing, the sawblade with its teeth corresponds to the breath with its air molecules, and the cut in the sawed wood corresponds to the nostrils. The meditator behaves like a qualified carpenter. He has learned to place the beam of wood (the body) immovably, he is familiar with the structure of the wood, he knows how to check the sawteeth, and, above all, he is well skilled in making movements of the saw that are even and require no undue expenditures of energy. These are all prerequisites. During the sawing, however, he checks neither the wood nor the sawblade, though he does perceive the contact between them. The point of his attention is on the point of contact between the saw and the wood and remains there as he gets deeper into the work.

You can see that the absorption of concentration is not to be conveyed by words, diagrams, and similes alone. The reality of the experience surely cannot be supplanted by words of description. We can only give indications and instructions on how to do the exercise. Practicing and learning can only be done by each person for himself or herself. Now we are running the risk that you may be getting "over-instructed." You are now familiar with two kinds of instructions: first, mindfulness of breathing as an exercise in reality anchoring, which was described in chapter 5; and second, the explanations for mindfulness of breathing as a meditative method of concentration. Only when compared with your personal experience will the foregoing explanations acquire practical value.

4. NĪLA-KASINA: THE WORLD IN BLUE

The faculty of thinking is generally so strongly promoted that it grows out of proportion to the other aspects of our makeup. Almost all those who have tried psychedelic drugs report that they have never heard music so vividly nor seen colors so clearly. Others say as much about feelings. But we do not have to cripple our thinking with drugs in order to bring sense perceptions and feelings into our consciousness. As you have already learned, it is possible to put to rest that (under certain circumstances) great helper, "Thinking," in order to train in feeling and true perception. Now we shall discover practically how to create supportive conditions for the development of pleasantly intensive seeing without thinking.

Traditionally, a *bhikkhu* or *samanera*[8] is first introduced to *kasina* meditation when his supportive basis of *sīla* has been faultlessly preserved for a long time and his relationship to his teacher has been firmly established. Then he receives the complete instructions, withdraws into retreat, and during his entire waking life keeps the meditative object that has been given him at the peak of the hierarchy of his objects of consciousness. At the same time, he keeps mindfully and with clear comprehension to a strictly regulated daily routine. All phenomena of the worlds that open during this strict meditation he regards purely as hindrances (*nīvarana*) and pays them no further heed. When he has advanced to complete *jhāna*, he talks over the whole experience with his meditation master.

But such strict precautions and security measures are not necessary if we use *kasina* meditation only as a concentration exercise with the specific purpose of intensifying sense impression and nonverbal feeling. It is important also here, however, to have clear comprehension of the experiential sphere and mindful management of the transitions from everyday experience to the sphere of meditation and back again, as we have already practiced in connection with mindfulness of breathing (see page 120). Practically speaking, this happens as follows:

As soon as you have made the necessary preparations and have sat down to meditate, speaking softly to yourself, make the following resolve:

> "Now I am sitting down
> in order to cultivate the perception of blue
> for the next fifteen minutes."

At the end of the decided time, stretch your arms upward with a deep inhalation and exhalation and say mentally:

> "Now I have set aside the meditative object 'blue.'
> Now, fresh and happy,
> I will return to everyday things."

Before we turn to the meditation process itself, we need some explanation on setting up the *nīla-kasina-mandala*, (literally, "the blue totality disk"), which we will be contemplating during the exercise. This blue disk should be about the size of a plate (eight to ten inches in diameter). For mentally restless persons, a smaller one is better, for more inert and slow-moving natures, a larger one. For irritable character types, a particularly brilliant blue is suitable according to the *Visuddhi Magga* (chapter 3, "Taking a Meditation Subject"). Take a piece of blue paper (not glossy) or cloth and tie it down around the edges of a plate or bowl in the manner of a drumskin. You have now made a portable mandala. You could also cut a disk out of some other blue material, transparent or opaque, and put this up on the wall or window. If you put it on the window, behind it you should be able to see only sky or a neutral landscape.

During the exercise, sit erect, relaxed, and comfortable so that you have the blue disk three to five feet in front of you, not too low and no higher than your head. The perception of the blue disk, to which—without effort, sitting comfortably and calmly—you turn your attention, is called *parikamma-nimitta*, the "preparatory image." The process at this stage of the exercise is similar to that illustrated in Diagram 10 (page 195). Speaking softly to yourself, label the inner arisings and clearly comprehend that the perception of the blue disk is the most interesting and rewarding one at this time. If your eyes become tired, this is a sign that you have been looking in a way that was not entirely composed and relaxed. In such a case, close your eyes for a while and recover your composure—for example, by means of mindfulness of breathing. If you feel heavy and lethargic, then it is a good idea to check your sitting posture, sit up straight and possibly stretch your arms above your head with a deep inbreath a few times. Then go back to the meditative object. If the preparatory image begins to shimmer or changes in other ways, this only means that the mind is a bit agitated. Calm yourself again with a few minutes of mindfulness of breathing or, if you can do it sitting up, *sayāna*. There should be no changes in the preparatory image (*parikamma-nimitta*); the most that is allowable is that with time it can become clearer and more vivid.

After having practiced in this way "a hundred or a thousand times or more," as the *Visuddhi Magga* says, perhaps it will happen at some point that with your eyes closed you see the same image as the *parikamma-nimitta*. This image seen with closed eyes is called *uggaha-nimitta*, or the "apprehended image"; it should be just as clear as the preparatory image. At this point comes a crucial transition, which is marked by a spatial displacement. The *Visuddhi Magga* describes it in the following words: "Beginning from the instant of its arising, one should no longer remain sitting in that same place, but remove to one's own dwelling place and sitting there, unfold the exercise further." In other words, we take the image home with us—we have it now. However, the apprehension and transfer of the *uggaha-nimitta* can fail repeatedly—the preparatory image can fall apart before we sit down again.

When we finally succeed in being able to sit down or possibly even lie down and develop the unitary image of blue with better detachment (*viveka*—cf. the eight stages of establishing ecstasy beginning on page 204). Then through the gesture of a spatial displacement, which represents an extension of the element of psychodrama, we also leave behind at the old spot our hindrances (*nīvarana*) and all other mental impurities. We now sit in a previously prepared place, which is better protected from outside light and noise than the old one, and work on the mental "corresponding image" (*patibhāga-nimitta*) through apprehension by means of thought (*vitakka*) and reflection (*vicāra*), as illustrated in Diagram 11. At this stage, all details of the background or the preparatory image have disappeared, that is, we no longer perceive the irregularities of the blue disk, the weave of the cloth, and so forth. We are now aware only of the unity of blue, which has clarified to a crystal-radiant vividness. We have now reached neighboring concentration (*upacāra-samādhi*). We now cultivate the five constituents of ecstasy and harmonize them until we attain the full concentration of *jhāna*. Later we can experiment with expanding and diminishing the unitary image and with diving under and popping up in the "world of blue."

Even if you should not succeed in obtaining the mentally apprehended image (*uggaha-nimitta*), you will still be able to acquire skills in this exercise that would not have come so easily with another object of concentration. Using these skills, the strategies of reality anchoring as well as the strategies of ecstasy can be approached more effectively in everyday life. If, however, you do succeed in attaining the full concentration of *jhāna*, then you have temporarily escaped the mortal world of manifoldness. Lasting liberation from the mortal world, however, requires perfection of *satipatthāna-vipassanā*, which is the goal of the strategies of power.

5. MARANA-SATI: CONTEMPLATION OF DEATH

The subject of death was until recently one of the taboos of our civilization. Lately, however, research—primarily in the area of psychotherapy—has succeeded in showing the benefits of conscious confrontation with death. Another critical contribution to this progress has been the reports of "after-death experiences" by people who were clinically diagnosed dead and then later brought back to life. The most important effect of these reports has been a rehumanization of the common attitude in our civilization toward the terminally ill and dying. It has also been recognized that people who die unprepared, distraught, or by violence, experience fright, horror, and confusion and therefore end up on a correspondingly painful existential pathway after death.

On the other hand, a person who meditatively contemplates death is not only shielded from these perils, but also derives profit for the present life. In conjunction with knowledge of conditioned arising (as discussed in chapter 3), meditation on death brings about revulsion toward greed, aggression, and delusion, the three roots of suffering (*dukkha*). If we know about death, we no longer crave ever more objects of use, and instead of clinging to the things of this world, we are able to use and enjoy them in a manner corresponding with their purpose. We then avoid evil in order not to defile the continuity of awareness that goes beyond death on account of impermanent things. What is most important, however, is that people who do not repress knowledge about death more easily activate their motivation and energy in striving for liberation. Thus this exercise is a basic element in the strategies of ecstasy and power, because it strengthens our ability to act and our will (*viriya*).

In the Abhidhamma tradition, numerous methods for the contemplation of death (*marana-sati*) have been elaborated. Some are used in direct confrontation with death, others are based on an idea of death; others still, very demanding ones, consist in direct awareness of the impermanence (*anicca*) of things, and of the birth and death of mental states. We shall now introduce a method of contemplating death that according to those who have used it holds up well in daily life as well as in meditation courses. This method is either practiced in full as an actual meditation or in an abbreviated form as a so-called protective meditation,[9] which can be inserted with benefit at the beginning of each practice session. Meditation on death is introduced in connection with the clear comprehension that its main points are nonrepression of this fact (which is part of life) and activation of our motivation for liberation. In its full form, this contemplation of death is divided into four stages:

1. Imagine a murderer standing in front of you holding a knife to your throat. This visualization of the approaching face of death is accompanied by reflections such as the following:

> "Just as this murderer is approaching,
> so death is coming toward me.
> My death is inevitable.
> That I will die
> is the only thing in my life that is dead sure.
> How long I will continue to live is unsure.
> That I will die is sure.
> It is certain that each day I get closer to my death."

2. Imagining a corpse, or remembering one you have seen, bring to mind the decay and rot that will inevitably come and create a vivid image of it. Visualize worms, insects, and bacteria devouring the corpse.

Bring to mind the fact that your "own" body is shared by many beings even while you are alive: bacteria that are continuously being born and dying in all the orifices of the body, and that feed on it; how your body serves them as a breeding ground, a latrine, a charnel ground. Imagine in the same way worms and other parasites that anyone might be prey to and the innumerable diseases they cause that lead to death.

3. In connection with the image of the corpse of a person you have known, reflect on the following in an inner dialogue:

"This dead person possessed so many things (enumerate them),
had prestige and status.
What good is it to him (her) now?
What was he able to take along?
The only thing that can persist in the continuity of his after-death consciousness are the karmic traces of his good and bad actions, the fruits of which he will reap in his future existence."

Reflect in the same way about your own existence. Visualize a symbol of death (the same one in each practice session) and realize: "This is a gateway into the uncertainty after death." For a period of time decided on beforehand, remain calmly contemplating this symbol with which all the previous reflections are associated.

4. Finally, try to perceive each present moment of consciousness in its impermanence. Notice your bodily sensations, feelings, and moves of mind, and try especially to apprehend wisely the phase of their ceasing and passing away (following the *Visuddhi Magga*, chapter 8):

"The life of a past consciousness (*citta-khana*) did live, lives no longer, and later will also no longer live. The life of a future moment of consciousness has not yet lived, at present does not yet live, and will only live later. The life of the present moment of consciousness previously did not yet live, lives only now, but later will no longer live."

In this realistic fashion, now proceed to reflect on the consequences of this for your own life situation. Now is the time to change something, to make and consolidate resolutions (cf. *abhisankhāra*, directive formations, pages 61 and 268f.), which, thanks to heightened mental concentration, will have greater effectiveness in daily life. Interesting in this connection is the following passage from Schopenhauer's work *The World as Will and Idea*:

The form of the appearance of will, that is, the form of life and reality, is really only the present, not the future, not the past; these only exist in the realm of knowledge. In the past no man has lived and in the future no man will ever live; rather it is the present alone that is the form of all life; it is, however, a secure possession, which can never be taken away.

You will find it helpful to practice the meditation on death in the full form described above a few times before trying the short form as a protective meditation. If you do *marana-sati* according to the instructions, no harm can arise. This meditation is not indicated in the case of the confusion, heightened sentimentality, and attachment to dead persons that can arise in the acutely depressive but also in normal persons shortly after the loss of a loved one. In these cases, the meditation can bring on further difficulties. Such people might then possibly slip into a deepened state of morbidity by losing clear comprehension of the two poles of the contemplation on death. One pole is the suffering of death (*marana*), the truth of which is acknowledged in the meditation. The other pole, however, is impartial, objective contemplation by means of liberating mindfulness (*sati*), which stands *beyond* death and leads to a liberated upliftedness.

The short form of *marana-sati* is used, along with the contemplation of the Enlightened One and with generation of kindness, as a protective meditation. This protective meditation has as its primary purpose ensuring the state of mental balance of a practitioner in an intensive meditation retreat; it also provides a framework for setting boundaries to particularly problematic contents of consciousness. Although it is tempting at this point to educe interesting psychological explanations—you can easily discover them in doing the practice—and in this way bring out the usefulness of the protective meditation, let us confine ourselves to just a few points related to clear comprehension.

The first point concerns clear comprehension of the sphere of experiencing (*gocara-sampajañña*) in connection with the transitions from everyday experience to the sphere of meditation altogether, then from the protective meditation to the main meditative object, and then from the main object to the sphere of disturbances related to *nīvarana*, which could also contain frightening material.

The second point concerns clear comprehension of the goal: liberation, concentration, release from suffering, and enlightenment. This goal was completely attained by the enlightened arhats and buddhas; thus it is within the realm of the possible.

The third point concerns anticipatory weakening of the impact of anything frightening we might encounter in the inner landscape, with the exception of the sphere of death, which we have intentionally resolved to contemplate with equanimity.

The fourth point is stabilization of consciousness through the soothing and pleasant harmonizing effects of radiating kindness (*mettā-bhāvanā*).

We need not give more than a minute each to the four parts of the protective meditation, because in each case we are merely calling to mind something that has already been attained in a corresponding systematic meditation. The procedure is as follows:

1. After we have sat down to meditate but before turning to the actual meditative object, we make the resolve first to do the protective meditation.
2. First of all, we develop clearly comprehended awareness of the supreme goal: release from suffering, liberation, happiness. It is helpful to visualize this goal as the personified form of the smiling Perfectly Enlightened One, who attained it.
3. Now follows a brief recollection of the four stages of contemplating death:
   a. Visualize inevitably approaching death.
   b. Visualize your body as shared by many beings.
   c. Bring to mind the image of the corpse and recall all the worldly things that a dead person cannot take along.
   d. Apprehend the uncertainty and impermanence of the present life and all the phenomena connected with it.
4. The short form of *mettā* consists in evoking a sense of well-being with the words
        "May I be happy!"
   and then radiating good will in all six directions. Finally, with the words
        "May all beings be happy!"
   visualize yourself as a radiant ball of light, which receives energy from all directions and diffuses love in all directions.

DEPARTURE FROM THE WORLD OF MORTALITY

The total absorption of *jhāna* is a temporary release from the manifold world of *papañca,* in which death prevails. But the "eternity experience" of *jhāna* is also impermanent, and we return again to the multiplicity of the everyday world. Moreover, a person who develops attachment to ecstatic experiences suffers as a consequence when ecstasy comes to an end. If such a person lets himself go further and fails to apprehend wisely the split between the open vision of ecstasy on the one hand and the ineluctable return to everyday-life occurrences on the other, then he increasingly loses access to the restorative calm and refreshing beauty that are enjoyed in the peaceful free spaces of concentrated awareness. As we saw in relation to the individual concentration exercises, the practice of ecstasy requires discipline and systematic organization to guard the gates and bridges leading beyond the world of mortality.

Entry into visionary freedom is thus only a step on the path to liberation. It is based on the previous steps[10] of developing reality anchoring and a reliable subjective basis (*sīla*). The further steps consist in bringing what has been seen visionarily into everyday life and ultimately realizing deathlessness by integrating both spheres. This is the goal of the strategies of power, to which we will turn in the following chapter. For the moment let us consider what has been accomplished in this chapter, for a disciplined method of reflection (*paccavekkhanā*— "looking at" (*ikkhana*) "with the help of the matrices of *akkheyya*" is part of this word) is a means toward firm establishment and further development of our capacity for ecstasy. Any improvement for the future only becomes realistic when it is based on a reflective evaluation of the past.

To put the results of a step-by-step retrospection—this is the meaning of *paccavekkhanā*—into writing here would be stealing your initiative, dear reader, and would hamper your creativity. So please note down yourself what you wisely apprehended in preparing for and carrying out the various exercises. Develop from this experientially ascertained vision of things your own worldview, which for you personally is more apt than all the worldviews of the most outstanding scientists, founders of religions, politicians, and writers. Take everything into account, including the inevitable limitations of any book and the widespread prejudices and misunderstandings concerning our subject matter. Do not let yourself be swept along; establish your own point of view, formulate your own position.

In spite of all the popular misunderstandings, I am convinced that the word "ecstasy" designates quite well what the strategies described in this chapter aim at. One definition of "ecstasy" is "the state of having stepped out of oneself." *Ex-stasis* is an overcoming of blockage, congestion, or rigidity and thus is closer to the intended state than "absorption," "state of attainment," "trance," or "meditation." "Meditation" especially is a very misused word that retains a many-faceted meaning even when it is used correctly. "Meditation" designates first of all, very generally, a method for working with inner experience; second, a technique for specific development of the mind; third, the actual flow of experiencing in a meditation session; fourth, the accomplished state of altered consciousness; and fifth, the effect of this last on knowledge and personality structure. I have already discussed how meditation accomplishes this and have pointed out that not every meditation leads to *jhāna*. We speak of total ecstasy only when a highly intense unity of awareness flows with a harmonious balance of apprehension and control of the object of consciousness, and of joy, happiness, and concentration.

In Abhidhamma the technical term *jhāna* refers only to the accomplished meditative state and the spheres corresponding to it. Related expressions such as Sanskrit *dhyāna*, Chinese *ch'an*, and Japanese *zen*, on the other hand, are used to refer to meditation in the broader sense. We may speak of ecstatic experience also in relation to the situation in which the five constituents of ecstasy are not yet harmonized but have been intensified to the point where the five hindrances (*nīvarana*) have been overcome. Critical here are energizing joy (*pīti*) and happiness-pervaded concentration (*samādhi*), which can arise either in meditation or in the midst of daily life. Thus strategies of ecstasy are those mindful, joyous undertakings that lead beyond the bounds of everyday experience without sacrificing our overview of the situation nor our control over events.

The concentration exercises in this chapter provide building blocks out of which programs can be constructed, and these can be coordinated into strategies. We became familiar with the main principles of Dhamma strategies at the beginning of this book (page 12f.) and then increasingly gained depth in our understanding of them, until in the previous chapter we were able to obtain a total overview of the structure of strategies of action (pages 162ff.) in connection with the strategies of sympathy. It would bore you, the reader, at this point to be put in the position of passive consumer of further descriptions of how to develop strategies of ecstasy in everyday life. Because of the competence you have gained through reading and the skills you have developed in the exercises, the task of devising your own strategies for daily-life situations will not be overwhelming for you. Rather it will very likely be a pleasant challenge and perhaps a bit of an adventure. The considerations that follow are meant to serve as an inspiration for that.

The strategies of ecstasy are intended to accomplish on the one hand a purification of the mind—we have already spoken of *citta-visuddhi* and catharsis—and a heightening of consciousness, in that they provide us with free space. From the perspective of that free space we are able to oversee our daily-life situation better and with greater detachment and eliminate unprofitable conditioning and alien programming. On the other hand, they make it possible for us to go beyond the bounds of the everyday and to have a vision of hitherto undreamed-of possibilities, as a result of which we can set new goals and devise the means to realize them. Such visionary goals go beyond therapeutic self-realization of frustrated potential. At the same time, they are free from the necessity of having to give up what is truly ourselves as a result of devotion to alien determinations by "higher intelligences" of earthly or otherworldly derivation. The liberational striving of the Dhamma strategies aims at self-realization of meditatively glimpsed and independently set goals. We can actualize these through mindful and clearly comprehended use of our abilities, skills, and techniques and in this way make them in their turn into a source of joy.

Ecstatic self-realization in daily life requires us to free ourselves from any tendency toward necrophilia (love of death). Necrophiliac tendencies take on, as part of an unwholesome way of life, two extreme forms, the common feature of which is denial and undermining of the flow of life. One extreme is rigidity, leveling conformity and opposition to any development—I have already mentioned several aspects of this form in another context (page 105). The other extreme is comprised of scatteredness, chaotic excess and overexpression. Both extremes bind our energies in a pathological way; by taking us away from the equilibrium of the middle path, they make any experience of ecstasy impossible. Scatteredness and overexpression in everyday life can be primarily ascribed to inadequate concentration (samādhi) and deficient self-regulation (sīla), and it is easy to see that the result of them is helpless exposure to determination from the outside.

The other extreme is worthy of more extensive consideration. The more we identify with rigid personality structures and avoid perceiving them impartially, the stronger becomes the fear of their dissolution and disappearance. Driven by ignorance (avijjā) and fear of death, we try to make up to death by killing all healthy initiatives toward change. In this perverted consciousness, we try to make morbidity seem harmless and to apprehend the mental defilements (kilesa) conditioned by greed, aggression, and delusion as welcome or even beautiful. We do not wish to recognize obvious perversions,[11] we shut our eyes to them or pass them over with superficial and distorted interpretations. In this superficial thinking, the perverted rationalizations reach the point where we find unwholesome material entertaining and interesting. We are even worried if anything at all worthwhile would be left if this morbidity were to fall away. Fearfully we think: "Will anybody still find me interesting when I no longer have any defilements?"

Actually in our civilization, the erroneous view that pathological behavior is interesting, that death is fascinating, that intrigues are exciting, is very deeply rooted. Such perversions are the motivating power behind much of our social life. The lower level of art merchandises these pathologies, offering a chimeric assortment of emotions without showing a way out. Even prestigious spokesmen of culture often fall prey to the illusion that artists have to be pathological in order to be sufficiently energized for their work. Apprehending wisely, however, we see:

Creativity does not arise from morbidity. Creativity is an expression of competence in solving problems and especially in creating that which is good, true, and beautiful.

The works of writers and painters capable of ecstasy, particularly because of their concentration and discipline of expression, are more delightful and of higher quality than the productions of morbid people. Imagine what concentration and visionary power a Michelangelo must have had in order to produce, for example, his David out of a block of stone, and what skills, techniques, and discipline were involved in the thousands of hammer strokes necessary to complete the work. Or the brilliant beauty of the works of a Mozart—would they have been possible without previous cultivation of the five constituents of ecstasy? Or, to take a contemporary example, would Joan Baez have been able to convey a (not always pleasant) truth with beauty if her insight had been obscured by some personal problem? It is always easy to make much of the problematic aspects of an artist's personality. We might also ask why Mozart's music was unable to soothe him, although it provides peace to most of us.

The great artists of our civilization have not in fact achieved *jhāna*, not to mention complete enlightenment. Some of the ecstatics were never able to give up their making up to death. Without clear comprehension and without the supporting basis of *sīla*, they were able to put up with neither the world of multiplicity nor ecstasy. Even a Jimi Hendrix, who during his ecstatic improvisations licked the strings of his guitar and tried to transcend the manifold world of music by having the rhythm of the improvisation culminate in destruction of the instruments—even he had worked his way up by means of joyful interest and practice apprehended and reflected upon with discipline. Even this level of ecstatic experience—one that was not very conducive to happiness, that was relatively disquiet and not very integrative—could hardly have been achieved by Hendrix by drunkenly walking around with the earphones of a Walkman over his ears.

People who see themselves as inferior tend to consume in an inferior fashion that which has little to do with their own reality. They are often not even able to attune their own experiential reality to beauty even as mediated from the outside. But you, dear reader, know the ways toward self-realization of the ecstatic, and you also have at your disposal the techniques and the ability to accomplish it. So take the above considerations merely as a spur for your own reflection. Creative absorption or creative ecstasy is not reserved for professional artists. The quality of the ecstatic experience of a noble person striving for liberation is also not to be determined by popular movements.

It is enjoyable to participate in the ecstasy-evoking experiences of others, especially if a product with artistic or some other kind of value is involved. Yet the most beautiful ecstasies of others remain outside, just a thing in the world of multiplicity that can in no way provide our own experiencing with integrative unity and fulfillment. No one else can meditate for us, and no one else can unfold the strategies of ecstasy in everyday life for us. Releasing our awareness from pathological defilements and making use of the perspective and creativity thus gained in everyday life—this one can only do for oneself. Dhamma strategies also are just means, which only when applied can make it possible for new visions to break out of the prison of old self-definitions and cause a richness of inner life to well up. As we develop our own strategies, dying powers can be reanimated and put to use toward inner fulfillment and liberational structuring of our way of life. Only liberation of awareness, only release from the fetters of manifoldness, can transform mind-killing daily routines into techniques, reshape them into a concentrated unity, and with their help perfect life into an ecstatic feast.

Strategies of Power

The will is the most important base of power, and it is in our power alone whether we have will, free will, or whether we make up our mind to give way to some form of determinism or dependency. When we, supposedly for the sake of simplicity, decide in favor of impotence, life becomes, without any further interference from us, more complicated and more filled with suffering. It is simple to be happy if we wish and if we have enough power to remain in control of life's constant new changes. We have dealt with the prerequisites for this power to master life in the previous chapters. We have saved only the subject of willpower (*viriya*) for last—and for good reason, as we will see, especially in regard to the technical aspects of training the will.

The greatest confusion reigns in our civilization concerning questions of power. Therefore it is appropriate to try, with the help of thorough wise apprehension, to cast some light on this muddle. First let us consider the sicknesses of the will, impotence, and caprice. Armed with the knowledge thus gained and aware of the dangers of abuse of power, we will investigate the components of our own will and consider their place in the harmonization of our mental energies. In so doing, we will also see in what ways training of the will leads far beyond so-called normality into the realm of magic. But we will not lose sight of the fact that our main aim is a happy life, which is attainable through transcending dependences and through development of integrative unity in our daily lives.

Questions of struggle and violence are closely bound up with the subject of power. Their presence in our lives cannot be denied. Dhamma strategies in no way seek to make the practitioner into a helpless victim of those destructive forces or in any way to diminish his warriorlike capacities. That it is possible to come out of a fight intact without using violence is documented by the martial arts associated with Zen Buddhism. They are an example on the bodily level of wise apprehension, mindfulness, and concentration (which must be free from aggression, greed, and delusion), as well as of willpower, wisdom, and mastery of technique based on self-confidence (*saddhā*). By contrast, raw violence and simpleminded cruelty are merely signs of the inner impotence of their perpetrators and of their lack of proficiency in right means.

Strategies of power cultivate the warriorlike spirit by directing it in a liberational direction and equipping it with the techniques of right means (*upāya-kosalla*). The battlefield of Dhamma strategies lies in our own inner world. The criteria for directing a battle attack are identical with the criteria for ethical evaluation in the framework of wise apprehension. Thus the hordes of countless formations of greed, aggression, and delusion are the enemy, against which the strategies of power are deployed in a greedless, aggressionless, and nondeluded fashion. The liberational struggle (*padhāna*) is not based on the principle of opposition and suppression, but rather on conquering by means of developing the good and the better. We do not fight against evil, but rather for liberation. The Abhidhammic metaprograms connected with this are based on the following matrix of wise apprehension, cited here after the *Anguttara Nikāya*,[1] a work I have referred to a number of times:

> There are four warrior-like, right efforts, O Bhikkhus. What four?
> Herein a Bhikkhu rouses his will not to permit the arising of evil, unwholesome states that have not arisen; he makes an effort for it, stirs up his energy, exerts his mind and strives.
> He rouses his will to abandon evil, unwholesome states already arisen. . . .
> He rouses his will to arouse wholesome states that have not yet arisen. . . .
> He rouses his will to maintain wholesome states already arisen and not to allow them to disappear; he makes an effort for it, stirs up his energy, exerts his mind and strives.

It is so simple, it sounds so obvious. But then why do we so often act counter to this self-evident truth?

SICKNESSES OF THE WILL: IMPOTENCE AND CAPRICE

People who have an unbiased attitude toward power are hard to find. Most people crave power, many quite openly; others hide their power-hunger behind apparent opposition to power and critiques of it; some people treat any conversation or reflection on the subject of power as taboo. There are also those who in their aversion to abuse of power, rather than purifying their mind from the greed for it, go so far as to convert their unprocessed power-craving into its opposite and voluntarily adopt impotence. But then impotence is also usually utilized as a weapon in achieving egoistic goals or, even worse, to make life miserable for their fellow beings, to punish and terrorize them. You certainly are aware of concrete examples from your own surroundings that would enable you to verify each one of the above attitudes toward power.

Let us look a little more in detail at what makes power seem so attractive. When questioned about this, most people react by explaining why they would not like to go through life helpless. Adults as well as young people, women as well as men, all are able to describe clearly what happens in concrete situations when a person is lacking in power. By contrast, the answers are less concrete and sometimes rather naive if people are asked to tell what they would do if they had enough power. They would use their power to "fulfill wishes," their own wishes and those of friends and relatives, to "be better off, to be able to organize things better and help other people," and not rarely also to "show power possessors a thing or two" and to "punish abuse of power."

It would be premature to look into these motives to see what is sick and what is healthy in them. Although those questioned tend to get carried away, usually emotionally, into unrealistic wishful thinking, still they are recounting their own experiences and feelings about events they have actually encountered. We are familiar with the matrix of conditioned arising (*paticca-samuppāda*), which we dealt with in such great detail in chapter 3, and thus we know that our experiences (*vedanā*) are largely conditioned by our previous actions, by karmic formations, and by the nature of our consciousness. We also know that it is not inevitable to slip immediately from experiencing something directly into craving (*tanhā*) motivated by greed, aggression, and delusion. Therefore, to begin with, let us attempt to apprehend wisely just as experiences or feelings (*vedanā*), these accounts of situations in which the desire for power arises. It would be helpful here if in so doing we could work with something that we ourselves have experienced.

With the help of wise apprehension, strategies of sympathy, and some of the techniques you have learned thus far in your reading, it is easy to deal with questions of power from the moment they appear in daily-life situations. We can also call upon the strategies of ecstasy, which make it possible for us momentarily to step out of the everyday world with all its problems of power, to lift ourselves above the manifold world of *papañca* in meditation. However helpful, disencumbering, and refreshing this may be, it does not offer any kind of definitive change or a lasting upliftedness. In order to bring about a significant change in our situation in the world and our attitude toward the world, we require the strategies of power, which make liberational use of our willpower.

Any person can arouse his or her will. Most people, however, lack the ability to direct their will. The will as a vehicle of power derails and shatters if no roads to power have been built and maintained. Shattering of the will is called impotence; its derailing is called caprice. Even if we have reliable roads to power, knowledge concerning impotence and caprice is still important for understanding the way in which other people apprehend and react and for taking this into account in our own clear comprehension (*sampajañña*).

Let us consider the responses to the questioning once more from the point of view of why power is attractive and what those questioned wanted to use it for. At this point let us set aside our insight that many of the problems of impotence and power abuse would never arise if those involved were able to apprehend situations thoroughly and wisely (*yoniso manasikāra*) and consequently work on their own greed, their own aggression, and their own delusion. This would certainly bring greater perspective and prevent helplessness. But we cannot get rid of all real difficulties and hostilities simply by "meditating them away" or—as most psychotherapists try to do—"analyzing them away." Such an unwise (*ayoniso*) approach would only take into account one side of the interplay between a person and his world and as a result deliver him once again into impotence with relation to his world. This is actually what the ideologies of "adjustment" try to accomplish. But how would it be if we did it the other way around—if we created an ideal environment and a just society, which would provide people with the power they are striving for?

Let us imagine that a person acquired all the power that, according to the results of our survey (as well as all possible further requirements), he or she needs. After all, it does actually happen in our industrial society that broad layers of the population have the power and means to get practically anything they want and certainly to fulfill all their needs. Many of them are independent of children that need care, parents, landlords, employers . . . Many are not excluded from interesting realms of experience and fashionable worlds of thought; they are integrated into groups of people of like views and are always tuned in to the latest developments . . . Many of them are subservient to nothing and do not even need to take their fellow human beings into account. Are these people happy? What do they do with their power?

In order to work through the questions raised here thoroughly and on the basis of concrete examples, let us bring to mind what people we know personally do with their power. An authoritative head of family who does not have the need to take out the frustrations created by his office superiors on the members of his family; a feminist fighting against lower status for women who enjoys the full support of her pliable male partner; a self-employed creative person who earns enough money . . . Are these people happy? What do they do with their power?

People often justify the actions of a powerful person by acknowledging that "He's just doing what has to be done." But how thoroughly thought out is his point of departure, how clearly comprehended his action, how conscious his goals? These things are seldom spoken of—and of the personal responsibility and will of the powerful, nothing is said at all. Whatever has to be done is fine; thus need and the absence of alternatives are the excuses of power. If somebody says, "He's doing what he wants," it sounds outrageous. Obviously, popular thinking does not want to get out of the conventional circle of power with active submission and power as a form of submission—even in looking at it from the point of view of the powerful and those who identify with them. From the point of view of the impotent, and of those who as a result of some unreflected-upon frustration identify with them, power is craved "to be able to do things better." We saw in our analysis of illusory solutions to social problems (page 30f.) how frustrated hunger for power is transformed into ideologies. The slogans "Dictatorship of the proletariat" and "Better dead than red" remind us that such frustrated greed can turn into aggression, regardless of whether the ideologies are formulated from the point of view of the powerless or the powerful.

It has also happened that people who really felt the need of power have actually acquired it (for example, within the strictly hierarchically structured institutions of the military, of industrial corporations, and so on). Characteristically, those who are trying to climb the ladder of power divide all others into power-possessors or non-power-possessors. They go by the bicycle-racers' rule: on the top, bend over; on the bottom, tread down. The psychologist Carl Rogers, whom I have already cited several times, discusses this subject, giving very penetrating accounts of how, for example, the leader of a holiday camp works with his newly acquired, outwardly assured power.[2] Incapable of wisely apprehending the realities of the situation, he imposes his injured "will" in acts of capriciousness. As the study indicates, he probably had no sense of his own will and in fear merely tried to subjugate those who were enjoying doing what they wanted. A person who does not respect his own will because he is completely unaware of it is also incapable of respecting the will of others. A person who is in a position of power, but who at the same time experiences himself as impotent (like the bicycle racer), tries by disdaining and bullying his subordinates to confirm the sense of power that he actually does not feel worthy of.

In training the will in the framework of the strategies of power, there is no formula for imposing one's will (by treading down) or for attaining a power position (by bending over); rather these strategies show us how to rediscover our own will as a vehicle of power if an unwholesome lifestyle threatens to dissipate it, and how we can cultivate our inner impulses of will so that we will be equal to the power we actually possess. Only then will we be able to use and develop our personal power in a liberational, happiness-furthering fashion.

THE PATH OF SEEING AND THE PATH OF POWER

"Knowledge is power": It's a phrase we heard even as schoolchildren. But later on we also discovered that not all knowledge is useful, and that some officially promoted systems of belief propagate untrue knowledge for political and economic reasons. In chapter 2, we approached these questions from a sociological point of view. Anyone can see that the externally powerful who are ethically blind spread half-truths or lies in the form of economic promotions, supposedly objective science, and political and religious propaganda[3] in order to make secure their external positions of power. The steady increase in suffering cannot be denied even by fanatical optimists. Anyone can see that what usually lies behind the aggressive acts that create so much suffering in the world is a ruthless greed on the part of the few who are externally powerful; this greed drives them to demand more power and to destroy in a blind rage everything that seems to stand in their way. And the power-hungry powerless ones ape them. In this way we befog our own sight and destroy the truth with its warning. This is done mainly by each one of us to him- or herself, because it is our own—more or less conscious—choice either to believe what we are told or to trust what we see. With this choice, the path of seeing, which leads out of the circle of mutually conditioning impotence and caprice, can begin.

The path of seeing leads to wisdom in the Abhidhammic sense of *paññā*. We have distinguished *paññā* from other types of knowledge (those consisting of mere technical know-how and accumulated information) and have seen how *paññā* can be developed. The exercises connected with Dhamma strategies described in these pages make it possible for us to discover *paññā* as well as the other abilities of mindfulness (*sati*), confidence (*saddhā*), concentration (*samādhi*), and will (*viriya*), and also to see them. We now know that *paññā* represents a holistic vision, which grows from wise apprehension that takes into account liberational potential. It became evident to us through detailed analysis that knowledge leading to a happy life is conditioned by ethical valuation and the ethical base of *sīla*.

This accounting of where we stand is not just theory for you, dear reader, but rather a concrete reflection on the building blocks of personal power that you have acquired through practice. This accounting can be done most simply and precisely in the terminology of *akkheyya*, which we understood as a liberational psycho-algebra. This Abhidhammic terminology designates precisely what your practice has defined as a process and has experientially worked through. In contrast we have the vague slogans of propaganda, advertising, and other means of manipulation, which purvey gullibility as belief, intoxication as ecstasy, and caprice as power. On the path of seeing, we mindfully and concentratedly test the reality of what we have heard, before giving credence to this secondhand knowledge. Such knowledge purified by seeing (*ñāna-dassana-visuddhi*) does not, however, become unshakable until realization of the path of seeing (*dassana-magga*); this point is referred to as "stream-entry" (*sotāpatti*).[4] Only after this point can we tread the path of power (*bala magga*) in the true sense.

Our goal is to see reality as it is, and to develop the faculties that we apprehend by means of *akkheyya* into the five powers, that is, mindfulness, knowledge, confidence, concentration, and will. As already mentioned, these five faculties are first developed into unshakable psychic powers (*bala*) on the path of seeing. In "seeing" in this sense, it is not views and philosophies about existence that matter—although we should also not put aside thinking and analysis, as some meditation schools erroneously teach. In our Dhamma strategies, we are concerned with knowledge that sees in the context of the five mental powers. In this regard the story of the blind men from the Theravada canon is very informative. A few extracts from it are translated below:

> This is the way a king had some men blind from birth try to grasp what an elephant was. . . . An elephant is like a jar, said the one who got hold of the head. The elephant is like a fan, said the one who grabbed the ear. The elephant is like a plow, said the one who took hold of the tusk. The

elephant is like a pillar, said the one that grasped a leg . . .
and persisting in their respective points of view, defending
them with sharp words, they disputed.

Some ascetics (only practitioners) and priests (only the-
oreticians) hold views about the eternality and finiteness
of the world (as well as on other philosophical questions) . . . ; on the body as identical with . . . different
from . . . neither identical with nor different from . . . the
soul, from the life-force . . . ; on the continued existence of
enlightened persons after death. . . .

The adherents of various ideologies are blind, they do
not see what is conducive and not conducive to liberation;
they do not see what the way (*dhamma*) is and what is a
false path. In their ignorance of these things, they get into
quarrels and fights and cling to words. . . .

Like those blind from birth are these ascetics and priests.
They do not see Dhamma. [From the *Jaccandha-Vagga*,
Udāna 6.4][5]

How current this twenty-five-hundred-year-old story still sounds
today, and how many-leveled its meaning is! It would go far beyond
our present subject matter to get into commentaries and interpretations or to consider what this story obviously has to say to the New
Age. Nonetheless, I will give a bit more here from the chapter in the
Udāna on the blind men, because it fills out the context of the cited
story and, beyond that, is of importance for the practice of Dhamma
strategies. The chapter on the blind men not only shows that the
whole truth about the path cannot be reached through a (so to speak)
"interdisciplinary" compilation of views and sciences, but also warns
of excesses that arise conditioned by

- reliance on supernatural abilities (page 62, Pali Text Society edition)
- absence of analysis (page 64)
- unverified adoption of others' statements (page 66)
- insufficient thoroughness (page 70)
- belief in an identity (page 70)
- ignorance regarding addictive mechanisms of sensual
  greed (page 71)
- insufficient staying power in the practice (page 72)

You will recall that we have already discussed all these dangers and
that the exercises are geared to deal with them. In your practice and
utilization of Dhamma strategies, you have very likely discovered
some of your own ways of overcoming these dangers. Instead of fighting them off, you have practiced mindfulness, concentration, confi-

dence, and knowledge. Before we get to the core subject of this chapter—discovering, seeing, and cultivating the power and will for a happy life—it is necessary to prepare the necessary tools. Doubtless you have guessed what these tools are: They are *akkheyya* as matrices of understanding, as meditative objects, and as the algebra of reflection on Dhamma strategies.

If we then proceed to train the will according to the microanalysis that it is an interplay of intention (*chanda*), resolve (*adhimokkha*), effort (*padhāna*), and exertion (*viriya*), we must not forget that any terminology, including that of the *akkheyya*, is a constructed apprehension of the mental processes. An apprehension that divides the flow of experiencing into units, thus making possible liberation and increase of the capacity for happiness, should not then impose a schema on liberated experiencing itself. In systematically practicing the exercises of power, we will nevertheless intentionally look for those aspects of experience that are part of the *akkheyya* to be learned. The everyday effect of this is comparable to what happens with a composer who hears melodies, rhythms, counterpoint, and chords not only in the songs of birds, but also in the noise of machines, the tumult of traffic, and so on. We have already considered such an approach in connection with the practice of clear comprehension in daily life.

In the psycho-algebra of *akkheyya*, the connections between the individual elements, as for example, intention-resolve-effort, are not produced by thinking; they arise at the level of experiencing conditioned by movements of attention, shifts of mood, and so forth. Since we have already been informed about the various levels of experiencing, we clearly comprehend how to distinguish between terminological (conceptual) thinking and experiential awareness. Conceptual order is timeless and experiential penetration happens in time—even if it takes the form of a retrospective experiencing or a meditative anticipation of not-yet-arisen, future abilities.[6] Our personal power is assured only by our competence and ability. Although the training of the will can take place only in present experiencing, it works with the terminology of the *akkheyya*, which have been experientially generated and verified in the past and are used in this training to create the conditions for the arising of a future that is free of suffering. In the *Khuddaka Nikāya*, the same canonical collection that contains the story of the blind men, there is the following key text on how to deal with *akkheyya* (terminology) while taking into account temporality (*addhā*—here translated as "time spheres"):

> Three time spheres there are,
> . . . past, future, and present
> (and in all three):

Beings who only perceive terminology,
who have their standpoint in terminology
and do not penetrate the terminology experientially,
end up beneath the yoke of death.

Experientially penetrating the terminology,
one no longer thinks of a namer (subject),
thus within freedom is attained
and one dwells in highest peace.

Though equipped with terminology,
still tranquilly enjoying timelessness,
on the path of truth he makes use of naming,
but enters no more into nameability—
the master of knowledge.

[ITIVUTTAKA 3.2.4][7]

THE WILL: INTENTION, RESOLVE, EFFORT

In connection with the example of goodwill (*mettā*), within the framework of the strategies of sympathy, we practiced discovering and developing the primary impulses of the will. At that point, we apprehended the nonverbal will as the intention to act (*kattu-kamyatā-chanda*), which is not yet resolved (that is, not directed toward any specific object or goal), but which has within it a particular quality and energy potential. To begin with, let us set aside the energetic aspect of the will and consider the structural aspect in a bit more detail. On the most elementary level, the will is present in every moment of consciousness as an intentionality (*cetanā*). This will determines in what context the experience is seen[8] and how it is apprehended by naming or labeling. But only by means of a resolve (*adhimokkha*) is the will directed toward a specific goal and can thus be fulfilled through an effort (*padhāna*). Here we recognize an example of conditioned arising, which is expressed in the fundamental matrix of *paticca-samuppāda* as follows:

experience → craving   → attachment → becoming
A. *vedanā*   → *tanhā*   → *upādāna*   → *bhava*
B. *cetanā*   → *chanda*   → *adhimokkha* → *padhāna*
experience → intention   → resolve   → effort

The difference between the two is that row A shows the apprehension of the conditioned arising of suffering, while row B shows the apprehension of striving for liberation. In understanding the movements of experiencing depicted in the two rows of *akkheyya*, we are helped by all the examples of concrete outer situations that were introduced in chapter 3 as illustrations of conditioned arising. The four links shown above repeat in lightning-fast succession, since each time effort conditions the arising of a similar experience. How a change of resolve happens, how we throw the switch on the tracks of power, is something we can discuss later. First let us try to gain a better understanding of the inner mechanism of will.

In practicing walking meditation, we examined the process of willing to walk after it had been instigated by thinking. In thinking, first we put the various images connected with standing and walking together into formations (*sankhāra*). Then we reflected on a program of walking, subsuming the images under the directive formations (*abhisankhāra*). Within this organization of images and thought formations, we resolved (*adhimokkha*) in favor of a particular direction and made an effort (*padhāna*) to mentally make the movement from standing to walking so as to arouse the experience of walking in the realm of the imagination. This same thing happens repeatedly until the voluntary aspect (*cetanā*) becomes so strengthened by the repetition that, as a voluntary impulse, it conditions an intention (*chanda*) on a higher level (see the lower part of Diagram 12, page 248). Thereby the conditioned arising of the will, as conceived of above in row B, is completed. It is challenging and amusing to follow this process with increasingly intensified mindfulness during *cankamana* meditation and occasionally to notice whether the other mental powers are present in a balanced way. After just a few weeks of regular practice, you will see that it is possible to take advantage of your understanding of this process in everyday exertions of the will. In this way your actions will gain in effectiveness.

The will must be systematically developed and stimulated (*vidhinā īrayitabbam*, literally, "systematically shaken," as a commentary to the Abhidhamma says) in interaction with the other mental powers in order to bring it to the status of the mental power *viriya*. This also brings to the fore the aspect of the will that we perceive as force vibrations or energy impulses. We dealt with this energizing trembling in detail in the context of joy and the sense of urgency (pages 100ff.) and later in connection with *cankamana* (page 127) we mentioned the observation of carrier waves. In the systematic training of the will, however, these interesting experiences in energy observation are important only insofar as they make us aware of stimulating the will through joy and a sense of urgency and thus bring out the personal autonomy of the will through its anchoring in the body. For practical purposes of will training, the structural understanding described above is more important, because it enables us to concentrate and direct the energy of the will. Willpower (*viriya*) concentrated and directed in this way is compared in a popular introduction to the Abhidhamma to a supporting beam that keeps the house from falling down. To this the following simile is added:

> When, O king, a large army has dislodged a smaller one, but the king of the small army then sends in reinforcements, thus united with them, the small army may defeat the larger. In the same way, O king, willpower possesses the quality of serving as a support, for as long as the good qualities are all supported by willpower, they cannot fade away.[9]

Thus the energy of the will available to a person expresses itself in greater effectiveness and influence. Such a person's actions not only gain in force and validity, but his or her mere presence in a situation represents a force not to be overlooked.

Willpower without the right-seeing understanding of *paññā* could easily lead to an abuse of power in our own inner household. For example, we might naively advance against the hostile armies of formations of greed, aggression, and delusion, instead of using the techniques of right means. Without *saddhā*, an overbalance of willpower would create doubt (*vicikicchā*) concerning the method and the goal and weaken the confidence that is based on trust and our reliance on our own autonomy. Willpower and concentration are directly opposed to each other, and if it is not balanced by concentration, willpower leads to agitation, restlessness, and impulsive excesses.

Without right mindfulness, an overbalance of willpower would lead to repressing unwholesome phenomena or leaving them unnoticed. Though this ostensibly brings about a temporary increase of power, it is quickly revealed as an undermining of personal integrity, since disregarded and repressed "demons" play their dirty tricks at just that moment when we are most vulnerable to them. Mindfulness (*sati*) is the most important power, since it alone can institute harmony among the other mental powers. Moreover, right mindfulness[10] is just as indispensable in creating the context for the highest application of the will on the four magical roads to power as it is in harmonizing all aspects of liberated existence.

The Four Magical Roads to Power

The techniques for the use of willpower for purposes of liberation are called *iddhi-pāda*. In the English translations of technical Abhidhamma texts, this term is rendered as "magical roads to power." *Iddhi* or *sid-*

dhi is a word that is hard to translate; in the colloquial language in narrative literature, it denotes all extraordinary, but especially supernatural, magical gifts. Abhidhamma does not deny the existence of such gifts and uses the word *iddhi* as part of its technical terminology. In the context of Dhamma strategies, we understand *iddhi* as a potentiality or ability that has ripened faultlessly and therefore has gone beyond the ordinary everyday level. Thus we will stick with the expression "magical roads to power," also by way of accommodating the widespread tendency to designate processes and powers that cannot be duplicated and are ununderstandable to the average person as "magic." In a commentary on the method for "guiding and directing the mind toward the manifold kinds of magic powers," Buddhaghosa explains the term *iddhi* as "self-fulfillment, succeeding, success, flourishing, ability, power, magical force, magical action, actualization, attainment" and as "the realization of a plan (*upāya*)" (*Visuddhi Magga*).

The great Burmese Abhidhamma master Ledi Sayadaw[11] classifies *iddhi* in connection with stages of mental purification (*visuddhi;* cf. chapter 4) and regards the following five as essential:

1. *Abhiññāsiddhi:* complete analytic apprehension of all phenomena in terms of the *akkheyya,* as contained in the Abhidhamma compendium *Abhidhammattha Sangaha.*[12]
2. *Pariññāsiddhi:* complete meditative penetration of impermanence and suffering, as well as the other aspects of the world of multiplicity.[13]
3. *Pahānasiddhi:* final overcoming of all mental defilements and pathologies (*kilesa*), which brings complete flexibility of mind on the roads to power.
4. *Sacchikiriyāsiddhi:* the power of realization, which leads to penetration of the Four Noble Truths (and thus to enlightenment), but which can also be used for worldly purposes.
5. *Bhāvanāsiddhi:* complete mastery in meditation and in carrying out all the strategies of the Dhamma.

The four magical roads to power (*iddhi-pāda*) thus lead to realization of the five groups of *iddhi.* They are only introduced here in order to make clear the actual goal of the *iddhi-pāda.* It would be irrelevant from a practical point of view to launch into a discussion of these high aims or even to theorize about those *iddhi* that have to do with telepathy, astral travel, and so on. The Dhamma strategies described in our book have as their goal an improvement in the quality of everyday life. Therefore we will concern ourselves with the four magical roads to power only insofar as they are helpful for our practice and way of life.

The most important prerequisites for cultivating the magical roads to power are already known to you from your work with this book thus far. They are the mental power of confidence (*saddhā*) and the reliable subjective basis of *sīla*. Perfection of the autochthonous personal ethics of *sīla* as morality is emphatically and repeatedly declared as the indispensible basis of magical power. In *The Questions of King Milinda*, the following comparisons are used to symbolize this:

> " . . . for morality (*sīla*) constitutes the basis of all good states of mind: the five mental powers, the foundations of mindfulness, the magical roads to power, and so on. As long as one has morality as a basis, all these good states are not lost."
>
> "Give me a closer explanation!"
>
> "Just as, O king, all kinds of seeds and plants in which a flourishing, growing, and unfolding is seen all flourish in dependence upon the earth, flourish, grow, and unfold just by having the earth as their basis, in the same way, O king, the practitioner of concentration—just by taking support from morality and taking morality as a basis—makes the five mental faculties unfold, namely, confidence, willpower, mindfulness, concentration, and wisdom."
>
> "Give me still another comparison."
>
> "Just as the builder of cities, O king, when he wants to build a city, first causes a place for the city to be cleared, frees it of tree stumps and brambles, makes it even, and after a time, goes on to divide it into streets, squares, crossroads, and so forth, and in this way builds the city, just in this way, O king, the practitioner of concentration—just by taking support from morality and taking morality as a basis—makes the five mental faculties unfold." [PTS ed., p. 33ff]

Immediately afterward the role of confidence (*saddhā*) is illustrated in similes: If a king wanted to drink from a body of water that had previously been roiled up by an army, then he uses a water-purifying magic stone (an item that can be purchased nowadays in pharmacies everywhere) to settle the mud. "By water we should understand the mind, by mud the mental obscurations and hindrances (*kilesa, nīvarana*), and by magic stone, confidence. As soon as confidence arises, O king, it makes the mental hindrances disappear. The mind without the hindrances is clear, pure, unsullied." It is interesting that confidence also has the characteristic of forward movement, of going ahead, like a man "who is aware of his own force and strength and reaches the other side of a flooded stream with a mighty leap." In this way such a man becomes a guide for other men (that is, the other mental formations), and in this way also, confidence shows the way. These similes adequately illustrate the prerequisites of the magical roads to power, which we shall now analyze from the point of view of their use in systematic practice.

On the roads to power, concentration and will, which oppose each other, are held in a dynamic balance. We learned in the meditation exercises that concentration brings things together, and equalizes and unifies them by dissolving all distinctions. By contrast, the will makes much of things and separates them by changing and moving them. The basic traits of concentration and will are present in every mental state. Energy potential only becomes available to the will if it is related to mindfully; otherwise, it falls into the hands of neurotic influences and drives (*āsava*). Whether a mental state is wholesome or conducive to suffering depends on whether or not it is free from the roots of suffering, greed, aggression, and delusion. Therefore, even states of mind that have arisen with these causes of suffering can undergo a wholesome transformation through wise apprehension of these states (that is, as defiled by greed or aggression or delusion). Thus wise apprehension (*yoniso manasikāra*) is already by itself an overcoming of evil, because it is free of greed, aggression, and delusion. If we furthermore wisely apprehend preconditioned unwholesomeness as conditionally arisen, then we can break the cycle and remove the basis for the continued arising of suffering. It is on this principle of liberational effort (*padhāna;* see the matrix of metaprograms at the beginning of this chapter) that the roads to power are also based. A mental state associated with wisdom is always free from greed and aggression. The presence of wisdom means that willpower and the beginnings of wise investigation are present as well. From any such good, wholesome state of mind, one of the four roads to power can be developed:

1. The road to power of intention (*chanda*)
2. The road to power of willpower (*viriya*)
3. The road to power of consciousness (*citta*)
4. The road to power of investigation (*vīmamsā*)

For each road to power, there is a psycho-algebraic formula combining three elements: the predominant principle, concentration, and the formations of effort. The formations of effort (*padhāna-sankhāra*) have the same structure in all four roads to power, that is, the matrix of the four right struggles introduced at the beginning of this chapter.

THE ROAD TO POWER OF INTENTION

The formula for the road to power of intention contains the following terms:

chanda-samādhi	–	*padhāna-sankhāra*	–	*samannā-gata*
intention-concentration		effort-formations		together-going

(For each of the roads of power the term with which the formula begins corresponds to the main principle of that road.)

Before developing the road to power of intention, the will aspects (*cetana*) of present wholesome moments of consciousness, that is, their intentionality, must be apprehended and repeated until they reach the status of an intention to act (*kattu-kamyatā-chanda*). Although investigation also takes place as part of this process, and willpower as well as specific properties exhibited by the given consciousness are present, in our apprehension we emphasize only the intention. In other words, the roads to power of investigation, willpower, consciousness, and intention are all made up of the same "raw material." But only one of these four aspects is cultivated at a time. Here it is intention (*chanda*).

Intention is definitely directed toward some object of the inner or outer world. However, we do not take this object as the object of our perception; rather we concentrate our awareness on the directedness of the intention. This mental movement itself (*chanda*) is the object of concentration. This is the practical way toward the realization of *chanda-samādhi*, the predominant principle of the road to power of intention.

The intention can be directed toward outer knowledge, action, or toward liberational alteration of awareness (cf. the distinction between the three types of knowledge in chapter 3). With growth in power, the danger of abuse of power also arises, which is different in each of these three spheres, and therefore requires different techniques to deal with it:

- In connection with outer knowledge, we protect the purity of the subjective basis (*sīla*) by guarding the gates of the senses (see page 257) so that our openness to reality is not obscured by sense craving and other distortions.

- In connection with action, we use the five criteria of *sīla* as found in the training resolve (see page 153).

- In connection with alteration of awareness, we prevent inner abuse of power by diagnosing the obscurations to insight (*vipassanā-upak-kilesa*), which arise in the form of supernatural phenomena during very intensive and highly advanced *vipassanā* meditation.[14]

Thus the techniques for maintaining quality and direction in cultivating intention are based on clear comprehension and early perception of deviations. We deal with these deviations in a manner similar to that in which we deal with distractions to concentration (we practiced this in the previous chapter). The difference is only that here we do not have a static content of awareness as the object of concentration, but rather the experiential dynamic of intention (*chanda*) is the focal point. Diagram 12 concisely illustrates the entire dynamic of the road to power of intention. Because this dynamic can most clearly be observed in the intention to act, the best actions for developing the road to power of intention are those in which generosity (*dāna*) or forgiving and protective nonviolence (*ahimsa*) predominate as motives. Daily life provides sufficient opportunity for the practice of this exercise. Using the same motives, the road to power of intention can also be practiced in the sphere of systematic meditation, radiation of kindness (see page 165ff.) being the best, and with meditative reflection (*paccavekkhanā*) on everyday situations.

Incidentally, there is nothing against your checking your own power of intention right now, before reading further.

The road to power of intention leads to an unshakable state of resolve. However, we use it only in those everyday actions that we have first wisely apprehended and reflected upon, and about the purpose of which we have clear comprehension. In other words, we do not let ourselves be diverted from our intention by incidental events and transitory shifts of mood, but rather, going beyond such things, we apply our entire power and succeed in what we have intended.

THE ROAD TO POWER OF WILLPOWER

In each moment of consciousness, an energy potential is present that determines its vitality (*jīvita*). In mental states that are filled with the energy of joy or urgency, the potential of the will is also activated. How the will is concentrated and cultivated to the level of mental power we examined in the chapter section entitled "The Will: Inten-

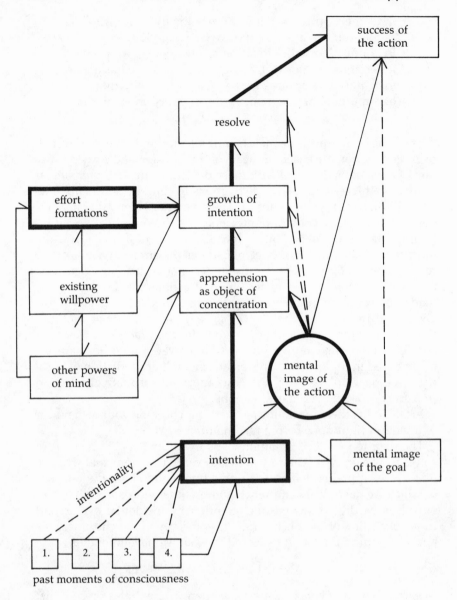

Diagram 12. The Dynamic of the Road to Power of Intention

tion, Resolve, Effort" (beginning on page 240), both from the point of view of energy and in relation to the structure of its conditioned arising. The road to power of intention explained subsequently concentrates on the structural dynamic of the will. The road to power of willpower, which I will now elucidate, takes as its object of concentration the growth of energy (*viriya*). Success in developing the road to power of willpower consists not in development of its dynamic, but rather in an intensification of its original form. Nonetheless, *chanda* and *viriya* are two aspects of a single phenomenon, the will, which are only seen as separate by means of *akkheyya* for purposes of practice. Thus the road to power of willpower can be depicted in a diagram similar to that in which the road to power of intention was depicted.

Meditative training of willpower stresses regularity and endurance in the correct execution of the exercises.[15] Accumulation of volitional energy can be brought about by any exercise related to any of the Dhamma strategies without any danger of going astray, since they have all been devised on the basis of liberational criteria. After all, we put together the program for our own practice out of familiar elements. We do not try to add things, but to improve and deepen what we are already working on and to increase our competence and power in relation to that.

In daily life, this power expresses itself as tirelessness in the accomplishment of a well-considered goal. It also means endurance in acquiring skills and is best used for endeavors related to self-knowledge and refinement of awareness, because, using available energies, it can bring about an intensification and liberational transformation of our nature. If we know what a happy way of life consists of, and if we have resolved to bring this about as far as possible, then the road to power of willpower will provide us with the power needed to do it.

THE ROAD TO POWER OF CONSCIOUSNESS

Abhidhamma investigates all states of consciousness (*citta*) as concerns their inner structure, their outer relationships, and also their potentialities.[16] Transpersonal psychology has recently begun to develop an understanding of the outer relationships, potentialities, and energies of consciousness by introducing the concepts of altered and alternate states of consciousness, as well as that of state-specific skills. For practical reasons, we cannot enter into theoretical discussions on these points here. For the purposes of our practice of Dhamma strategies, we need distinguish only the groups of consciousness (*citta*) as shown in the accompanying table.

	Suffering-producing: *Akusala*	Beautiful: *Sobhana*
With right-effort formations		Joyful or indifferent experiences of generosity and forgiveness, connected with knowledge. Wise apprehension of all states. Overcoming of pathologies and entry into *jhāna*.
Spontaneous	Sad, rooted in aggression. Indifferent and joyful, rooted in greed. Indifferent, connected with doubt, rooted in delusion. Indifferent experiences with agitation, rooted in delusion.	Joyful or indifferent experiences free from greed, aggression, and delusion with or without knowledge. Pleasant fruits of wholesome *kamma* causes, smile of the Enlightened One, etc.
With pathological formations	Sad, connected with resentment, aggression, and prejudice. Indifferent and joyful experiences, rooted in greed, with or without prejudice.	

The methods of Abhidhamma make it possible to understand the states of consciousness microanalytically, that is, to experience the differences in their inner structure, as well as to distinguish macroanalytically eighty-nine states of consciousness according to their external relationships and potentialities.[17]

During practice, it is sufficient at the beginning if we note only the following qualities of the experienced consciousness:

tending apart	drawing together, rigid
concentrated	scattered, restless
free	defiled by greed, aggression, delusion
undeveloped	become great (*mahaggata*)

Mindfulness and clear comprehension (*sati-sampajañña*) with regard to the quality of consciousness makes possible the development of the road to power of consciousness. This follows the same principles as those illustrated in Diagram 12. The most suitable objects and goals of consciousness are the liberational themes and objects of concentration with which we have become familiar in our previous practice of Dhamma strategies. In daily life, we can more intensively experience conditionality and impermanence, the inclination to simplify things, the arising of kindness and compassion, the breathing rhythm of other beings, and so on. In the advanced practice, in apprehending the quality of consciousness, we will make use of the constituents of ecstasy and the paradigm of the conditioned arising of freedom (which will be explained at the end of this chapter) as additional criteria.

The road to power of consciousness is characterized by the practitioner's trying, during all his free time (that is, time that is not taken up by everyday business and obligations), to maintain his experiencing on higher levels of consciousness through connection with a chosen meditative object. Artists, writers, composers, and inventors might speak in connection with something like this of "times of inspiration." The creative and beautiful in the sense of a road to power of consciousness is beneficial for all undertakings that we perform of our own free will and with joyful interest; it could be an educational project, preparing for an examination, planning a vacation, or anything of that nature. The road to power of consciousness can transform any sphere of life into a field of consciousness-culture. Even an all-embracing organization of everyday life could provide content for the heightened consciousness if it were apprehended as a creative project.

THE ROAD TO POWER OF INVESTIGATION

The road to power of investigation can be briefly characterized as the high art of asking questions and solving problems. Investigation (vīmamsā) emphasizes the discriminating aspect of consciousness, which is already present in less developed states of consciousness as the noticing of dissimilarities and oppositions. But investigation is not based on views whose contents are conveyed by means of concepts and images; rather it has to do with wise apprehension (yoniso manasikāra) of immediate experiencing and thus precludes any distortions or perversions (cf. page 68). Wise investigation uses the various paradigms of Abhidhamma explained in this book as matrices (yoni), which apprehend experience holistically in a liberational perspective. Vīmamsā is thus more than merely pondering or reflection. Wise investigation knows suffering (the First Noble Truth) and penetrates it experientially and apprehends it wisely. It thereby also knows the cause of suffering (the Second Noble Truth) and its conditioned arising (*paticca-samuppāda*); it aims at liberation and is informed concerning the liberational Dhamma strategies. Thus the road to power of investigation guides awareness away from the ugly spheres tainted by aggression, greed, and delusion. It frees from the entanglements of the manifold and leads to the simple beauty of liberation.

Through the exercises of wise apprehension, you have acquired the basic skills for wise investigation (*vīmamsā*) and are already familiar with some paradigms of the Abhidhamma, which you have tried to apply as matrices to your own experiences. You have already made use of investigative reflection to coordinate your skills and experience in devising your personal strategies. The structure of strategies of action illustrated in Diagram 9 on pages 166–67 is the field on which the road to power of investigation is built—with the minor change that here strategies of action become strategies of knowledge and purification. In the true Abhidhamma sense, the road to power of investigation (*vīmamsā-iddhipāda*) divides and orders the mental field in such a way that wise apprehension by means of *akkheyya* becomes possible. Thus it is the road to magical power mentioned at the beginning of this chapter section as *abhiññāsiddhi*. *Abhiññāsiddhi* is the power of high knowledge (*abhi* = high; *ñāna* = knowledge), which is related to the following six fields (cited following the *Visuddhi Magga*):

1. Moving in various spheres. "Being one, he becomes many, and having become many, he again becomes one. He makes himself visible and invisible. Unobstructed, he passes through walls, enclosures, and mountains, just as though in the air. On water, he walks along without sinking, just as though on the earth. In the earth, he comes up and dives under, just as though in the water. With legs crossed, he moves through the air. . . ."

2. Telepathic perception. "With the divine ear, the pure superhuman one, he perceives both sounds, the divine as well as the human, the distant as well as the near."

3. Reading thoughts. "Seeing through the minds of other beings, other persons, with his mind, he knows. The greed-tainted mind he knows as greedy, the greedless as greedless . . . etc. . . . aggression-tainted and without aggression, deluded and undeluded, tense and scattered, concentrated and unconcentrated, developed and undeveloped."

4. Remembering previous births. "He remembers many earlier forms of existence, one birth, two, three, four, and five births . . . , and many world-arisings and world de-

clines: 'There I was, such a name I had, such a clan I belonged to, such an appearance I had, such-and-such joys and sorrows were my lot. . . .'"

5. Insight into the conditions of rebirth. "With the divine eye, the pure and superhuman one, he sees the beings pass away and reappear, common and noble, beautiful and ugly, happy and unhappy, he sees the beings reappear in accordance with their deeds."

6. Liberation from the power of all evil influences, which as neurotic motivations and drives (āsava) obstruct freedom of the will and capacity for happiness. "After conquering the defiled motivations, while still alive he comes into possession of the deliverance of mind and deliverance through wisdom free from defiled motivations, in that he himself sees and realizes them."

As we can see from the psycho-algebraic formula of the road to power of investigation, the will and concentration are coordinated in the service of paññā. The liberational wisdom of paññā also has within it the ability to go forward on the path to freedom. The road to power of investigation thus not only directs awareness toward the true and beautiful, it also frees us from the causes of suffering, distortion, and repression. For this reason, it is combined—as becomes much clearer in relation to the vipassanā exercises—with the other roads to power. The road to power of investigation opens the way to transcendence by ordering, cleansing, and harmonizing the mental household. It provides the power to deal with all the projections of the inner world properly, and this obviously also has its effect on the quality of our relationship with the facts of the external world. Thanks to the Dhamma strategies based on vīmamsā, we can accomplish the following in meditation and in everyday activity:

- dissolve and eliminate blockages of the flow of experiencing
- break down seemingly solid masses of obstacles and possibly use them as building blocks for the roads to power
- see through, simplify, and set in order hampering entanglements and complications
- deal skillfully with enemies, either transforming them into helpers or holding them at a distance
- uncover demons of neurotic motivations and repressed complexes and tame them
- divest menacing energy concentrations of their explosivity and crippling force, even out the pressure they exert,

use the energy in them in a happiness-furthering manner, while still preventing new ones from arising
- protect and cultivate unharmful energy sources and
  currents
- cultivate and spontaneously bring into play the inclination toward the true and beautiful

We have looked into the properties of all four roads to power and
seen how, in a broader context, they harmonize the mental powers of
will and concentration. We have acquired a technical understanding
of how they become powers whose applications have a magical quality.
In the tradition of Abhidhamma, we are emphatically warned against
taking a frivolous approach toward these powers, especially against
using them for selfish purposes or making them an occasion for boast-
ing and arrogance. Though we can make pragmatic use of the techniques connected with them, we should not make our happiness dependent on their efficacy. It is important to understand how their
power functions and what effects it has, as well as to cultivate clear
comprehension of whether and when to use it. This is a kind of noble
humility in perceiving our own power and deciding whether or not to
nourish it with further energies.

The only guarantee that we will not go astray on the roads to power
is right thought, free from greed, aggression, and delusion. This
flawless way of thinking is a component of the eightfold path to liberation.[18] In cultivating right thought on the everyday level, we can utilize the five criteria of *sīla,* which we described in detail in the context
of the strategies of sympathy. It has become evident in various contexts how important the reliable subjective basis of *sīla* is for experimentation and opening up of new spheres of experience. This is even
more the case in the sphere of the strategies of power, because here
the protection and support of *sīla* is essential both for setting goals
and for decisions concerning the means to be used in reaching them.

Satipatthāna-Vipassanā Exercises

High success (*iddhi*) with Dhamma strategies can be achieved, at least
to some degree, by any person who has gained a basic experiential
understanding of Dhamma through the exercises described up to this
point in this book. Thus you already have at your disposal the con-
stituent elements and the metaprograms for the systematic practice of
satipatthāna-vipassanā. The exercises described below represent a selection of techniques that have particularly proved themselves with a

great number of participants in intensive meditation courses. A qualified meditation teacher chooses during a meditation course a technique for each practitioner that corresponds to his or her personal makeup.[19] The majority of meditation courses offered today, insofar as they have liberational goals at all, unfortunately present what could be called "spiritual ready-to-wear" that every participant has to fit into. Thus many meditation teachers who, though they do inspire through their charisma, have no ear for the most personal concerns of practitioners, could with benefit have their teachings complemented or even replaced by a good practice manual. In view of this, the strategies and exercises we have investigated in these pages have been worked out in such great detail that every practitioner should be able to make his or her own selection. Your personal power, dear reader, consists to a great extent in continually experientially checking and verifying the teaching relationships and methods that you place your trust in.

The following exercises are connected with the five realms of *satipatthāna-vipassanā* that should be taken into account in any complete meditation course.

Basic Exercise: Contemplation of Impermanence. This exercise aims for clearly comprehended awareness of the true nature of all real things and clear discrimination between reality and the apprehension of reality. This is a mindfulness exercise in the most real sense, and it is performed with a minimum of effort. From the point of view of the four right struggles (*padhāna*—see page 232), it is the most nonviolent method for overcoming arisen evil, unwholesome things. It is the basic exercise of *satipatthāna-vipassanā*—not a preliminary exercise— because it provides the basis for all the other exercises, is contained in all of them, and also represents the final step to enlightenment and liberation.

Guarding the Sense Gates is an exercise that protects and maintains the good.

Reshaping of Suffering-Producing Processes is a method of breaking down unwholesome material and structuring incipient wholesome alternatives.

Turning Away from Suffering is the way out of the circle of conditioned arising and thus an opening toward the absence of suffering, that is, toward the peace of complete liberation. It is the right struggle of causing not-yet-arisen wholesome things to arise.

Experiencing Emptiness is the supreme method for transcending both unwholesome and wholesome things.

In the following pages instructions will be given for the exercises that lead to realization of these five realms or stages of *satipatthāna-vipassanā*. In each case, in order to begin with the higher stage of the practice, the previous stage must be mastered to the point where in case of mishap one can definitely fall back on it. Indispensable for all advanced practices of *satipatthāna-vipassanā* is the ability to distinguish between directly experienced bodily events (*rūpa*) and mental apprehension of them (*nāma*) by means of feeling, perception, labeling, and so on. Otherwise the practitioner runs the risk of carrying on experiments of thought and imagination that have no directly experienceable bodily anchoring in reality. This especially happens with meditators who have little practice in walking meditation (*cankamana*) and in noting physical postures (*iriyā-patha*). They frequently talk enthusiastically of their spectacular meditation experiences, of "body vibrations and sensations," for example. They prize their "choiceless awareness" or "altered consciousness" and throw around a lot of other catchphrases. In fact, however, one quickly sees that they are physically unmindful and interpersonally disturbed, in spite of perhaps having sat through several meditation courses. In order to hold such dangers at bay, a great deal of space is devoted in these pages to reality anchoring.

At the beginning of every *satipatthāna-vipassanā* exercise, we are conscious with clear comprehension of the high goal that has been described as the power of experiential knowledge (*abhiññāsiddhi*) and liberational penetration (*pariññāsiddhi*). But during the exercise, full mindfulness should go to the immediate experience of reality as it is. In order to guard ourselves from digressions into imaginary and thought worlds, we should return, even in the most advanced exercise, to physical rootedness in reality, that is, to our physical posture or to the sensations of breathing. The most suitable techniques for the practice of *satipatthāna-vipassanā* are the techniques of mindfulness of body that we have already discussed. The practitioner should behave like a cat hunting a rat, according to the simile in *The Questions of King Milinda*:

> As, sire, the cat, in caves and holes and the interior of large houses, seeks only after rats, even so, the yogin . . . should constantly and continuously and with diligence seek only after the food of mindfulness that is directed in the body (*kāya-gatā-sati*).
> And again, sire, the cat seeks after its food only in what is near, even so . . .
> Not far from here you need to look!

Highest existence—what can it avail?
Here in the present being,
In your own body overcome the world!

1. THE BASIC EXERCISE: CONTEMPLATION OF IMPERMANENCE

The basis for contemplation of the impermanence (*anicca*) of all phenomena is the advanced level of mindfulness of breathing as described
on pages 119–20. If you have mastered *ānāpāna-sati* as a technique of
concentration (cf. page 215), this can also serve as a basis. You should
especially take care, however, that it is not the unitary image connected with breathing but rather the tactile sensations that constitute
the primary meditative object. The noting and labeling of observed
processes as well as the process-oriented apprehension of breathing
and the five elements of *jhāna* focused on it all belong to apprehension
of mental reality (*nāma*). In *satipatthāna-vipassanā*, however, we take
the physical reality (*rūpa*) of the rising and falling of the belly or the
passage of air against the rim of the nostrils as the primary meditative
object. There is indeed no experiencing of *rūpa* without *nāma*, and it is
certain that there is no progress in *vipassanā* without the experientially
penetrating knowledge of the difference between the two (*nāma-rūpa-
pariccheda-ñāna*).

The best way to learn the difference between *nāma* and *rūpa* is
through the mistakes that inevitably are made by every practitioner:
We observe the breathing and label what we experience until we notice that the labeling "Breathing in, breathing in . . . breathing out,
breathing out" or "Rising, rising . . . falling, falling" is actually no
longer synchronized with the actual physical process. It would be extremely unintelligent to quickly skip over the mistake with shame or
even to try to "retouch" what happened. In *satipatthāna-vipassanā*, the
point is to note things the way they really are, however mistaken,
painful, or unfavorable they may seem.

It is common to all things that they are impermanent. This is true
for experiences and all the things of the inner world as well as for
things of the outer world—from the biggest concrete blocks to atoms
and their particle-waves. Understanding and accepting this intellectually probably creates little difficulty for the person of average intelligence—even if his emotions and actions are remote from this truth.
The point of *satipatthāna-vipassanā* is to overcome this alienation from
the truth, this "normal" madness.

The practical procedure is already known to you, dear reader, to a
great extent. We put our relationship to the world in order and also

generate the reliable subjective basis *sīla*. Then, like the cat in the simile, we practice reality anchoring in our bodily experiencing and acquire clear comprehension concerning the status of our mental powers, will, confidence, concentration, wisdom, and mindfulness. Prepared in this manner, we enjoy joy and peace in dwelling on our meditative object and learn to deal wisely with disturbances and distractions, even turn them into supports and helpers of concentration. When the practitioner has progressed to this point, he behaves like the leopard in another simile,[20] which, "lurking in ambush, attacks its quarry—so also, dwelling in solitude, the yogi attains . . . mastery in the six higher mental powers (*abhiññā*)." And the fundamental paradigm for the development of abhiññā is provided by the four foundations of mindfulness (*satipatthāna*):

1. Contemplation of the body (*kāyānupassanā*)
2. Contemplation of the feelings (*vedanānupassanā*)
3. Contemplation of consciousness (*cittānupassanā*)
4. Contemplation of mental contents (*dhammānupassanā*)

As concerns preparation for the meditation session and attunement to the primary meditative object, the procedure for *satipatthāna* meditation is the same as that for mindfulness of breathing, which we have already practiced. The key difference lies in the attitude toward distractions, which are apprehended as secondary meditative objects. Their appearance is no longer a problem that is difficult to deal with. As a leopard lurks in ambush waiting for its quarry, the meditator dwells on the primary meditative object and waits for secondary objects to crop us, which he grasps with one of the four *satipatthāna-akkheyya* (body, feeling, mind, mental contents) by noting and labeling them. This grasping must be precise, without vacillation or offhandedness. The power consists in this. Only the grasping is important, not the properties or details of the object.

When a more specific label imposes itself, assign it immediately to one of the four foundations of mindfulness. Because of previous practice, you will probably assign things to the four foundations of *satipatthāna* in a second step, having first apprehended them as belonging to any of the following categories:

Light, color, sound, noise, warmth, movement, trembling, itching, stinging, pressure, lightness, etc.	*kāya* body
Pleasant, enjoyable, pleased, amused, bored, sadness, pain, indifference, etc.	*vedanā* feeling

Concentrated, scattered, tense, greedy, hate-filled, freed, etc.	*citta* state of mind
Thinking, wishing, planning, intending, trust, doubt, knowledge, etc.	*dhammā* mental content

As soon as you have apprehended the secondary object with one of the four *akkheyya*, hold it firmly in your grasp and observe its changes (not what and how it changes, but rather the change itself), its fading, falling apart, transforming—at some point its existence ceases. Experiencing this directly is the contemplation of impermanence (*anicca*), the most important component of *vipassanā* meditation.

2. GUARDING THE SENSE GATES

This exercise continues a subtle analysis of body and mind; through this, it enables us to prevent distortions of perception and blockages of the flow of feeling caused by craving and attachment. Moreover, it represents at the same time the experiential confirmation of a whole segment of the circle of conditioned arising:[21]

viññāna	→	*nāma-rūpa*	→	*āyatana*	→	*phassa*	→	*vedanā*	→	*tanhā*
conscious-ness	→	body-mind	→	sense bases	→	contact	→	feeling	→	craving

We know, even when our still imperfect mindfulness does not see it, that our discriminating consciousness (*viññāna*) is conditioned by bodily and mental formations (*sankhāra*). When, in the basic exercise of *satipatthāna-vipassanā*, we observe the quickly arising elements of consciousness, we become able with time to see directly how the experience of mind and body (*nāma-rūpa*) is conditioned by consciousness; this was spoken about earlier as the key experience of the basic exercise. In the contemplation of impermanence, we do not concern ourselves any further, however, with the connection of the individual *nāma-rūpa* moments to particular outer and inner spheres of the senses (*āyatana*), because there we are mainly concerned with training our awareness of process.

Guarding the sense gates, *indriyesu-gutta-dvāratā*, aims at training sense-perception. We learn to distinguish by which of the six sense bases a given experiencing is supported, which of the six *āyatana*, conditioned by an initially indeterminate impulse of *nāma-rūpa*, is activated. Modern experimental psychology investigates this process externally as an "incipient orientation reflex," which precedes the perception of the object by a specific sense organ. We, by contrast, are training in the inner mastery of subjective apprehension of the manifoldness of things through the six channels of information processing, which condition the contact (*phassa*) between the inner and outer bases of experiencing. The quality of the contact—that is, discrepancy, absence of interference, or concordance—is experienced as an unpleasant, neutral, or pleasant feeling, which triggers a craving (*tanhā*) based either on neurotic motivations or on an intention (*chanda*) of liberational will. The structures on which these cybernetic-epistemological processes are founded are illustrated in Diagrams 1 and 2 (pages 10 and 11) and then, in their liberational transformation, further explained beginning on page 240. But before going on to the actual exercise instructions, it would be an enjoyable experiment for you just now to have another look at the pages concerning our biocomputer. Turn back to page 9 and try to represent to yourself the difference between "the person who read it then" and yourself here and now!

We guard the sense gates with the purpose of bringing under conscious control the processes (not the contents) of perception and thus of maintaining their reliability. Whatever we perceive—whether pleasant, neutral or painful, ugly or beautiful—we must apprehend it truly and thoroughly (*yoniso*), so that we can deal with it realistically. As a result, we should be able to notice distortions that arise in sense perceptions owing to greed and aggression (also in their very subtle forms of attraction and repulsion) and so would provide encouragement for delusion-tainted information processing (*ayoniso manasikāra*). To bring deluded thought processes to a halt after they are already under way, however, we need further skills, which can be acquired through the exercise of reshaping suffering-producing processes; this will be explained later (see page 262). As already explained, according to Abhidhamma mental apprehension is also an entry into the sense gate of the mind. To reiterate, we gradually learn through practice to distinguish, first, which of the six inner bases (*āyatana*) has been activated in the sense contact (*phassa*), and later also what feeling quality (*vedanā*) the experience has. As with the previous exercise, it is beneficial to begin this exercise with mindfulness of breathing:

1. Remain for a few minutes with the breathing and then begin to watch for the arising of other contents of awareness.
2. Every experience that arises is quickly labeled and its fading away noted.

3. Experiences that last longer or repeat are assigned to one of the following bases (say the name of the base mentally):

Outer Multiplicity:	Āyatana:
pressure, warmth, etc.	body
images, color, light	eye
sounds, noises	ear
odors	nose
taste	tongue
thinking, planning, imagining, wishing, etc.	mind

4. As you make progress in the exercise, try to accomplish assignments to the inner bases with increasing speed.

As soon as we are able to assign all experiences to the inner six bases effortlessly, we can try, even without anchoring ourselves beforehand through the breathing, to note which of the six *āyatana* is activated each time. In complex situations that require coordination of several senses, sometimes the impression is created that two or more *āyatana* are activated at the same time; then we simply choose the most prominent. It is important to stick with the respective perceptual processes (for instance, seeing). The *Visuddhi Magga* tells us that we should cling neither to a detail of the visual object (for example, hand, foot, smile, speaking, looking away of the person seen), nor to the total appearance (*nimitta*) and evaluations of it, such as beautiful, ugly, impermanent, and so on. We stop as soon as we have seen something. Then we carry out the steps of the exercise described above. Experience shows that it is quite easy also to note the pleasant, neutral, or unpleasant feeling tones, once distinguishing among the six sense gates has been learned well.

To begin with, then, we learned to order the things of the sensual world (*kāma*) according to which sense bases they activate; then we learned to note which of the six inner *āyatana* is activated on each occasion, in doing which attention was placed on contact (*phassa*), that is, on the traffic at the sense gates. Finally, we note the feeling quality (*vedanā*) of the contact (without evaluation of the object, its details, or its mental representations). Now we are ready for the actual guarding of the sense gates. We also know that *satipatthāna-vipassanā* does not take a visualized image (*nimitta*) as its meditative object, but rather the bodily reality (*rūpa*) and the process of apprehending (*nāma*) its arising and passing away. Mindfulness as the guard of the sense gates notes and identifies arrivals with the help of wisdom, knowing about them that they can provoke an aggressive upheaval in the city of the mind if their advent is unpleasant and that they can trigger waves of greed if their advent is pleasant. To this extent, for mindfulness all objects that enter by the sense gates are suspicious. On the other hand, in the city of the mind itself (to pursue the simile), there are patently bad elements that only cause harm—greed and aggression. Therefore, mindfulness as guardian of the sense gates also looks inward to see if these bad elements are seeking to make an alliance with one of the arrivals. This is the essence of the exercise of guarding the sense gates.

Since mindfulness holds such a high status in the mental hierarchy, its presence at the gates of the five physical senses is enough to prevent collusion of the pleasant with greed and the unpleasant with aggression. At the mental gate, however, arriving objects that are neutral from the point of view of feeling can still enter into collusion with mental objects (*nimitta*) that bring an endless succession of suffering-producing processes in their train. For this, mindfulness must get help from the formations of right effort via the roads to power. How this takes place you will learn in the next exercises. Already in guarding the sense gates, we gain power, since systematic repetition of this method brings development of endurance and willpower (*viriya*), as we learned in the explanation for the road to power of willpower.

Guarding the sense gates is practiced both as a systematic meditation and as protection for our mental household in everyday situations by combining mindfulness with discriminating clear comprehension and with the right application of will. This strategy is composed of the following techniques:

1. Pause during the process of perception.
2. Apprehend the experience through the use of the *ak-kheyya* of the sense bases (*āyatana*).
3. Check to see if there is a tendency for pleasant to connect with greed and unpleasant with aggression.
4. Persevere forcefully with the apprehension through *ak-kheyya* and in this way affirm the power position of mindfulness as guardian of the sense gates.

3. RESHAPING SUFFERING-PRODUCING PROCESSES

This method is explained in detail in Sutta 20 of the *Majjhima Nikāya* (Theravada canon) under the name of *vitakka-santhāna*. *Santhāna*, "reshaping," means both a harmonious bringing together and a soothing process of unburdening. It relates to apprehension by means of thought (*vitakka*). The method consists of the paradigmatic unity of the following five techniques, which aim at an undisturbed flow of experiencing:

1. Replacement of the suffering-producing mental representations (*nimitta*) with others that are free from greed, aggression, and delusion and are therefore realistic
2. Interruption of the unwholesome processes through analysis of their perilous consequences (*ādīnava*)
3. Withdrawal of attention (*amanasikāra*) from spheres of suffering-producing thoughts and elimination of their traces in memory
4. Dismantling of unwholesome formations (*vitakka-sankhāra*) and neutralization of their energy
5. Clearly comprehended taming of the suffering-producing, hardened mental habit patterns by a higher consciousness (*cetasa*) and energetically crushing them until they melt away (*abhisantāpeti*)[22]

Dear reader, by now you are acquainted with the various *akkheyya* that make it possible for us to see how the apprehension of reality by means of mental representation (*nimitta*), thought (*vitakka*), and consciousness (*citta*) takes place. In the context of the strategies of ecstasy, we developed by means of thought apprehension that was free from greed, aggression, and delusion and that fitted together with the other constituents of ecstasy (joy, etc.). We cultivated concentration by using unitary images (*ekattārammana-nimitta, uggaha-nimitta*, etc.), which served as gateways to absorption. Later, in connection with the road to power of consciousness, we learned to distinguish between beautiful and suffering-producing *citta*. With the help of the same criteria (see the table on page 250), we can also distinguish between a kind of apprehension by means of thought that leads to beautiful consciousness and suffering-producing thought-apprehension (*vitakka*).

We may characterize *vitakka* as the mind's approach to reality, which it apprehends and labels. This thought-connection between word and reality can, however, if seen from the other side, also appear as a verbalization of reality or as a symbol or image formation. We saw this clearly in the analysis of levels of experiencing (pages 87ff.). When the sense gates are not guarded, mental representations (*nimitta*) can arise that are distorted by greed, aggression, or inadequate apprehension (*ayoniso manasikāra*). In the method of *vitakka-santhāna*, this possibility is reflected upon, and the first of the five techniques then provides the solution: to generate a mental representation that does not distort experiencing. The canonical text[23] gives a simile for this replacement of a suffering-producing representation by one that does not distort experiencing:

> As a skillful carpenter replaces a rough peg with a finer one, in the same way, the monk, when because of a mental representation unwholesome thoughts arise that are connected with greed, aggression, and delusion, should generate another mental representation that is connected with what is wholesome . . . then the unwholesome thoughts fade away and dissolve. With their fading away, his consciousness becomes firm in itself, settles, becomes unified and concentrated.
>
> When the monk generates another mental representation connected with what is wholesome, and those unwholesome thoughts still continue to arise for him that are connected with greed, aggression, and delusion, then he should look into the perilous consequences of these thoughts.

And with this the text goes on to the second of the five techniques, which should only be applied when it is clear that simple replacement does not work. We then wisely apprehend (*yoniso manasikāra*) the unwholesome processes, label them and very concretely weigh their painful consequences. Through mental representation of these dangerous, painful consequences (*ādīnava*), we arouse in ourselves revulsion toward the unwise apprehension by means of thought that would cause them and shake it off "as a handsome young person, decked out in good clothing, would, with horror and disgust, throw off the decaying carcass of a snake or a dog if someone would hang one around his neck."

The use of the third of the five techniques is in turn only appropriate when it becomes clear that the unwholesome thinking also cannot be stopped through the wise thinking of the second technique. We encountered a similar state of affairs when we were dealing with skepticism in chapter 7. Here too, the solution consists in leaving the sphere of thought by simply noting and labeling the fact that "thought processes are taking place" without getting involved in the content of the thoughts. We then pointedly pay the thought processes no more heed (*amanasikāra*) and direct mindfulness toward the awareness of bodily processes, movements, and everyday business. For this we use the strategy of reality anchoring described in chapter 5 and allow the overly excited thought processes plenty of time to wind down. In other words, we extinguish the traces in memory of the senselessly ever-recurring thoughts by ignoring them. This technique cannot be accounted for by either logical or psychological-theoretical considerations; its effectiveness, however, has been confirmed by many years of experience of countless meditators. The canonical text illustrates this technique with the following similes:

> As a man with very sharp sight who no longer wishes to see pictures that are in his field of vision either closes his eyes or looks away, in the same way, the monk, when he looks into the perilous consequences of unwholesome thoughts and nevertheless these unwholesome thoughts arise, should withdraw his attention from these thoughts . . . then the unwholesome thoughts fade away and dissolve. With their fading away, his consciousness becomes firm in itself, settles, becomes unified and concentrated.
>
> If he withdraws his attention from the unwholesome thoughts and still these thoughts continue to arise, then he should dismantle the formation of these thoughts.

The dismantling and pacifying of formations of apprehension by means of thought (*vitakka-sankhāra-santhāna*) is the fourth of the five techniques, which now—in contrast to the three discussed before—consists of painstaking work on the level of microanalysis. Now we concern ourselves neither with the objects of apprehension by means of thought nor with its consequences. Also we do not take any position with regard to the totality of its functioning (*amanasikāra* = withdrawal of attention), as we did in the third technique. In dismantling the formations of *vitakka*, we investigate the inner structure of the consciousness present at the time of the unwholesome apprehension by means of thought, as we did in developing the road to power of consciousness.[24] For the purposes of our Dhamma strategies it is enough to use those *akkheyya* with which you are already familiar. We check especially to see what currently present formations are wholesome, neutral, or unwholesome, what kind of status (for example, in connection with intention and resolve or as directive formations) they have in the present structure of consciousness, and how much energy (for example, joy, interest, sense of urgency, excitement, etc.) they have bound up in them. In brief, this fourth technique dissolves the seemingly solid totality of the disturbing thought-apprehension and brings its continued appearance to a stop. The canonical text illustrates the process with the following simile:

> Just as if a man was hurriedly walking along and the thought came to him, "Why am I walking along in such a hurry? I want to go a bit slower," and he went slower. And the

thought came to him, "But why am I walking altogether? I am just going to stop," and he stopped. And the thought came to him, "But why am I standing up? I am going to sit down," and he sat down. And the thought came to him, "Why should I be sitting? I want to lie down," and he lay down. And in this way this man discontinued the coarser movements and gave himself over to the more subtle ones. Just in this way, a monk, when he immediately stops thinking with that thought-apprehension, pays it no heed, and still evil unwholesome thoughts with greed, aggression, or delusion arise, should direct his attention to how this thought-agitation is composed and thus set it to rest. While directing his attention to how the thought-agitation is composed and setting it to rest, the evil unwholesome thoughts with greed, aggression, and delusion fade away and dissolve. And when they are done away with, the heart (consciousness) becomes still, settles, becomes unified and concentrated.

Although the five techniques of *vitakka-santhāna* are presented in a canonical text about advanced meditation, we can certainly use them in everyday life. They can be applied in several spheres of experiencing. In the framework of the basic exercise of *satipatthāna-vipassanā*, we can apply the techniques we have mastered well and so eliminate distractions. In contrast to eliminating disturbances to concentration (*nīvarana*; see page 202), in this case the disturbances to *vipassanā* are not suppressed, but rather neutralized and dissolved. Though we do take the distractions as secondary objects of *vipassanā*, we do not give them too much weight, but get rid of them as quickly and lightly as possible by using the techniques in order to remain uninterruptedly in the sphere of the main object.

If the distraction is too great, then we find ourselves in any case outside the sphere of the main object, that is, the four foundations of mindfulness and their impermanence. In such a case, we take the unwholesome apprehension by means of thought as the main object and investigate its structure through the systematic application of all five techniques. Such an investigation of structure (*vitakka-sankhāra-santhāna*) is also appropriate when a particular suffering-producing thought-apprehension stubbornly repeats itself in daily life. Then we should allow enough time for a thorough confrontation with this stubborn material in a meditation session especially devoted to it. Otherwise we must try within the practical limits of everyday-life situations to replace the suffering-producing processes, to dismantle them or consider their consequences, and to stop them.

It can be seen from the explanations up to this point that the technique of dismantling and neutralizing formations requires special circumstances: the well-regulated context of systematic meditation. You have certainly noticed in reading the accounts of these techniques that you have already used the first three techniques of *vitakka-santhāna* in the strategies of sympathy, both in meditation and in pausing between daily-life actions. Then you chose how you wanted to act on the basis of apprehension and reflection. In the kind of situation in which this fourth technique is applied, the approach to outward action is: "Don't act!" and "Don't draw any conclusions for daily-life matters from current apprehension and reflection!" With clear comprehension of the sphere of experiencing (*gocara-sampajaññā*), which at the moment has nothing to do with outer reality, we avoid decisions for action. In this way we prevent inappropriate actions and rest in a seeing nonaction.

The canonical descriptions of the techniques of *vitakka-santhāna* especially cast light on the energetic aspect of *vipassanā*. We have already dealt in detail with the epistemological aspect of *vipassanā*. For this reason, we shall only recall at this point that *vipassanā* means an analysis, a dismantling, and an experiential penetration of the impermanence of all phenomena. Literally, the word *vipassanā* means "discriminating seeing" (*vi* = "apart," "in two," but also "intensification" and "clarity"; *passati* = "seeing"). Practice of *vipassanā* makes us capable of sharp sight, as though our inner eye were equipped with a magnifying glass and a slow-motion apparatus. To illustrate with a simile: The light of mindfulness, which is like sun rays, can be focused and directed by the magnifying glass of concentration, so that the eye of wisdom (the sun) can also see in the shadows of unwholesomeness. And beyond that—this relates to the energy aspect of *vipassanā*—in this intensified light, obstructive rigidities will melt and ugly growths will be burned out in the seed. Unwholesomeness grows from the seeds of greed or aggression and proliferates in formations of suffering-producing thought-apprehension (*akusala-vitakka-sankhāra*).

We have already discussed at various points how action is generated from consciousness. As the most subtle form of minimal action, we described the smile (*hasita*) of the Enlightened One, which is a bodily expression (*kāya-viññatti*) of the joyful consciousness of having overcome suffering. We also saw how thought-apprehension (*vitakka*) as "verbalization" is a step in the direction of verbal utterance (*vacī-viññatti*). We also looked into the way in which truthfulness and genuineness mean a concordance between word and reality, conscious-

ness and action. In the discussions on the development of *sīla*, we
saw that, nevertheless, genuineness and truthfulness do not mean
a compulsion to manifest our experience in words and deeds that
would bring suffering. Thus we saw that it is not necessary for us to
speak or act in a problematic way—or at all—when our inner situation is problematic. And working with our own greed or our own aggression is a highly problematic inner situation! Not acting, not saying anything: that may seem to you to be a cheap piece of advice. How
is one supposed to achieve that, especially when in a state of inner
upheaval?

In daily-life situations we could use the tactic of retreat, which was
explained as part of the *brahma-vihāra* strategies (pages 177f.), or some
other means of controlling and composing ourselves. If we do not
wish to speak, we could press our hand over our mouth or clamp our
teeth tightly together to lend emphasis to our resolve. Such external
aids actually evoke corresponding inner movements of the mind.
Here we find a reversal of the principle of the simile, whereby inner
mental movements are expressed in terms of outer events. Before we
go ahead to the explanation of the fifth technique of *vitakka-santhāna*,
try to find in your own treasury of experience a few examples of how
you sometimes express your moods in terms of similes. (For example:
"I've had it up to here!" or "I feel like running away," and so on.) Also
recall a few occasions on which you changed your mood through
an outer action. (For example, by adopting an upright posture you
evoked a sense of moral uprightness, or by holding onto an object
you found an inner reference point.)

The fifth technique of *vitakka-santhāna* tames suffering-producing
processes by raising and imposing a goal-directed consciousness
(*cetasa*):

> My resolve is: to be free from suffering and the causes of
> suffering!
> May I be happy, may all beings be happy!
> This high consciousness learned in *mettā-bhāvanā* is what
> I want!
> With full force I now subdue the energy of this impulse
> recognized as unwholesome and restrain it!
> I direct this energy exclusively into the happiness-
> furthering, beautiful, and peacefully flowing experiencing
> of freedom!

Taken out of context, the above sentences would be no more than
a meaningless soliloquy. The mindful reader, however, will recognize that they are a verbal formulation of directive formations (*abhi-*

sankhāra) through which some of the skills explained and learned through practice in this book are being coordinated into a Dhamma strategy.

The complete practice of *vitakka-santhāna* leads to liberation in many ways, according to the canonical text—through release from being driven by craving (*tanhā*) and through independence of thought processes ("He is now a master of thought processes; whatever thoughts he wants to think he will think, whatever thoughts he does not want to think he will not think"). With clear comprehension of this purpose (*attha*) and with clear comprehension of the suitability (*sappāya*) of the five techniques of *vitakka-santhāna*, this method will only be used when the suffering-producing thought-apprehension resists treatment by the first four techniques. In this connection, the canonical text illustrates the fifth technique in the following way:

> When the monk apprehends the thought-apprehension associated with greed, aggression, and delusion dismantled into its formations and this unwholesome thought-apprehension still continues to arise for him, then, with teeth tightly clamped together and tongue pressed against the gums, he should subdue the arising of this unwholesome consciousness, suppress it, and eradicate it.[25] Then the unwholesome thought-apprehension fades away and dissolves. With its fading away, his consciousness becomes firm in him, settles, becomes unified and concentrated.

It is not at all true that there would be "nothing left" if you, dear reader, were to destroy all forms of greed, aggression, and delusion in your mind. To destroy something, to eradicate it, incinerate it—do you, perhaps, shrink from the task? What do you do with your garbage? For many people it is taboo to think about destruction, although in actual fact they participate in the torment and destruction of many sentient beings through their unconsidered lifestyle. In eradicating the roots of suffering from our minds, strictly speaking, we are destroying nothing at all. We can only tame the energy of unwholesomeness, suppress it, and drive it out of the suffering-producing formations in order to release it for wholesome use. Also, a thought cannot be destroyed: the unwholesome apprehension by means of thought was there, after all, and we cannot make that unhappen. What was no longer exists when something else exists. What is present in consciousness when the fifth technique of *vitakka-santhāna* is used is a wise apprehension and a liberational resolve of will to disapprove of the unwholesome consciousness just past and to generate a wholesome one to come. In other words, we incinerate the unwholesome thoughts and split the suffering-producing thought-apprehension, which would otherwise harden in our minds into a nucleus. And something else: in such nuclear fission and incineration of unwholesome thoughts, there are no waste products, and the radiation from the process only does us good!

The first half of the reshaping of suffering-producing processes by *vitakka-santhāna*, the dismantling and subduing of unwholesomeness, has been presented in detail here. The skills for bringing forth wholesome material have already been communicated previously in this book. The second half of the reshaping, the development of the causes of happiness, I leave with confidence, dear reader, to your own personal richness of ideas, to your free discretion and your creativity.

4. TURNING AWAY FROM SUFFERING

Through the power of *satipatthāna-vipassanā* no reality is suppressed and no energy destroyed. All things are wisely apprehended and all energies liberationally utilized. Even energies connected with suffering as well as things that are not beautiful are made use of for liberational purposes—and indeed very purposefully in the process of turning away (*nibbidā*), which eventually leads to a complete conquest (*pahāna*) over all the causes of suffering. Turning away from suffering is not turning toward something, but rather opening up to the realization of happiness. This principle holds true even for attainment of the supreme happiness of enlightenment: turning away from suffering-producing distortions of reality and opening up to the happiness of the supreme reality.

In the practical exercise of turning away, we use right techniques of working with emotions and mental movements such as fear, horror, disgust, aversion, boredom, yearning, pining, and longing, which for the most part are all too real to be easily made to fade away. The repelling experiential quality and energy of such emotions and movements of the mind can, however, quite suitably be directed against the causes of suffering. On the other hand, the energy of attraction can serve as a force working upward toward liberation and openness once it is freed from its connection with suffering-oriented objects and images. The practical execution of techniques of turning away involves a combination of methods known to us: guarding the sense gates, thorough investigation (*vīmamsā*) of objects and images, and development of longing for liberation on the road to power of intention. The techniques of turning away can, however, only be successful if they are carried out within the framework of the following paradigms of the three experiential penetrations or *pariññā:*

1. Penetration of the known (*ñāta-pariññā*)
2. Penetration of the common characteristics (*tīrana-pariññā*)
3. Penetration that overcomes (*pahāna-pariññā*)

The first penetration is thorough wise apprehension by means of the terminology of *akkheyya* of all phenomena as what they really are— bodily sensations, feelings, states of consciousness (mental events or shifts), and objects of consciousness. It is helpful not to let this process of cognition become too detailed. We should keep the classification of the known as simple as possible, so as to be able, without distraction, to make the transition to the penetration of common characteristics. Part of the penetration of the known is thorough apprehension (*yoniso manasikāra*) of the relationships between phenomena and investigative reflection (*vīmamsā*) in their way of functioning. Total penetration of the known is at the same time a transcendence of the sphere of phenomena and of the terminology of *akkheyya*, which is pithily portrayed in the canonical verse on page 269.

The penetration of common characteristics (*tīrana-pariññā*), the second of the three penetrations, is no longer related to the experiential manifoldness of *papañca*. All *akkheyya* that are used to order the manifoldness have by now fulfilled their function, and we now let go of them. During the penetration of common characteristics, awareness is exclusively concentrated on a characteristic that is common to all phenomena. Such a characteristic is, for example, impermanence (*anicca*) as we experienced it in the basic exercise of *satipatthāna-vipassanā*.[26] The transition to penetration of common characteristics is an experiential change of epistemological level, which was elucidated in another connection on pages 82ff. Ripened penetration of common characteristics changes smoothly into penetration that overcomes (*pahāna-pariññā*). These transitions constitute turning away from suffering. As a result of this turning away, the evil influences (*āsava*) that are the driving force perpetuating suffering dwindle away. Turning away is at the same time an opening, an opening full of confidence that release from all suffering is near.

The whole process of turning away (*nibbidā*) can be neither accomplished intellectually nor determined by will. To attain turning away, uninterrupted intensive practice of *satipatthāna-vipassanā* for weeks is sometimes necessary. At that point the three experiential penetrations develop as a by-product of progress in the systematic practice of *satipatthāna-vipassanā* meditation. All that we can do intellectually is to assimilate knowledge concerning the three penetrations. This is the purpose of the exercise in turning away from suffering explained here. Complete turning away leads to disengagement (*virāga*), which in turn makes possible the liberational leap (*abhisamaya*). This happens at the moment (*samaya*) when the world of manifoldness (*papañca*) as a whole is ordered epistemologically by the three *pariññā* and experientially penetrated.

When progress in liberational insight takes place through systematic practice of *satipatthāna-vipassanā*, then the experience of fright, boredom, and longing also make their appearance. Such experiences, however, are not related to individual things in the everyday world of manifoldness. Rather they are an expression of progressive turning away from the suffering-tainted manifold world (*papañca*) as a whole. Thus we become frightened when suffering-ridden phenomena repeat themselves in our own lives, we feel a sense of urgency (*samvega*), penetrate our own ignorance, and let go of the craving that binds us to the repetitions. When we pervasively recognize the constant repetition of the circle of conditioned arising (*paticca-samuppāda*) and penetrate in a way connected to our own experiencing, then there is nothing left but to find it boring. Disgusted, we turn away. The meaning (*attha*) is clear: we no longer wish to suffer, we also do not want any cheap consolations or provisory satisfactions—we long for liberation (*vimutti*). Such experiences of fright, disgust, and longing are further inspirations in working toward the conditioned arising of freedom, which will be discussed in the last chapter section of this book.

5. EXPERIENCING EMPTINESS

Turning away from suffering, once successfully accomplished, leads to the peaceful experiencing of an emptiness that is called *suññatā*. The attainment of *suññatā* is the highest fruit of liberational progress in *vipassanā*, which can also be described as perfected clear comprehension of nondelusion; on page 140 we also described it metaphorically as a kind of evacuation that stopped the building of castles in the air. The experiencing of *suññatā* is considered a gateway to supreme liberation, to entry into the stream of enlightenment (*sotāpatti*). A person who succeeds in entering emptiness is always able to realize the experience later as an object of meditation. But then also, the way into the free space of *suññatā* is conditioned by the regular procedure of *satipatthāna-vipassanā*, the steps of which we know from previous exercises. Now let us try to make clear, at least in broad outlines, what *suññatā* is, and also, particularly, what experiences of emptiness have nothing to do with *suññatā*.[27] To begin with, let us look at some rather widespread false interpretations of emptiness, which stem from inadequate understanding.

A first type of false understanding of *suññatā* is based on experiences of gaps in perception or memory. These are experiences of an empty consciousness, or rather a nonconsciousness, in which all awareness of any phenomenon is absent. Such gaps in experiencing appear often in the meditation of a beginner but are also known to many who have never meditated. After starting more advanced meditation, it usually happens when the attention is fatigued and someone "succeeds" in soothing the mind by means of a lapse in mindfulness.

Another false notion of *suññatā* arises when the perceived emptiness of an object is fixated upon. This could be the emptiness of a container, an empty window, or an empty sheet of paper. When a person solidifies such an experience of emptiness by believing in its ontological reality and then thinks about it, then he might perhaps think he is meditating on *suññatā*.

Another type of false understanding is the mere thought of emptiness as a word without any connection to reality or any ontological attribute. Emptiness can also be a result of philosophical deduction, a conceptual abstract. Such an abstract concept can afterward have signs or symbols attributed to it that can be meditatively visualized. In this visualization, the abstract concept becomes a mental representation or image (*nimitta*), which then exists as an autonomous object of consciousness.

Sometimes very advanced meditative experiences that are very intense and extraordinary are wrongly held to be experiences of *suññatā*. These could be ecstatic experiences of bliss, of a seemingly ontological unity of all things, profound peace, or pure light. Even a person who is experienced in meditation might develop craving-filled attachment to such spectacular and intense experiences. This leads to exclusion of the connection to reality and thus hinders real progress toward liberation.

A combination of the last two false interpretations of emptiness actually appears in the younger schools of Buddhism, which were predominantly mystically or philosophically oriented. *Suññatā* is then presented through a kind of mental acrobatics as identical with *samsāra* and *nirvāṇa*. However, the original tradition of Abhidhamma, which is practically based on liberational way of life, recognizes such spectacular experiences and deductive results caused by attachment as obscurations of insight (*vipassanā-upak-kilesa*). Abhidhamma teaches the basic attitude of openness toward all experiences. This is an openness free from any attachment and any belief in an identity.

Suññatā is emptiness of mind that is without any interpolation of mental representations (*nimitta*) or concepts (*akkheyya*) and that is free from distortions resulting from greed, aggression, or arrogance. Thus it makes possible a direct experience of reality. When awareness is free from all obscurations (*kilesa*), then reality is fully experienced.

THE CONDITIONED ARISING OF FREEDOM

It is simple to be happy when we know the Dhamma strategies and use them in everyday life. The Dhamma strategies make possible more than just skillful dealing with the facts of life; they are methods for liberating our way of life, for increasing our capacity for happiness. In daily practice, that means on the one hand that we apprehend events wisely and integrate them harmoniously into our mental ecosystem, and on the other hand that we use them as a field of practice to develop our mental powers and to free ourselves from any dependence on inner and outer evil influences. Both lead to an increase in our competence and freedom of choice in acting as well as in our capacity for happiness in experiencing. In meditation we learn the skills that are the prerequisites for competence in everyday life. All the instructions for exercises and other explanations in this book are there for these purposes. They unite the two goals of freedom of choice and capacity for happiness into a single efficacious methodology that provides you with the power to do what you really fundamentally want and to live happily with all and everything, no matter what comes to you from the outside.

In looking back at this point over all our practices and the knowledge that we have gathered, the question might easily arise, what is most important in all this? This question can only be answered by each person for him- or herself. And even then the answer will come out differently depending on where we are in our lives and how we are currently viewing reality. If we were compelled to organize everything into concepts intellectually, we would now attempt to draw up a theoretical system about the Dhamma strategies. But to what end? As if theories and philosophical ideas produced happiness or were themselves wise! We devoted an entire chapter to finding out the importance of knowledge for a happy life, and it would be inappropriate to repeat all that now. But let us return to the question of what is of greatest importance among the Dhamma strategies and try to bring out the principles essential for the practice. If we think about the Dhamma strategies in this way, we encounter two motifs that run through the whole book: wise relationship to reality and openhearted joy.

I would like to invite you, dear reader, to try a further experiment in which the presence of reality anchoring and taking joy in experiencing is compared in two persons. Bring to mind two comparably problematic situations that actually happened, one of which was lived through by a "control" person with no knowledge of the Dhamma strategies and the other by a person who had practiced the Dhamma strategies. In order to meet the criteria of scientific experiment, the best would be to use yourself, just as you are now, as the person experienced in the Dhamma strategies. As the "control" person, take the person you were before you became acquainted with the Dhamma strategies.[28] The evaluative criteria for anchoring in reality could be how holistically, how thoroughly, and how free from preconceptions the situation was experienced by both persons—in other words, to what extent wise apprehension (*yoniso manasikāra*) was present. For the evaluation of openhearted joy, the criteria could be to what extent joyful interest (*pīti*) in innovative solutions and in the improvement of one's own skills was present and how much energy the joy mobilized to loosen up attachment to the "good old familiar" repetitions. Do take the time now to carry out this experiment—which will be more relevant for you personally than all other scientific experiments put together—in peace and quiet.

In evaluating and reflecting on our experiment, we may, if we like, use the technical concepts and methods of the Abhidhamma that we have worked with thus far. The following expositions are meant to provide you with support, stimulate your capabilities, and awaken the treasury of experiences connected with the paradigms you have learned. To begin with, let us focus briefly on that which is most important—what wise apprehension means for us in problematic situations and how to experience joy in finding solutions to problems and in shaping the causes of happiness. We will subsequently turn our attention to wise apprehension in situations that are not problematic.

Wise apprehension is thorough and total. We are familiar with this thoroughness from the practice of bodily anchoring in reality and from the analytic penetration of seemingly solid mental and emotional complexes and recognition of their motives and roots. We practiced thoroughness in dismantling things and events into their component parts, in experiencing their impermanence, and in distinguishing between word and reality. Thus we do not permit ourselves to be overly impressed when something major, lasting, overwhelming, or promising presents itself, nor do we let ourselves be led into error by biased, abstract, comprehensive, or purely logical general statements. We practiced apprehending reality in all its concrete component parts, relating to all parts with mindfulness, and observing real connections and conditional links—that is, those not composed of conceptual associations. Therein consists the total or holistic quality of wise apprehension. Wise apprehension uses only global paradigms as knowledge matrices (*yoni*), ones that do not exclude parts of reality and do see things in their contexts. This total approach also takes into account the ethical aspect of each event, that is, its significance for happiness and for the liberation of awareness.

Most explained and most practiced was the circular paradigm of conditioned arising (*paticca-samuppāda*), which fulfills all requirements of thoroughness and totality. Thorough and total apprehension happens with the purpose of overcoming the repetitious patterns of suffering that are apprehended and opening a way to the absence of suffering. There are several exits from the circle of the conditioned arising of suffering. In this book, I have intentionally dealt only with those that are usable in the everyday application of Dhamma strategies. The one exit that is shown in Diagram 5 (page 58) consists of attempting, whenever possible, to keep the realistically flowing process of experience (*vedanā*) free from defilements and blockages resulting from greed and aggression. We practiced subduing the various formations of greed and aggression, which are the instinctive expression of craving (*tanhā*), by guarding the sense gates and reshaping suffering-producing processes. We became acquainted with the four magical roads to power and thus discovered in the liberational intention, in the will to freedom, an alternative to being driven by *tanhā*. Thus we have means at our disposal to weaken suffering-producing formations and so increase our power to make free decisions.

The strategies of power represent neither a way of acting against other people nor techniques for controlling and changing the environment; rather they aim at raising the level of power we have over ourselves and at making us independent of determination from the outside. This goal is realized by cultivating trust (*saddhā*) in our own competence and capabilities, stopping evil influences (*āsava*), and broadening our liberated freedom of choice. For this, we use the exercises of *satipatthāna-vipassanā*. These are methods for analytic penetration of the conditions of suffering and for transcending the sphere of suffering. From a technical point of view, this amounts to purification of the mind, seeing through suffering-producing programs, dissolving greed- and aggression-tainted program elements, to the point of discriminating insight into consciousness and the mind-body (*nāma-rūpa*). This leads to complete overcoming of all causes of suffering, to enlightenment. This overcoming of suffering by meditative dissolution of its causative conditions is, however, a result of very advanced practice, which requires mastery of wise apprehension (*yoniso manasikāra*) and experiential investigation (*vīmamsā*) both in everyday life and in systematic meditation. This overcoming then ripens in *vipassanā* meditation as a fruit of repeated insights into conditionality. We know with the clarity of our own experience that only that suffers, is subject to disease and disorder, declines and dies, which arises or is born as an individual. We know that the condition for the suffering and death of every being, every formation, and every consciousness is present in its birth. In this way we gradually gain insight into all the conditional links of *paticca samuppāda* (see Diagram 13). In meditation we investigate the conditioned arising of suffering in the reverse order, until we also gain experiential knowledge concerning the mutual conditionality of individual consciousness (*viññāna*) and the mind-body (*nāma-rūpa*). We wisely apprehend this mutual conditionality and as a result are able to transcend it. Such a transcendence dethrones ignorance (*avijjā*) in our experiencing once and for all, as well as the formations conditioned by it. With this the circle of conditioned arising is broken through and the victory over death achieved. Until we have experienced certainty about this in our own realization, this meditative way out remains a hypothesis for us—but a hypothesis in which we can trust (*saddhā*), because the steps that confirm it are known to us.[29] This exit consists mainly in wise apprehension of suffering (*dukkha*) and cultivating trust in the proven steps to liberation.

The wise apprehension of suffering and the growth of trust in our own competence and capabilities into a confidence that permits a liberational unfolding of joy—these are fundamental conditions for any real liberation. All the Dhamma strategies discussed in this book were chosen with the intention of providing you, the reader, with concrete procedures that open a way practicable in everyday situations to a happy life. Let us next apprehend the way to greater happiness as an exit from the spheres subject to suffering. This exit will be explained using a paradigm that incidentally has also proved itself in the framework of psychoanalytic and client-centered psychotherapy. In psychotherapy, the concrete process remains limited, however, to particular threads of suffering that are determined by the client him- or herself. But this same approach, as broadened by especially talented people, can be used by itself as a liberational strategy. For this, we must be capable of reaching a comprehensive understanding of the entire matrix of *paticca-samuppāda* for apprehending everyday events and of systematically developing joy (*pīti*) in our meditation exercises.

In setting up this Dhamma strategy independently it is extremely important that a balance of wise apprehension of suffering and meditative unfolding of joy be constantly maintained, because without the guidance of someone experienced in Abhidhamma and without the

Diagram 13. Meditative Penetration of Conditioned Arising

noble friendship (*kalyāna-mittatā*) of a wise companion, a person could, in spite of the best knowledge, easily slip into an extreme of timidity or foolhardiness, depending on whether suffering or joy dominate experience in the long term.

All necessary techniques and knowledge are available to you in this book. You need only add the metaprogram to devise the strategy for the conditioned arising of freedom. The metaprogram is illustrated in Diagram 14 (pages 280–81) so that wise apprehension of suffering is on the left side and the stages of the unfolding of happiness are on the other. Wise apprehension (*yoniso manasikāra*), which we practiced for the first time in chapter 3 as a practical application of liberational wisdom (*paññā*), takes place here in the following steps:

1. In connection with events experienced as unpleasant, unsatisfying, and painful (*dukkha*), we understand the causes of suffering, which consist of reality-distorting ignorance (*avijjā*) and frustrated craving (*tanhā*).
2. Next we recall the paradigm of the Four Noble Truths (cf. page 49) and at the same time our own liberational capabilities.
3. Thinking over the painful event, we try to see it as globally and completely as possible and in so doing, we especially try not to detach our own subjective part from the whole. For this we use the paradigm of conditioned arising.
4. After apprehending the event with the help of the paradigm of conditioned arising, we see the effects of previous karmic formations and of the ignorance that conditioned them on the interaction of the individual parts of the event. We also see the repetition of similar events, and we know how their (re-)birth is already conditioned by the attachment and becoming in the preceding events.
5. After having holistically investigated the repetitions in this manner, we purposively work out the fact that that which begins by birth (arising) is necessarily subject to dysfunction and ends in decay and death. What has arisen and died and not been wisely apprehended only perpetuates a similar ignorance and leaves behind formations that in turn condition a similar suffering.

Thus in these five steps suffering is wisely apprehended. As soon as this has taken place successfully, the key experience for conditioned arising of freedom has been prepared. This key to the exit from

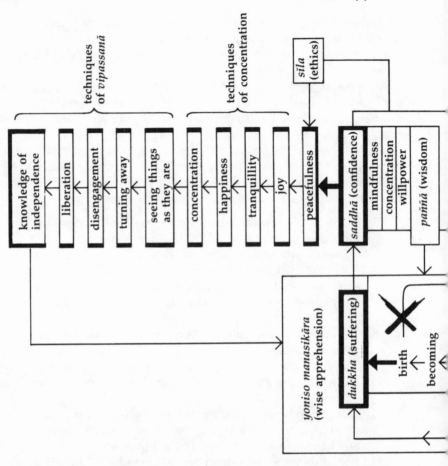

the circle of conditioned arising consists in not permitting a further similar event characterized by suffering to simply die without having used this birth for the experiential penetration and overcoming of suffering. In this way, the birth of every event, every being—our own birth as a human—can provide the condition for liberation.

No longer to die into ignorance, no longer to be reborn into the same kind of suffering-tainted consciousness, but instead to wisely apprehend *dukkha* and steer toward the exit, to find *saddhā*, confidence, in the liberational Good Dhamma- -this is a key experience that cannot be arrived at simply by thinking. It cannot be conceptually constructed, but must arise out of wise apprehension; it must grow organically. At this point please look once again at Diagram 14.

On the left side of the diagram is the cycle of suffering, which—apprehended in its totality as *dukkha*—brings us onto a higher level of

Diagram 14. Conditioned Arising of Freedom

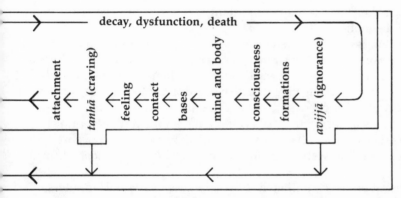

experience on which the conditioned arising of freedom develops. On the right side of the diagram, the actual conditioned arising of liberation is represented. Let us now look at the individual relationships of conditionality. First, let us notice that the strived-for liberation itself is in the next-to-last place and still higher above it is the knowledge of independence. This is because liberation is a freedom of which we are aware. We know that we are independent, that all compulsive motivation is extinguished, that all influences have dwindled away. Now the will is free. When liberation has been realized, we also recognize our freedom, (*āsava-khaya*, literally, "dwindling away of influences"). This knowledge of independence (*āsavakkhaya-ñāna*) is only all-pervasive, however, in the case of a fully enlightened buddha or arhat, because only through complete enlightenment do we become free from all compulsive motivation. A freedom fighter who is treading on the path of seeing or the path of power recognizes stage by stage from what evil influences he has freed himself and to which ones he is still sometimes subject. The degree of knowledge of independence is thus conditioned by the level of liberation.

Liberation (*vimutti*) is conditioned by disengagement (*virāga*). Disengagement is the fading away of longing, the cessation of drivenness. In complete enlightenment, even the longing for liberation ceases. Enlightenment is thus not only a fading away of longing, but finally also a fading away of fading away.

Disengagement presupposes turning away (*nibbidā*). Turning away from suffering was presented in detail as an exercise of *satipatthāna-vipassanā* on pages 270ff.

Turning away is conditioned by seeing-things-as-they-are (*yathā-bhūta-ñāna-dassana*). When we know through direct experiential clarity what things are suffering-tainted, then we let go of them, turn away, and open to the cessation of suffering. Such liberation-oriented "seeing wisdom" is the most important task of all the exercises of *vipassanā* meditation.

Seeing-things-as-they-are is conditioned by concentration (*samādhi*), since only concentrated awareness is free from distractions and is thus able to investigate a given directly apprehended phenomenon thoroughly. This investigative direct seeing does not—by contrast to some concentration exercises—take a mental image (*nimitta*) as object; it consists in seeing the reality of mental and bodily (*nāma-rūpa*) processes. This is where the transition from the practice of concentration exercises to the systematic practice of *satipatthāna-vipassanā* takes place.

Concentration is conditioned by happiness (*sukha*). Happiness means here the pleasant feeling of serenity and the happiness of contentment resulting from success of the meditative exercise. It is the happiness of that contentment through which miscellaneous tendencies to become conscious of new contents or to achieve something have subsided. Evenly flowing awareness only further intensifies in relation to what is present, thus the mind becomes concentrated in happiness.

Happiness is conditioned by tranquillity (*passaddhi*). This is the twofold tranquillity that follows high-flying ecstatic rapture: tranquillity of the body (*kāya-passaddhi*), which maintains a fullness of energy free from all intractability and tension, and tranquillity of consciousness (*citta-passaddhi*), which is characterized by wakefulness, mobility, and flexibility of mind. Such tranquillity cannot be fabricated; it comes about as a by-product, so to speak, of successful concentration practice.

Tranquillity is conditioned by joy (*pīti*). Here it once again becomes clear that for the conditioned arising of liberation a high energy potential must be present. Such energy-laden tranquillity arises from the harmonization of joyful impulses, which are first increased in ecstasy and then become refined and harmonized. This twofold liberational tranquillity is conditioned by the refinement of ecstatic joy; it is the transcendence of ecstasy.

Joy is conditioned by peacefulness (*pāmojja*). This inner peace is characterized by the absence of all self-accusation and bad conscience, because we know that the ethical principles of *sīla* have been fulfilled. We have generated a flawless subjective basis, which guarantees us sovereignty in our own inner household as well as harmony in the mental ecosystem. This is partly the result of applying Dhamma strategies in everyday life, and partly the result of conscious reliance on the wisdom (*paññā*) of the Good Dhamma as it is taught in the Abhidhamma. *Pāmojja* is the composed and joyous contentment of everyday consciousness, which has been freed from greed, aggression, inertia, agitation, and doubt and therefore makes possible unobstructed unfolding of more intensive levels of joy.

Peacefulness is conditioned by confidence (*saddhā*). The capacity for trust and how it is developed into a mental power by testing and verifying trustworthiness, how it then, in the form of confidence, stabilizes and clarifies the mind—this we have already considered in various contexts. We illustrated the effects of confidence in the similes about the magic stone that makes water clear. At this point, let us recall once again that trust in the liberational teaching that reaches to the point of confidence can be cultivated only in balance with the other mental powers.

Confidence is conditioned by wise apprehension of suffering, *dukkha*. Wise apprehension (*yoniso manasikāra*) is a technique of the mental power *paññā* in which the powers of will, concentration, confidence, and mindfulness (which harmonizes them all) also participate. These relationships are shown in the lower right-hand section of Diagram 14; they represent the inner context of the key experience of the conditioned arising of freedom.

Happiness can be lived; it cannot be theoretically thought out and cannot be technically fabricated. The art of living happily consists in being free to allow happiness in ourselves and others. The better things are going for the people around me, the better the outer conditions are for things going well for me as well. My happiness, however, is not only conditioned by outer circumstances that cause short-lived experiences of happiness. Rather the quality of my life is determined by my capacity for happiness. Capacity for happiness is a result of maturity as a human being that is experienced as personal power. This power gives us freedom from determination from the outside and freedom for liberational shaping of inner and outer circumstances, which we can make into conditions for happiness. Happiness itself, however, cannot be fabricated; we can only let it arise as a fruit of wholesome action. The conditions for a happiness-filled, liberational way of life can be created through the application of Dhamma strategies in everyday life and in systematic meditation. The paradigm of conditioned arising of freedom just explained makes it possible for us to unify all the Dhamma strategies introduced in this book into a self-determined way of life. This liberational way of life also gives us the power for effective political involvement, for culturally significant creation, and for making recognized contributions to society. But the greatest power consists in our maintaining an overview of our own experience and not losing ourselves in the manifoldness. The manifold Dhamma strategies also have the single simple goal of helping us find confidence in ourselves, because being happy is simple. The Dhamma strategies open up the freedom for this happiness.

Appendix: Basic Concepts

Practical application of Abhidhamma in everyday life requires a familiarity with these six basic concepts:

1. *Sīla* is the reliable subjective basis for all strategies. It gives us support and protection in forging ahead into the unknown and in experimenting with new things. *Sīla* is practiced concretely as self-regulation according to the principles of a liberational ethics.

2. *Wise apprehension (yoniso manasikāra)* is practiced as a holistic epistemological technique and a systematic method for training mental skills. Wise apprehension utilizes matrices (*yoni*) that test the total framework of relationships of events and the reality anchoring of awareness (*yathā-bhūta*).

3. *Clear comprehension (sampajañña)* of the respective spheres of experiencing (*gocara*), as well as clear comprehension of suitability and purpose (*attha*) of ways of apprehending and acting, contributes toward systematic training of the mind and a meaningful way of life.

4. The four foundations of mindfulness (*satipatthāna*) make it possible for us experientially to divide the inconceivable manifoldness of the world into four realities, and as such to master and transcend them: (1) bodily awareness, (2) feeling, (3) states of consciousness, (4) contents of awareness.

5. *The five mental powers (bala)* are present in every person as faculties of knowledge, trust, will, mental concentration, and presence of mind, which can be cultivated meditatively into the mental powers of wisdom (*paññā*), confidence (*saddhā*), willpower (*viriya*), concentration (*samādhi*), and mindfulness (*sati*). The unfolding of these powers is an important condition for a way of life liberated from all outer as well as inner forms of suppression and distortion.

6. *Conditioned arising (paticca-samuppāda)* is the basic paradigm of the Abhidhamma. Experiential recognition of the conditioned arising of suffering permits us to break out of and transcend the cycle of suffering-producing repetition. Knowledge of the conditions of happiness gives life orientation and meaning.

Notes

INTRODUCTION

1. This liberation means that we make ourselves independent of outside influence and limitations and yet preserve responsibility within the framework of the whole. (Editor's note)
2. A theoretical overview of Abhidhamma as compared with the paradigms of science is given in M. Frýba & B. Vogt: Sīlabbata: Virtuous Performance, The Empirical Basis for the Science of Buddhist Psychology, *Sri Lanka Journal of Buddhist Studies* 3 (1989), 1–44.

1. IT'S SIMPLE TO BE HAPPY

1. The neglected outlines for a psychology of experience put forth by the nineteenth-century German thinker Wilhelm Dilthey are now being slowly rediscovered by modern psychotherapy. The Austrian-born American psychologist Eugene Gendlin has made a contribution of major importance to modern psychology by reinstating "experiencing" as the experimentally verifiable variable. Eugene Gendlin and I have agreed in private conversations that his theories are closely akin to the Abhidhamma.
2. Epistemology goes beyond the domain of psychology in that it also concretely investigates the subjective experience of the contents of knowledge and the processes from which they result. It is distinct from theories of knowledge in science and philosophy, which primarily organize knowledge in logically formal terms. Epistemology also cannot be reduced to psychocybernetics, regardless of the very refined understanding of the processes of experience gained from the metaphor of the "biocomputer," which was elaborated particularly by John Lilly, *The Center of the Cyclone: An Autobiography of Inner Space* (New York: Crown, 1985). For modern epistemology, the works of Gregory Bateson are of key importance. I refer to them several times (see pages 22, 47, and 81ff.).
3. Mindfulness (*sati*) is the most important of the mental powers, because it harmonizes their input. The techniques for training described in this book are based on the as yet unsurpassed book of Nyanaponika, *The Heart of Buddhist Meditation* (York Beach, Me.: Samuel Weiser, 1988).

2. NEW AGE POLITICS: PERSONALLY EXPERIENCED?

1. A good overview is given in *Transpersonal Psychologies*, ed. Charles Tart (El Cerrito, Calif.: Psychological Processes, 1983).

2. For a brief description of the principles and procedures of Freud's method of meditation, see Mirko Frýba, "Traum, Trip, Ekstase—in psychoanalytischer Sicht," *Psychotherapie, Meditation, Gestalt,* ed. Hilarion Petzold (Paderborn: Junfermann Verlag, 1983).

3. Agehananda Bharati, *The Light at the Center: Context and Pretext of Modern Mysticism* (Santa Barbara, Calif.: Ross-Erikson, 1976).

4. "The writings of Nyanaponika Thera are a 'Guide for the perplexed' in the last quarter of this century. They are exactly the opposite of the popular cults. In his book on Buddhist meditation mentioned above, he has succeeded in describing the method of genuine meditation so clearly that it is accessible to anyone who is serious and does not shy away from the effort. . . . I am convinced that Nyanaponika Thera's work may become one of the most important contributions to the spiritual renewal of the West, if it can only reach the knowledge of a sufficient number of people" (Erich Fromm, Foreword to Nyanaponika, *The Vision of Dhamma* (York Beach, Me.: Samuel Weiser, 1986).

5. Claudio Naranjo and Robert E. Ornstein, *On the Psychology of Meditation* (New York, 1971). This book gives a reliable transcultural overview of spiritual training methods that go beyond meditation in the narrow sense.

6. "I said earlier that nothing is developing here that could be compared to yoga. That is not quite accurate. There has developed among us, in accordance with European prejudices, a medical psychology that occupies itself specifically with the *kleshas.* We call this the "psychology of the unconscious." C. G. Jung, *Gesammelte Werke,* vol. 11, p. 618 (Olten, Switzerland: Walter Verlag, 1971).

7. Ales Wotruba and S. Wotruba, "Existenzialpsychologisch-Meditative Therapie," in *Wege zum Menschen: Methoden und Persönlichkeiten moderner Psychotherapie,* ed. Hilarion Petzold (Paderborn: Junfermann Verlag, 1984), vol. 1, pp. 531, 537.

8. C. S. Hall and G. Lindzey, *Theories of Personality* (New York: Wiley, 1978).

9. "The Hopi Prophecy and the Chinese Dream," an interview with Frank Waters by Tom Tarbet in *East West Journal* 7, no. 5 (May 1977), pp. 52–64.

10. Fritjof Capra, *Turning Point: Science, Society, and the Rising Culture* (New York: Simon & Schuster, 1982).

11. Thaddeus Golas, *The Lazy Man's Guide to Enlightenment* (Palo Alto, Calif.: Seed Center, 1971), appeared under this title in German.

12. In *The Medium, the Mystic, and the Physicist* (New York: Viking, 1974), Le Shan does not limit himself to a comparison of worldviews, but also provides insight into similarities of epistemological approach. This interesting book was the groundbreaker for a number of later popular-scientific publications on these themes.

13. Laing has been able to profit from, among other things, intensive training in Abhidhamma-based *vipassanā* meditation in Sri Lanka. He is considered a pioneer in nonviolent treatment of psychotic patients.

14. *Karma,* the teaching of the causation of present suffering and happiness

through previous action, is discussed in chapter 3 in connection with conditioned arising.

15. As a basic psychological element or faculty, trust is present in all human beings. Only through training in the Dhamma strategies does this faculty become the psychic power *saddhā*, which in the form of confidence has a stabilizing effect on one's character.

3. THREEFOLD KNOWLEDGE AND THE ECONOMY OF THE MIND

1. *Papañca* means proliferation, dissemination, dispersion, diffusion, prolixity, appendage, indulgence, thicket, interdependence, ramification, manifoldness, multiplicity; it is a term for the manifoldness of the changing world of *samsāra* in which suffering cyclically perpetuates itself.

2. These obscurations and defilements (*kilesa*) of mind are not necessarily pathologies in the narrow psychiatric sense. See chapter 2, note 6.

3. The meditative way of dealing with obstacles or hindrances (*nīvarana*) to spiritual progress is explained in chapter 7. These hindrances are outgrowths of *kilesa* (see previous note).

4. *Samsāra*, the manifoldness of the world of change, which is often compared with a house that is on fire.

5. This presentation simplifies the facts in two ways: First, when we say that a matrix determines the frame of reference in terms of which we perceive the world, that means that it structures the experiential realities or cognitive correspondences (*nāma*) of the world. Thus corporeal things (*rūpa*) are not ordered in this fashion. For example, the outer *āyatana* do not mean "things-in-themselves out there," but rather the given experience of the object of perception. Correspondingly, the inner *āyatana* refers to the subjective registering of a sense perception (i.e., the software) and not the sense organ of flesh and blood (i.e., the hardware). See Diagram 1.

   Second, a simplified version of the matrix of *paticca-samuppāda* is sufficient for the explanation given here. The complete matrix of the cycle of suffering is given in Diagram 5.

6. In meditative training of willpower or exertion (*viriya*), awareness is protected by mindfulness (*sati*) from the suffering-producing influences of craving (greed, aggression), thereby making possible the development of happiness. A more detailed explanation is given on page 240f.

7. S-R (stimulus-response) and S-O-R (O for organism) are paradigms of behavioristic psychology.

8. Some groups in Europe have actually organized such courses. See also chapter 8, note 12.

9. For a more detailed explanation of the use of *akkheyya*, see page 239f. *Akkheyya* as technical terms are nonetheless indispensable for structuring Dhamma strategies.

10. *Vibhanga*; English translation, *The Book of Analysis* (London: Pali Text

Society, 1969); Buddhaghosa, *The Path of Purification*, trans. Ñānamoli (Berkeley: Shambhala, 1976), p. 484.

4. INTELLIGENCE OF THE BODY AND JOY

1. Bodily experience creates a continuum in the world (*kāma-bhava*); thinking constructs relationships in our picture of the world. The differentiation and connectedness referred to here has nothing to do with digital and analog representations and communications.
2. From *Anguttara Nikāya* 1.21, translated in Nyanaponika Thera, *The Heart of Buddhist Meditation* (York Beach, Me.: Samuel Weiser, 1988), p. 158.
3. As presented in his *Entwurf einer Psychologie* (1895).
4. A detailed evaluation of this contribution on the part of Lacan is found in A. Wilden, *System and Structure* (London: Tavistock, 1980). Wilden provides a critique of epistemology that has significant implications for social questions. However, he fails to recognize the liberational value of individual training in awareness.
5. Nyanatiloka, *Buddhist Dictionary* (Kandy, Sri Lanka: Buddhist Publication Society, 1980).
6. The shortest definition of "double-bind" is: "Whatever you do, it's wrong." In double-bind situations conflicting messages are communicated on two levels (for example, physical and verbal) requiring an action and at the same time prohibiting it. Both nonexecution and execution of the action are punished.
7. Once one has experienced the fullness of reality in an experiencing that is free from all distortion, one never again loses oneself in attachment to delusive projections. In the *Visuddhi Magga* (English translation, *The Path of Purification* [Berkeley: Shambhala, 1976], p. 220ff.), this is called "stream-entry" (*sotapatti*). See also the chapter section "Experiencing Emptiness," p. 272ff.
8. This is an application of *akkheyya* to the apprehension of units of experiencing. By contrast, reflection by means of *akkheyya* does not belong to this type of experiencing, even though all Abhidhamma concepts are anchored (*yathā*) in concrete experience (*bhūta*). The Canon (Sutta Nipāta, v. 808) defines *akkheyya* as "the pointer":

> From the beings seen and heard,
> previously called by a name,
> only this name remains,
> as the pointer to departed being.

9. *Anguttara Nikāya* 10.58. Professor E. Hardy, the editor, says in the foreword to volume 5 (London, 1900, p. 9f.): "If I do not refer here to the individual books of the Abhidhamma, the reason is simple . . . that here special research would be necessary, since they are all entirely dependent on the Anguttara."

10. See note 7, above.
11. See the exercise in apprehension of elements beginning on page 123.
12. English translation by Nyanamoli, *The Path of Purification*. Translates *pīti* as "happiness" (p. 149ff.).
13. Treated in detail by Erich Fromm in *Man for Himself*.
14. Aristotle, *Poetics*. See also note 15, below.
15. A good overview is given by Z. Moreno in her article "Über Aristoteles, Breuer und Freud hinaus: Morenos Beitrag zum Konzept der Katharsis," in *Integrative Therapie* 5 (1979), nos. 1/2. The theories of J. L. Moreno, like those of Bateson (as discussed on page 81f. of the present book), have paved the way for a scientific assimilation of Abhidhamma.

5. STRATEGIES OF REALITY ANCHORING

1. Cf. page 77: "Intelligence fundamentally refers to comprehension of relationships and meanings . . . reading what is taking place between really existing things."
2. See Diagram 12 (page 248).
3. Precisely this kind of situation is very valuable for cultivating the path of willpower (see page 247ff.). As we will understand later from a technical point of view, the training of the will (*viriya*) involves not the use of force in any form, but rather persistence and perseverance.
4. See the simile of the saw on page 217.
5. Or ten minutes, or thirty minutes—whatever you personally decide. If you are practicing before breakfast or before going to bed, you can increase the period of practice up to the ideal length of forty-five minutes.
6. English translation by Soma, *The Way of Mindfulness* (Kandy: Buddhist Publication Society, 1981), p. 55.
7. This observation by the Abhidhammikas offers an introspective empirical solution to the so-called mind-body problem, which modern science has attempted to solve externally and theoretically. (See, for example, *The Understanding of the Brain* [New York: McGraw-Hill, 1973] by the Nobel Prize winner John Eccles.)
8. The explanation of the four magical roads to power—*chanda-, viriya-, citta-,* and *vīmamsā-iddhipāda*—in the framework of the strategies of power clarifies the differences between these mental movements. See chapter 8.
9. First translated into English as *Psychological Ethics* (London: Pali Text Society, 1900).
10. We will deal with this question in greater detail in chapter 7 in connection with meditation instruction.
11. J. H. Schultz, *Der Weg zur Seele* vol. 4/1 (1953), p. 19.
12. This ritualization should be simple and playful. In the psychotherapeutic treatment of sleep problems in compulsive personalities, however, quite complicated rituals have proved most effective.

6. STRATEGIES OF SYMPATHY

1. For the scientific foundations, see C. R. Rogers, "The Necessary and Sufficient Conditions of Therapeutic Personality Change," *Journal of Consulting Psychology* 21 (1957).
2. *Vibhanga* 712, 713; English translation, *The Book of Analysis* (London: Pali Text Society, 1969).
3. Translated in Nyanaponika Thera, "The Roots of Good and Evil," in *The Vision of Dhamma* (York Beach, Me.: Samuel Weiser, 1986).
4. Translated (except for verse 133) in W. Rahula, *What the Buddha Taught* (New York: Grove Press, 1974).
5. Translated in *Buddhist Scriptures*, ed. Edward Conze (Baltimore: Penguin, 1959), p. 186.
6. Several meditation students have told me that they were unable to recall any situation in which they were really happy. If this should also be the case with you, think first of a problematic situation and then of the subsequent situation that provided relief and was characterized by a subsiding of anxiety.
7. The principles of Dhamma strategies are recorded in the technical terminology of *akkheyya*, the use of which is explained in detail beginning on page 239.

7. STRATEGIES OF ECSTASY

1. The method for doing this is described in detail in the context of the exercise for transforming suffering-producing processes (page 262).
2. *Jhāna* is sometimes translated into English rather imprecisely as "ecstasy"; ecstasy is actually a preliminary stage of *jhāna*, and *jhāna* is the transcending of ecstasy. Nyanatiloka, in his *Buddhist Dictionary* (Kandy: Buddhist Publication Society, 1980), gives the following definition: "Jhāna, Absorption, refers chiefly to the four meditative Absorptions of the Fine-material Sphere (*rūpajjhāna*). They are achieved through the attainment of Full (or Ecstatic) Concentration (*appanā samādhi*), during which there is a complete, though temporary, suspension of fivefold sense-activity and of the five Hindrances (*nīvarana*). The state of consciousness, however, is one of full alertness and lucidity. Jhāna in its widest sense denotes any, even momentary or weak absorption of mind when directed on a single object."
3. A detailed description is found in the third chapter of the *Visuddhi Magga* (*The Path of Purification*).
4. See *Anguttara Nikāya* 3.70, 6.10, etc.
5. In the commentary to the *Anguttara Nikāya* as well as the *Papañca-Sūdanī* (English translation by Soma; see note 6 of chapter 5), *sayāna* appears as a preparation for analysis of the elements. The *Dhammapada* (271, 272) says that rituals (*sīlabatta*), scholarship (*bāhu-sacca*), concentration (*samādhi*),

and detached relaxation (*vivicca sayāna*) are not by themselves sufficient for enlightenment.

6. The *ālaya-viññāna* is also known as the "cosmic storehouse consciousness," in which all defilements (*kilesa*) are latent and out of which the cosmos unfolds (*Sūtrālankāra* 11.44). A description of the advanced stages of *yoga-niddā*, which lies beyond the framework of strategies of ecstasy under discussion here, is to be found in M. Frýba and W. Bliss, *Antar Mouna* (Monghyr, India: B.S.Y. Press, 1968). This method includes among other things the meditative procedure for grasping the cosmos as a hologram.

7. This is not a reference to some kind of *unio mystica* or any other kind of numinous or ontological entity.

8. *Samanera* (literally, "little shaman") is the term for a novice who has entered homelessness, but has not yet received full ordination as a monk, or *bhikkhu*.

9. The traditional form of fourfold protective meditation is described in a little book by Mahasi Sayadaw, *Practical Insight Meditation*.

10. Cf. the swinging back and forth in the steps of *yoniso manasikāra* on page 178f.

11. The four principal perversions were introduced in the framework of the algebra of *yoniso manasikāra* on page 71f. For a detailed explanation, see *Anguttara Nikāya*, trans. Nyanaponika, *The Wheel*, no. 155/158, pp. 86f and 118 (Kandy: Buddhist Publication Society).

8. STRATEGIES OF POWER

1. *Anguttara Nikāya, The Book of Fours*, Sutta 13, trans. in *The Wheel*, no. 155/158 (Kandy: Buddhist Publication Society). The Abhidhammic metaprograms for struggle are elaborated in detail in *Vibhanga* 390–430 (English translation, *The Book of Analysis*; see chapter 6, note 2). Cf. the explanation of "proficiency in right means" (*upāya-kosalla*) on page 74 of the present book.

2. *Carl Rogers on Personal Power* (New York: Delacorte, 1977).

3. A penetrating analysis of these themes is given in Aldous Huxley, *Brave New World Revisited* (London: Panther Books, 1983), p. 170f.

4. In the *Anguttara Nikāya*, which I have cited above in note 1, the form of *paññā*, which is characterized as knowledge that sees (*ñāna-dassana*), is declared to be a result of specific meditation exercises, present happiness (*sukha-vihāra*), mindfulness, clear comprehension (*sati-sampajañña*), and conquering of blind drives (*āsava-khaya*). This goes far beyond the scope of the present book.

5. *Udāna, Khuddaka-Nikāya*, Pali Text Society ed. (London: Luzac, 1948), pp. 67–69.

6. These principles of Abhidhamma, which are especially clear in the paradigm of *pariññā*, or experiential penetration (*Patisambhidā-Magga* 1.87), have never been taken into account in the purely philological translations

that have been made up to now. Proficiency in the terminology of *ak-kheyya* makes possible only the first of the three *pariññā* and thus is insufficient for overcoming suffering. (Cf. the practice-related discussion on page 271.)

7. *Itivuttaka, Khuddaka-Nikāya*, Pali Text Society ed. (London: Luzac, 1948).

8. The interpretation of intentionality by the German phenomenologists Franz Brentano and Edmund Husserl corresponds to a great extent to that of the Abhidhamma. In the *Vibhanga*, it is shown how confidence (*saddhā* or *pasāda*) arises conditioned by intentionality.

9. *Milinda Pañha*, p. 36 of the PTS edition (London, 1962).

10. In its most comprehensive formulation, the path of release from suffering, which we introduced on page 49 in connection with the Four Noble Truths, is composed of eight factors. Each factor represents the supreme instruction for the happiness-furthering, right (not wrong) organization of a particular aspect of life. This classification is exhaustive; thus these eight factors represent the necessary and sufficient conditions for liberation: (1) right knowledge, (2) right thought, (3) right speech, (4) right action, (5) right livelihood, (6) right effort, (7) right mindfulness, (8) right concentration.

    A systematic discussion is found in Nyanatiloka, *The Buddha's Path to Deliverance* (Kandy: Buddhist Publication Society, 1982).

11. Ledi Sayadaw, *The Requisites of Enlightenment* (Rangoon: Kaba-Aye, 1965); rev. ed., Kandy, Sri Lanka: Buddhist Publication Society, 1984.

12. Translated by Narada as *The Manual of Abhidhamma* (Kandy, Sri Lanka: Buddhist Publication Society, 1984). Chögyam Trungpa mentions in his *Glimpses of Abhidharma* (Boston: Shambhala Publications, 1987) that learning the *Abhidhammattha Sangaha* by heart was a fundamental part of the education of a Tibetan lama.

13. For an elucidation of the paradigm of *pariññā*, see the chapter section "Turning Away from Suffering" (page 270ff.).

14. The obscurations of insight are treated in detail in the *Visuddhi Magga*, trans. Ñanamoli, p. 739ff. Cf. our discussion of *suññatā* on page 272ff.

15. Cf. the discussion and examples regarding dealing with distractions on page 116f.

16. Treated in detail in Nyanaponika, *Abhidhamma Studies* (Kandy: Buddhist Publication Society, 1976), pp. 101ff.

17. Tabular overviews of these can be found at the end of Nyanatiloka, *Buddhist Dictionary* (Kandy: Buddhist Publication Society, 1980). According to the classification in the *Abhidhammattha Sangaha*, of the 89 states only 54 appear in daily life, of which 12 are suffering-producing, 18 neutral, and 24 are considered beautiful (*sobhana-citta*).

18. See note 10 to chapter 8.

19. The liberation-furthering relationship between the teacher and the student has the qualities of a noble friendship (see page 152). On the distorted ideas concerning the teaching relationship common in Western countries, which have developed to the point of sectarianism, see Mirko

Frýba, "Dhammaduta in the West and Its Hindrances," *Buddhist Quarterly* (London) 13, no. 1, 13–17.

20. In the *Visuddhi Magga* (trans. Ñanamoli, p. 289ff.), this simile stands just before the detailed instruction in mindfulness of breathing (*ānāpāna-sati*).

21. See Diagram 5 (page 58).

22. *Abhi* = "from above," *san* = "together," *tāpeti* = "to heat up." Philologically, *tāpeti* is related to the Sanskrit word *tapas*, which refers to the Hindu practice of self-torment through the practice of austerities. The Abhidhamma tradition rejects self-torment and austerities as useless and harmful.

23. See *Majjhima Nikāya* 20 (London: Pali Text Society, 1979), vol. 1, pp. 119ff.

24. In the table on page 250 we use only the unwholesome formations of greed, aggression, resentment, delusion, prejudice, doubt, and agitation; however, to this group belong also arrogance, miserliness, envy, as well as lust, rigidity, and dullness—these last were discussed on page 201f. as hindrances (*nīvarana*) to concentration. According to a table ("The Formations in Connection with Consciousness") in an appendix to the English translation of the *Visuddhi Magga*, an unwholesome consciousness is composed of between thirteen and twenty formations; a wholesome consciousness contains up to thirty-six formations.

25. This simile is taken completely out of context by the American psychologists D. H. Shapiro (*Meditation: A Scientific/Personal Exploration*, 1980) and P. Carrington (*Freedom in Meditation*, 1978) and passed along as a "Buddhist meditation instruction": "With teeth clamped together and tongue pressed against the gums, with sheer mental effort one should restrain, suppress, and incinerate the thoughts" (Shapiro, p. 14).

26. The other common characteristics are suffering (*dukkha*) and absence of individuality (*anattā*, "egolessness"), which are discussed in connection with the overcoming of perversions on page 76.

27. For a detailed explanation of *suññatā* meditation, see Mirko Frýba, "Suññatā—Experience of Void in Buddhist Mind Training," *Sri Lanka Journal of Buddhist Studies* 2 (1988).

28. Although this experimental design may seem amusing, it is actually in many regards more scientific than the majority of experiments that scientific theories have been based upon. Even in the area of the so-called exact natural sciences, researchers work with introspective experiences, either their own or those of others (often uncritically adopted), that have been evoked by externally observed events. The researcher formulates his experiences in so-called "basic premises," and when he no longer wishes to analyze his epistemological processes, he simply sets them down as "data." The data and basic premises are then processed by means of complicated statistical procedures in order to distract attention from their origin. Actually many scientists behave like the schoolteachers who without much reflection evaluate their pupil's performances in terms of "grades" and afterward, with the help of a computer, calculate the grade averages out to two or three decimal places. In any case, we must acknowledge

that the results of scientific mass calculations are often more impressive than those of individual creativity. Take a few minutes to consider two examples: the boomerang and the atom bomb.

29. These steps of wise apprehension, investigation, and experiential penetration are described in detail in the *Nidāna Samyutta*, particularly Sutta 65 of the *Samyutta Nikāya*. See Bhikkhu Bodhi, *Transcendental Dependent Origination* (Kandy: Buddhist Publication Society, 1980). For a detailed treatment of all elements in the formula of conditioned arising of freedom.

Index of Technical Terms